SOCIAL SCIENCE EDUCATION

This book provides an introduction to social science pedagogy in India. It delves into the interrelationships between society, social relationships, education, and learning.

Social science education in schools helps build a critical understanding of social processes and institutions. This book critically examines school spaces and approaches to social science teaching and pedagogy in Indian schools. It outlines distinguishing features, differences, and similarities in pedagogical models and also explains how these varied approaches can be applied in the teaching process. The book also addresses the challenges and possibilities of integrating technology in teaching social sciences.

Part of the series, 'Principles-based Adaptive Teaching', this book will be of interest to students and teachers of education and the social sciences. It will also be of interest to teachers, educators, curriculum designers, policy makers and social science course developers, NGOs, and public and private sector bodies who focus on teaching and learning practices.

Yemuna Sunny is a researcher, teacher and writer who has been engaged with social science education for nearly three decades. She has been a senior fellow in the Eklavya Foundation in Madhya Pradesh. She has been part of the focus group for social science for the National Curriculum Framework, 2005, and played a pivotal role in guiding teachers to write social science text books in Kerala state in 2008. She was central to the evolution of the course 'Pedagogy of social studies' in the Masters of Arts in Education (Elementary) (MAEE) programme at the Tata Institute of Social Sciences, Mumbai, which she taught for nine years. She has vast experience in writing for teachers, students, and curriculum developers. Her research and publications are based mostly on social geography, politics of knowledge, and critiques of curriculum and educational policies, tribal issues and sustainable development. She has authored a number of articles and books. Her recent writings, along with innovative cartographies, are being published as books for young readers.

Simantini Dhuru is the Director of the Avehi Abacus Project, Mumbai – a unique educational initiative devoted to strengthening and transforming public education. She has played a key role in policy-making and curriculum development bodies at state and national levels (particularly actively contributing her experiences and insights in the capacity of a member to the National Executive Committee for Sarva Shikha Abhiyan, NCERT and Maharashtra SCERT). She is a visiting faculty with the Centre of Excellence in Teacher Education (CETE, formerly CEIAR), where she developed and taught the integrated B.Ed. M.Ed. course, and the School of Education at the Tata Institute of Social Sciences. She also developed and taught a course in Indian Education at the Department of Asian Languages and Cultures, University of Michigan, Ann Arbor campus. She is also a documentary filmmaker with national and international awards to her credit.

Principles-based Adaptive Teaching

Series Editors: **Mythili Ramchand** and **Nishevita Jayendran**,
Tata Institute of Social Sciences, Mumbai, India

This series bring together critical discussions on educational practices and pedagogies in India. The teaching profession has undergone rapid changes and advancements in recent years. The books in this series will identify the changes which are affecting teaching-learning practices in schools and the range of knowledge development required for educators to develop and adopt innovative pedagogical practices to adapt to uncertain futures. The books in the series include worksheets, vignettes, emerging classroom discussions, case studies along with other additional resources for teachers and students. The series caters to a range of teacher education programmes and the volumes are envisioned as resources, primarily for teacher educators and student-teachers and others engaged in the education sector. It focuses on topics such as adolescence in India, pedagogy of language (English), pedagogy of mathematics and pedagogy of science, the nature and purpose of education, philosophy of education, knowledge and curriculum, learners and learning, educational policies and practices, teachers and teaching, inclusive education, pedagogies of language, social sciences and assessments and evaluation, within the themes of education.

Language Education
Teaching English in India
Nishevita Jayendran, Anusha Ramanathan and Surbhi Nagpal

Adolescence in India
An Interdisciplinary Perspective
Gomathi Jatin Shah and Sybil Thomas

Science Education
Developing Pedagogical Content Knowledge
Shamin Padalkar, Mythili Ramchand, Rafikh Shaikh and Indira Vijaysimha

Social Science Education
Developing Social Scientific Perspective
Yemuna Sunny and Simantini Dhuru

For more information about this series, please visit: https://www.routledge.com/Principles-based-Adaptive-Teaching/book-series/PAT

SOCIAL SCIENCE EDUCATION

Developing Social
Scientific Perspective

Yemuna Sunny and Simantini Dhuru

LONDON AND NEW YORK

Designed cover image: Cover image by Vrushali Joshi

First published 2025
by Routledge
4 Park Square, Milton Park, Abingdon, Oxon OX14 4RN

and by Routledge
605 Third Avenue, New York, NY 10158

Routledge is an imprint of the Taylor & Francis Group, an informa business

© 2025 Yemuna Sunny and Simantini Dhuru

The right of Yemuna Sunny and Simantini Dhuru to be identified as authors of this work has been asserted in accordance with sections 77 and 78 of the Copyright, Designs and Patents Act 1988.

All rights reserved. No part of this book may be reprinted or reproduced or utilised in any form or by any electronic, mechanical, or other means, now known or hereafter invented, including photocopying and recording, or in any information storage or retrieval system, without permission in writing from the publishers.

Trademark notice: Product or corporate names may be trademarks or registered trademarks, and are used only for identification and explanation without intent to infringe.

British Library Cataloguing-in-Publication Data
A catalogue record for this book is available from the British Library

ISBN: 978-0-367-70642-5 (hbk)
ISBN: 978-1-032-56846-1 (pbk)
ISBN: 978-1-003-44934-8 (ebk)
ISBN: 978-1-032-56845-4 (eBook+)

DOI: 10.4324/9781003449348

Typeset in Sabon
by Deanta Global Publishing Services, Chennai, India

To teachers and students of the world...

CONTENTS

List of figures   *xi*
Series editors' note   *xiii*
Foreword   *xvi*
Acknowledgements   *xviii*

Introduction   1

PART 1
SOCIETY, STATE, AND CONSCIOUSNESS   5

1 Studying society   9

2 State formation and social consciousness   36

3 The modern state and citizenship education   60

PART 2
DEMOCRACY, EDUCATION, TECHNOLOGY   81

4 Approaches to teaching social sciences: Why, what, and how?   85

5 Technology, teaching, and the practice of social sciences   131

PART 3
CHALLENGES AND POSSIBILITIES 159

  6 Can classrooms transform? 161

  7 Teachers, society, and the classroom 185

Bibliography 229
Index 237

FIGURES

1.1a	In search of clay	16
1.1b	Creating life	17
1.1c	Making of tools	18
1.1d	The granary	19
1.2	A sketch of the Arabian Sea trade region (eleventh-to-twelfth century)	23
1.3	A sketch of the silk trade route (eleventh-to-twelfth century)	25
1.4	A sketch of megaliths	28
1.5	Migrations, mixing of people, and the Harappan culture	32
2.1	Monarchies in the North Indian River plains (1200–500 BCE)	38
2.2	Interfaces of the tribal and the brahmanical systems: the north-eastern and southern regions	42
4.1	Factory model of education	98
4.2	Web-map democracy and education	100
4.3	Disciplinary approach textbook index	101
4.4	Integrated approach example 1	102
5.1	Education in the digital age!	137
5.2	Pedagogical content knowledge (recreated with reference to Shulman, 1986)	141
5.3	The TPACK framework (recreated with reference to Mishra and Koehler, 2009)	143

5.4	TPACK framework, modified to address contextual factors (recreated with reference to Mishra and Koehler, 2012)	146
5.5	TPACK for social studies (recreated with reference to Hammond and Manfra, 2009)	147
6.1	Different sides of a development story	164
6.2	Collective creation of knowledge in the classroom	173
6.3	The reactions to a film	174
7.1	Community of learners	219

SERIES EDITORS' NOTE

The last two decades have seen developments of national importance in school education in India. With the Right of Children to Free and Compulsory Education (RtE Act, 2009) and the National Curriculum Framework (NCF, 2005), changes have been afoot to enable access to quality education for children at scale. Responding to the concurrent need for teacher education to support the vision of a robust education system, the National Curriculum Framework for Teacher Education (NCFTE, 2009) recommended substantive changes in curriculum and practice of teacher education in the country. Subsequently, the high-powered committee on teacher education set up by the Hon. Supreme Court of India (Justice Verma Committee, 2012) endorsed these curricular reforms and called for an overhaul of the sector. Notably, similar shifts have been observed across the world, as teacher education programmes discuss pathways for professional development to enable teachers to work as transformative professionals in the twenty-first century. UNESCO's Sustainable Development Goals (SDGs) call for transformative pedagogies, with a shift towards active, self-directed participatory and collaborative learning, problem orientation, inter- and trans-disciplinarity, and the linking of formal and informal learning (UNESCO, 2017, p. 7). Acknowledging the need for gearing up the Indian education system to meet SDGs, particularly SDG 4 to ensure inclusive and equitable quality education and promote lifelong learning opportunities for all, the recent National Education Policy (2020) has proposed re-envisioning teacher education in multi-disciplinary institutions that can prepare teachers to meet the needs of learners in the twenty-first century.

With the rapid advances in science and technology and the pervasiveness of ICT and media in our lives, the education sector stands witness to radical changes that are affecting teaching/learning practices in schools. Arguably, the onset of the Fourth Industrial Revolution requires preparing learners for a range of competencies, including effective communication, intercultural sensitivity, analytical and critical thinking, and problem-solving skills and creativity, which extend beyond content knowledge. In this context, educators are required to gain adaptive expertise to prepare themselves and their students for uncertain futures.

A dearth of good curricular resources has been consistently identified as a key lacuna, from the first national commission on education in independent India, in preparing teachers as professional educators. In the light of the present education policy calling for substantial changes to teacher education, there is an urgent need for quality teaching/learning materials that can trigger critical inquiry, invoke a sense of adventure, and provoke the curiosity of both student teachers and teacher educators to embark on the complex task of learning to teach.

To this end, the Centre of Excellence in Teacher Education (CETE) at the Tata Institute of Social Sciences, Mumbai, has developed a series of textbooks under the theme 'Principles-based Adaptive Teaching' that make inroads into the content and pedagogical domains of study relevant to teaching/learning practice. The titles for these books have been identified based on a consideration of the NCFTE 2009, emerging understandings from comparative studies of teacher education curricula in the international context, and demands from the field to address the needs of preparing teachers for the twenty-first century. Drawing from current research in education, the titles adopt an innovative, practice-based approach to deal with the selected topics. The themes covered in the series include adolescent learners in India, titles on subject pedagogies (English, mathematics, science, and social science), knowledge and learning, ICT and new media in education, and state, education, and policy.

Each book covers key concepts, constructs, theories, conceptual and empirical frameworks, and contemporary discourses around the topic. The content and discussions are meant to broaden and deepen readers' understanding of the topic. Cases, narratives, and vignettes are used for contextual illustration of ideas. It is desirable that educators bring supplementary illustrations to problematise local issues. The references, range of activities, and discussion triggers provided in each volume are meant to enable readers to explore issues further. The books are meant to be used as one among many 'resources' rather than 'a book'.

It is hoped that this book series will help readers gain nuanced perspectives on the topics, along with relevant skills and dispositions to integrate into their teaching repertoire.

Dr. Mythili Ramchand
Dr. Nishevita Jayendran
Centre of Excellence in Teacher Education, Tata Institute of Social Sciences, Mumbai, India

FOREWORD

The discipline of education and professional development of teachers in India and the broader South Asian region has been undergoing radical redefinition over the past thirty years, with significant advances in its conceptual base, approaches to theory and practice, and the formation of practice of teachers. Policy documents such as the National Curriculum Framework (2005) and the National Curriculum Framework for Teacher Education (2009) in India lay out for us the scope and depth of ideas that are of contemporary disciplinary interest. Resources that enable students of education to engage with these ideas relevant to the developing world contexts are, however, very few. This has been a key problem for widespread dissemination and for the ideas to take root in disciplinary discourses and practices in the universities and colleges of teacher education. While planning the scope of work of the Centre of Excellence in Teacher Education at the Tata Institute of Social Sciences, supported by the Tata Trusts, therefore, we included the development of resources as one of the major activities that would be needed to revitalise the sector. Dr. Mythili Ramchand and Dr. Nishevita Jayendran, as series editors, have laid out the scope and vision of such resources built around a series of textbooks to be developed in English and major modern Indian languages. Recognising the importance of such an initiative, several colleagues from universities in India have joined this effort as collaborators.

Textbooks are essential to support the formation and advancement of disciplines. Important scientific ideas become integrated into disciplinary thinking through textbooks written by scientists themselves. In the colonised world, textbooks came to represent 'colonisers' knowledge' and the cornerstone of the examination system, defining 'official knowledge' and strongly framing academic discourse from the world outside. Many of us trained in education, therefore, retain a suspicion of textbooks that may come to dominate the intellectual mental mindscape of students and have sought out 'original writings' to include in our course reading compendia. Important as the reading of original texts is, particularly in the social sciences, they do not address what good textbooks can do and need to do for their students: performing a disciplinary landscaping function that is contextually relevant, drawing on contemporary research and practice, putting ideas to use as tools for thinking, scaffolding engagement, and stimulating inquiry. In developing the textbooks in this series, authors have drawn on their experiences of teaching, research, reading, and field engagement. We hope that the faculty of education, students of education, and teachers will all find the resources useful.

Padma M. Sarangapani
Chairperson, Centre of Excellence in Teacher Education
(formerly, Centre for Education, Innovation, and Action Research)

ACKNOWLEDGEMENTS

The book has partially drawn from the classroom transactions of the course Pedagogy of Social Studies as part of MAEE, that was initiated in 2006 in the Tata Institute of Social Sciences (TISS), Mumbai. We hold happy memories of our students, and deeply acknowledge their contributions, many of the writings of whom have been utilised in Chapter 6. These were outcomes of the course in which Yemuna Sunny and Manish Jain were co-teachers for several years. We deeply acknowledge Dr. Manish Jain, for his contributions to the course. From 2015–16 onwards, Simantini Dhuru has been teaching the course, in which she has expanded the course material and medium, drawing from multi-media sources, being a filmmaker herself.

We are grateful to Prof Padma Sarangapani, Chairperson of CETE (formerly CEIAR), TISS, Mumbai for her vision on the need to write books that can fruitfully gather from the blend of subject knowledge and pedagogy. We express our gratitude to Nishevita Jayendran of CETE who has been always available to help out with all our queries regarding the final manuscript. We also thank Mythili Ramchand of CETE, who, along with Nishevita, has improved us as series editors.

We take the opportunity to thank the Routledge team, namely Lubna Irfan, Shloka Chauhan, and Shoma Choudhary, for their discussions and reminders of deadlines, for enhancing the review process of the draft manuscript, and for all other requirements that led to the final shaping of the book. We are also indebted to the reviewer of the manuscript, whose critical eye has helped in finetuning the document.

We thank Vrushali Joshi who has patiently and carefully attended to all the requirements of illustrations in the book. Thanks are also due to Honoch

Samuel for his generosity in conceptualising some of the visuals and Amir More and Mahendra Devle for refining and executing them. Thanks are also due to Sanjeevi Nagarajan, Project Manager at Deanta Global Publishing for helping us with the copyedit and final formatting.

Our long-time associations with institutions of educational innovations have helped us to bring in reflections of practices which have made their way into Chapter 6, in particular. These include Eklavya in Madhya Pradesh with which Yemuna has had around twenty five years of engagements, and Simantini's over three decades long involvement with the Avehi Abacus Project.

We thank our families and friends for their support, especially when the writing demanded intense time commitments.

INTRODUCTION

There are several reasons as to why we set out to write a book on social science education. The premise is of the need to unravel the complexities of learning about society in which all of us are located. Conventionally, school textbooks and training materials do not encourage us to think critically about social processes. Moreover, social science literature, often rich in expressions of jargon, fail to arouse a desire to decipher social processes. So, students and teachers are overwhelmed while making sense of the world with reference only to their day-to-day experiences, which, more often than not, are deeply embedded in practices of class-caste-gender.

How can a teacher or an educationist help to build critical thought processes? This concern is contradistinct from the popular concepts of 'good' teachers and 'good' students, as what is good is generally decided by the most powerful strata of society. These issues can be unpacked by social science as it throws light on the processes of power and dominance, and on the processes of reshaping for social justice. How can these premises, so essential for a democratic society, flow between the textbooks and other resources, the classroom processes, and the larger society?

Social studies that derives from Social science, and anchors citizenship education, is formulated as three different components in school books – history, geography, and civics/social and political life/political science. The interconnections and linkages between them are usually not explored through possibilities of integration.

Most modern disciplines, like social science, governed by a European contextual vantage, continue to impact the nature of institutional knowledge creation. The need for reinterpretation is recognised and built on in various

DOI: 10.4324/9781003449348-1

parts of the neo-colonial world. In neo-colonial states like India, internal dominance and marginalisations bring to the fore several crucial questions. Whose story is being told? Where are the silences? Reinterpretations try to throw light on the silences and also to create perspectives by which to interpret anew the dominant stories that are written.

We need evidence, data, and perspectives for social interpretations. From the cave paintings of prehistoric people to the evolution of language and letters, society developed into a stratified one, and not everyone was handling the letters. We have a long history of the toiling people, bereft of leisure time, space, and technique to pen their thoughts or resistance. That is why the oral traditions of songs, poems, and performances are rich in folk expressions of pain, resistance, pleasure, and acceptance, which become important sources from which we can learn about social relationships of different time space.

It is from the concreteness of society that abstractions are inferred, paving the way for social theories. Theories could also change depending on new evidence and research. It is not only our vantage that matters in social theory, but the evidence, data, and methodologies for interpretations. Nevertheless, as vantage plays an important role in matters of social justice, it also becomes political. So, social science has different vantages, debates among them, and dissent become continuing processes of contestations and negotiations in knowledge creation.

It is notable that social studies in schools do not deal with different points of view. They give us only a single dominant view. Moreover, many aspects of social science enquiry, that are crucial, interesting, and important for knowing about society, do not become part of school texts. That is why we often hear someone remark: 'This is very important. I did not ever read about this in my schoolbooks!' We have tried to write of those important absences in this book, that are crucial for getting a feel of the flow of society.

In contemporary times, and more so after the COVID-19 pandemic, an increased usage of technology has made way into education. How do we assess this intervention, and how can we tune it according to the realities of society in the country? Technology is human-made and it can be shaped according to human needs. But human needs are not uniform. There are some things that are accessible for certain strata of society, but not for others. Other than the issue of accessibility, the challenge also extends to the pedagogic realm, in which teacher-student relationships, and analysis would need to open up critical and creative possibilities.

It is in the midst of the various issues coming together that are mentioned above that teachers deal with social studies. Even as many of the institutional aspects are a 'given' to teachers, they could equip themselves with social science as a process embedding their own lives and thoughts and that of students and institutions governing them in a deeply interlinked world. In the light of this perspective, this book is organised within three connected themes.

In Part 1, Yemuna Sunny brings together a historic and socio-geographic examination of relationships between society, state, and consciousness. These relationships are foregrounded so that the readers would be encouraged to connect their day-to-day experiences to a larger canvas of space–time. The recognition of such linkages between the concrete and the abstract build consciousness that holds the key to education. Social studies can aspire to fulfil this by enriching (a) democratic spaces promised by the modern school and (b) critical reinterpretation of society to create democratic praxis. The possibility of enlivening the promise of democracy is examined in Part 1 in the form of three chapters that look into (1) social scientific ways of studying society, (2) dialectical relationships between state formation and collective consciousness of people, and (3) critical examination of social studies which anchor citizenship education in the modern school.

In Part 2, Simantini Dhuru examines, the intricate relationship between pedagogy and the content. Within a democratic perspective of education, this relationship can change the classrooms, and also helps teachers and students to collectively create knowledge. In post-COVID contexts, the reliance on technology to build offsite practices of schooling continues to make a trajectory. Today as technology has taken over almost every aspect of our life, we need to understand the historical processes in which the politics of knowledge creation is embedded. Can technology be utilised to enhance content and pedagogy in the pursuance of democratic classrooms? How do questions of equity and justice affect technology and education? These are some of the main issues examined in Part 2 through the two chapters that focus on (1) approaches to pedagogy of social studies and (2) technological utilisation for democratic pedagogy.

In Part 3, the process of schooling is examined as an outcome of educational policies, learning-teaching materials, and examinations and evaluations. The perspectives on citizenship education impacts on how social studies actually play out at concrete levels in the school. Through concrete experiences of classroom transactions, and by examining the possibilities of enriching content and pedagogy in social studies, the section brings to the reader the concrete challenges as well as the rich possibilities that teachers, educationists, and policy-makers can make to transform the classrooms democratically. Part 3 elaborates these through two chapters that examine the possibilities of (1) classroom transformations (Yemuna Sunny), and (2) the collective role of teachers (Simantini Dhuru).

PART 1
Society, state, and consciousness

How are societies formed and how do they change? Most significantly, these processes happen through the relationships evolved by humans with nature and with each other. In studying society, we try to know these processes evolving across time–space. In the journeys of human societies, consciousness plays an important role whose reflections are seen in early cave paintings and creation legends, the latter continuing to come alive through oral traditions of communities.

The earliest development of urbanisation, traced to the late fourth millennium BCE (between 4000 BCE and 3001 BCE) and which continued to 1750 BCE, the Indus Valley Civilisation, was one of the most widespread river valley civilisation of the ancient times. The cities of the Indus Valley were built from surplus production of the river plains and mining carried out from sites like Baluchistan and Rajasthan. Evidence shows a high level of efficient management of land, water, produce, and labour in the construction and maintenance of the cities. In contradistinction to other ancient civilisations, the Indus Valley Civilisation does not depict religious buildings or elaborate burials. The decline of the cities has been interpreted through multiple possibilities, ranging from the environmental (linked to the geological changes in the Himalayas and therefore the shifting of river courses) to the spread of diseases and to the invasion of people from other areas.

It was much later, in the sixth century BCE (600 BCE–501 BCE), that urban centres emerged in the subcontinent again, this time in the Ganges Valley. This was the period of emergence of kingdoms or states and the gradual organisation of society through the varnas of the brahmanical order. Across time, these expanded their spatial controls into distant regions of the

DOI: 10.4324/9781003449348-2

subcontinent like the Deccan Plateau and the Brahmaputra Valley. What emerged in these regions are stories of negotiations and contestations that changed, not only the social systems in those regions, but also the brahmanical system that itself metamorphosed into regional heterogeneities.

The transitions of society, from the collective tribal/*Adivasi* formations to the brahmanical/feudal state, implies a change in which the control of women's sexuality became a central feature. The mode of production (MOP), defined by the way in which production is carried out, through processes of human labour, tools, land and other resources, control of property and resources, relations between people and the objects of their work, and the relationships among the social groups, were changing to form – the four *varnas* in this case.

The above-mentioned social transitions entailed changes in people's consciousness. On one hand, creation legends were reconstructed by the emerging brahmanical powers to legitimise the hierarchical structure based on the *varna*, which, in turn, was a social and economic structure that synchronised with the changing mode of production. On the other hand, the consciousness of people in the social classes that were controlled, marginalised, and deprived in the brahmanical order, manifested in the form of resistance to the ordering of society. The resistance took cultural forms of expressions and/or reasoned articulations. These were often non-materialistic, very rarely materialistic.

The migrations of people from place to place across time form an important process of human history and social geography. The movements of people from Africa and Central Asia into the Indian subcontinent, the movement and conquest of state powers from the Ganges to the Deccan and the Brahmaputra Valleys, the forced movements of Adivasi people from the river valleys of these regions to the forested hilly lands, and so on are examples of time–space mobility of people. But, unlike all earlier movements and conquests of state powers in the subcontinent, the colonial British rule marked a differently hued imposition, the trajectory of which is linked to imperialism.

The British entry into the Indian subcontinent began with the East India Company that obtained permission from local authorities to procure land and to conduct duty-free trade. But gradually, it became involved in overthrowing the rulers of different parts of the subcontinent and also in sidelining other European presence in the region. They occupied forest lands, and some of the very first consciousness and resistance against the British emerged from the Adivasi people in the eighteenth century. The Pahariya Sirdars in 1778, the Tamar revolt in 1789, the Santhal rebellion led by Sidhu and Kanu, and the revolts led by Birsa Munda are some prominent examples. In the nineteenth century, the freedom struggle or the anticolonial movement began and grew across the subcontinent in organised ways. In

1947, the subcontinent became independent of colonial rule, giving way to two independent nations, India and Pakistan.

The modern state is one in which the MOP has transitioned from the feudal one to one of capitalist production. Capital and labour, as distinct categories, produce goods through machines in the capitalist MOP. The neo-colonial modern states like India had a lot of transitions to do in order to emerge from the impacts of colonialism as well as from the feudal dominance in the larger expanses of the countryside. The modern state had also evolved the modern school to develop people to be citizens of the modern state and also as labour in the modern industries. On one hand, schooling assists the above-mentioned requirements of orienting the people to the requirements of the modern state and production system. But, on the other hand, it also becomes a ground in which consciousness builds resistance to marginalisation in the new system and those that are continuing from the brahmanical feudal system in India.

Consciousness is a running thread in Part 1 of the book in which a historical-geographical foregrounding enhances the search for democratic possibilities that could be built in the modern school. This is seen as an important space that brings together people from all walks of life into common classrooms and which therefore holds a number of dialectical possibilities. The contemporary phase of increased privatisation and commodification of education has surely limited the scope of interactions by giving way to stratified schools, based on the varying buying powers of the people.

Chapter 1 delves into the processes of studying society and the sources that are used for the purpose, picking up traces that lead us to interpret society across time–space, the methods used to search for evidence, and to make interpretations, are examined.

Chapter 2 examines the transitions of society through state formation in the Indian subcontinent. It also traces the changes that happened in regions of the subcontinent that are away from the Ganga Plains and to which the brahmanical state order made conquests.

Chapter 3 is an examination of democracy in the modern state vis-à-vis ground realities in India and how the modern school continues to both uphold and to confront the reproduction of brahmanical relationships. It also examines some possibilities of democratic learning that have emerged in social studies.

1
STUDYING SOCIETY

Introduction

Societies are formed on the basis of two important relationships made by human beings, namely, with nature, and with each other. These create patterns of economic and social practices, evolving a form and a structure to society.

A 'community' is not a society. For instance, communities like Bhil, Naga, and Bodo belong to tribal society. This implies that people belonging to very different geographies, languages, and customs could have the same social structure. Whereas language and customs are concrete practices that differ from one community and geography to another, the social structure could be more or less the same. Structure is an abstraction derived from the concrete practices of communities evolving from the relationships with nature and of people with one another.

Do people across the world live in the same sort of societies? Have societies been changing across time, and are they still changing?

Human beings had been hunters and gatherers to procure food from nature. They shared food, like meat after hunting, and moved from place to

DOI: 10.4324/9781003449348-3

place. This form of human society with social ties of a loose pattern is called a **band**. Territories and ownerships, that indicate social control of nature, as well as sexuality, developed much later in human history.

Changes started to happen around 10,000 years ago with human beings sowing seeds to yield grains. As the 'cultivation' of food grains evolved through the sowing of seeds, the need to stay in a place perhaps became more pronounced, compared with foraging. Domestication of animals also evolved a relatively more on-site procurement of food, like milk and meat. Animals also became sources of power for labour, like pulling a plough. The production of food as a geographically on-site activity brought changes in the practices of society. This is the beginning of a **tribal society,** that evolved changes in geographic, cultural, and social practices. Cultivation of crops required a synchronised sort of labour, as did hunting of large animals, and such contexts could have paved the way for collective actions and thoughts:

> Whether it is hunting, gathering, or cultivation, the building of houses, the rearing of children, or the celebration of festivals, in a tribe, these activities are done together as a community.... There is no private property and there is a shared understanding of nature and cultural expressions. For instance, the tribal dances are expressions of togetherness. The religious understanding is one of nature worship.
>
> *Sunny, 2022; 52*[1]

Traditional fishing and nomadic communities also show similar social relationships. Changes started to happen in the tribal social formation around 2,500 years ago with the selective breeding of crops and animals. This marked interventions into and control of the productions of nature. The family emerging as a fundamental unit of society, and its stability getting linked to the stability of the changing society, paved the way for the control of women's sexuality. The family as a microcosm of both production and reproduction, stabilised through brahmanical rituals, played a crucial role in creating and maintaining the caste system in the Indian subcontinent. Chakravarti (2002) underlines the nuanced relationships between production, reproduction, labour, and caste hierarchies. Engels had in 1884[2] described this relationship in society in the formation of the state and private property.

Whereas many people laboured to produce food grains and goods, a few others started to assert by procuring 'ownership' of land and the produce thereof. The fruits of labour thus became separated from those who laboured. The practice of slavery emerged. The labouring people had very little to eat as only meagre amounts were shared with them. The landowners sold the excess grains through trade to create wealth for themselves.

In the state, territories in which nature, people's labour, and their produce were controlled by the rulers, the latter sought to acquire more land, people, and power, and so wars were fought. Armies became an integral part of the state. Some men were freed from production of food and goods and reserved for use as soldiers and army personnel.

The king did not directly control the people. There were intermediaries who were given the responsibility and power to execute these jobs and held direct power over the people. They also provided troops for the king. Generally, it was the norm that land in the state belonged to the king, and people were tenants who cultivated the land and paid tax to the king. The powerful intermediaries collected tax from the people on behalf of the king. The intermediaries were the officials of the king who were granted land. They were expected to pay the king a small fraction of their revenue from the land. They held more wealth than people at large. They were known variously as feudal lords, fiefs, *Samants*, and so on.

The society that changed in this way from the tribal one and took the form of the state in which controls on sexuality, wealth and power were executed through feudal lords, and where the king was supreme and the labouring people a less powerful mass, is called the **feudal society**.

In the Indian subcontinent, this system evolved into a complex system of 'castes'. It defined the nature of labour as well as the location within the social structure. For instance, in the **caste system**, there were shoemakers, carpenters, barbers, potters, and so on who were each placed within a hierarchy, and whose offspring were obliged to continue the same production or service as their father. The carpenter's son became a carpenter and the potter's son a potter. This pattern cannot be changed. The labouring castes of people became a class who did not own land and who had no say in their own labour. Thus, sexuality and labour were controlled along with the relationships with nature (ownership of land and production).

The structure of unequal societies under feudalism had ensured a distinct, deep, and hierarchical relationship between women and men in society. This structure is described by the presence of inequality at every socioeconomic level of society and is most basically played out through the hierarchy in families. These hierarchical relations between women and men, which is socially created, are not a matter of biological difference between females and males in nature but a matter of power and control. A number of social practices then emerge like gender-based ownership and inheritance of land, and the lineage following on from the male family line. These denote the alienation of women from nature (land) and from claims to their own bodies. Through the changed processes of production and reproduction, women are relegated to contexts of less power and wealth across all the hierarchical levels of wealth and power.

Private property brings in the issue of inheritance. The control of women's sexuality plays a crucial role. Women's reproduction through men from the same social strata is the key to ensuring social hierarchy in the changing social order of feudalism. This practice, termed as **patriarchy,** denotes a social system in which men predominantly hold power in familial and political leadership, control of property, authority, and social privilege. These changes contradict the tribal society that mostly trace their lineage through women. Private property, surplus production of wealth, and a hierarchical social structure and the state are not usually the characteristics of the tribal society.

Changes happening in the production process developed the trade of grains and goods among places, different peoples, and kingdoms. Transportation by land and water was continuously innovated. Bullocks, horses, camels, mules, and donkeys were utilised to pull carts. Ferries, boats, and ships were made to transport goods across rivers, lakes, seas, and oceans. From the early fifteenth to the early seventeenth centuries, traders from Western Europe travelled to the continents of Africa, North and South America, Asia, and Australia in search of people to be enslaved as labour, for trade of goods, and in search of produces. These also led to territorial control of lands in different continents by European feudal states.

Territorial controls led to many lands being transformed into 'colonies' of European states. Colonialism is a process by which peoples and lands are controlled and their produces extracted to benefit the lands and peoples of the colonists. That is why colonists remain as foreigners. It is distinct from the expansion of territories and the enlargement of kingdoms/states that was discussed earlier. The Western European economy went through an historic economic surge through the extraction of resources and control of people of other continents. The massive wealth that accumulated in the states of Western Europe through these processes of colonialism was utilised for the innovation and creation of machines and factories. Factory production made profits through greater and more rapid production of goods and expanded markets across the world.

These changes happened approximately three hundred years ago. The expansion and development of new cities as the sites for factory production and as nodes of transportation, like new ports, became marked geographic features. Large-scale production and markets evolved infrastructure for transport and continuing technological innovations for greater production.

The factory workers who assisted the machines were paid wages for their labour. The society now became divided hierarchically into the capitalist and the labour classes. The former owned the land, the capital, and the machines and equipment for factory production. The latter sold their labour to earn wages for a living. These developments led to historic changes in society and did away with the feudal society in Western Europe. The transition was to a **capitalist society** in which a new set of hierarchical relationships evolved.

These changes separated production from the arena of the family. The products of the potters, carpenters, handloom weavers, and others began to be produced in the factories of the cities. The separation of the workplace from the home led to bifurcation of labour largely based on gender. Domestic labour became focussed around food processing, upbringing of children, and the caring of the aged. These developments not only restructured gender spatially but also created a dichotomy of paid and free labour. The capitalists paid the labourers only just enough to be able to buy the raw materials with which to cook food. This does not take into count the labour done by women, that is necessary to maintain the family of the labourers through domestic labour as well as through reproduction. Thus, women subsidised the wages that the capitalist paid to the factory workers.

Capitalism created a contrast between the industrial cities and towns on the one hand and the agricultural villages on the other hand. It also changed the nature of the state in Western Europe. People, who were called the subjects of the king in the feudal state, now became 'citizens' of the modern state who elected their administrators for a fixed period of time. Political parties emerged that competed through elections. Modern institutions of legislature, executive, and judiciary evolved. Modern nations emerged in different parts of the world. Armies were upgraded and the nature of warfare changed. Weapons were manufactured in factories and these were also traded between nations.

The world saw two 'World Wars'.

- What makes these wars very different from wars fought among feudal states?
- Find out from other sources why these wars were fought.

14 Society, state, and consciousness

- Find out about the atomic bomb and where it was dropped during the Second World War.
- What are the continuing impacts of the atomic bomb on the world?
- Find out about the concept of 'world peace'.

The inequality in capitalist society has often been critiqued. The establishment of a more equal society was pursued in many parts of the world. This is the aspiration for a **socialist society**. The idea is largely inspired across the world by the writings and works of Karl Marx and Friedrich Engels.[3] The world has seen conflicts of ideas between capitalism and socialism. This is because the uneven distribution of wealth in society through the structures of the capitalist state is sought to be changed by those who support socialism. Many countries have declared themselves as socialist countries, the meanings of which show a range of possibilities. While some have been led by the left political parties inspired by Marxist and communist thoughts, there are others like India who are multi-party republics and stand by socialism. In the Preamble to the Constitution of India, it is stated that "we, the people of India, having solemnly resolved to constitute India into a Sovereign Socialist Secular Democratic Republic and to secure to all its citizens."

A very brief sketch of the historic transitions of human society is given above but it has to be noted that geographically different types of societies exist at the same time, as you can see across the Indian subcontinent. These societies are not insulated from each other. There has been trade and relations of co-existence between tribal communities and princely states. As land becomes owned, and ceases to be shared, co-existence becomes challenged, and some people are marginalised. The capitalist extraction of resources through mining, tourism, and other activities in contemporary times is dispossessing tribal communities, traditional fishing communities, and others from their habitats, livelihoods, and relationships with nature.

In studying about societies, a significant question is focussed on the social processes that continue across time and geographies. What continues, what changes, and why? What are the practices that have tried to change the social and economic inequalities? Social science studies the concreteness, the abstractions, and the linkages between the two.

In making sense of the world

Long ago, people wondered how the world began, and how life evolved. We can find creative explanations from stories of indigenous/tribal peoples. They are known as 'creation myths' or 'creation legends'. The word 'creation' refers to the ideas of the creation of the world, either by some supreme power or in some other way.

Communities across the world have created such legends. They can be seen as the beginnings of the awareness of human beings about themselves in relationships with the world and with other living beings. Broadly, there are two types of creation legends – one that describes how the world was created and how everything originated and the other that describes how specific techniques or cultural life evolved. Given below is a creation legend from which you can gather both components. This is from the Gond tribal community of Central India (Figure 1.1)[4].

In the legend, we can see two important ideas: (a) the original creation by a supreme power, and (b) toolmaking by human beings. It also throws light on how humans observe and learn from nature. There are specific tree names mentioned which have significance in that particular geography.

16 Society, state, and consciousness

FIGURE 1.1A In search of Clay.

Studying society **17**

Kekda mal found the earthworm.

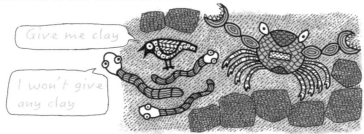

Kekda mal squeezed out some clay from the earthworm. The crow grabbed it.

Baba was happy to recive clay and asked Makda dev, the spider to spin a web across the water.

Baba spread clay across the web and released animals, birds and other living beings on the earth.

FIGURE 1.1B   Creating Life.

18 Society, state, and consciousness

The Gond man came to the baba.

Baba plucked three hairs from his head and threw them on the earth.

They took roots and grew as the mango, the teak and the kassi trees.

Man began to chop a tree.
A woodpecker imitated those actions.

Man was distracted and the pieces of wood became crooked in shape.

Angrily he threw the hatchet at the woodpecker. The hatchet disappeared in the sky.

Man went to Baba for help.
Baba gave him some ash.

FIGURE 1.1C Making of Tools.

Studying society **19**

Man placed the ashes on the roots. The trees flowered
and the earth was filled with forests.

He threw the crooked wood on the earth.
A bamboo maiden emerged from that place and
spread herself all over the earth.

The crooked piece of earth became
the first plough with which man
learnt to cultivate crops.

The Gond woman thought...

The goddess of grain should not disappear. What should I do?

She watched the white ant, and
learnt to make a lillar kothi (granary).

She filled up the granary with
grains and fed the whole world.

FIGURE 1.1D The Granary.
Source: Created by Vrushali Joshi.

The world is rich with creation legends on every continent and country. Long (2020)[5] writes that the names given to plants, trees, animals, and birds, as well as to landforms, are a part of human relationships in space. The legends have been communicated orally from generation to generation. Moreover, they extend their influence to community rituals like dances, folksongs, and masks. For instance, in the book on Mizoram[6] in the series 'People of India', Sengupta et al. writes on the Lusei tribe:

> The Lusei have a variety of folksongs and folktales. Many of these songs depict the history of their origin, descent, and routes of migration. A good number of legends deal with the creation of the world and the first appearance of mankind and other natural phenomena.
> *(1995, p. 90)*

If you know of such folktales and folksongs in your area that can be linked to creation legends, please record them.

Do you find any commonality with the creation legend narrated above? Can you write about them?

The creation legends also influence the artistic designs of crafts. Thus, a living relationship exists between the legends and the cultural practices of communities. The celebration of the legends in these ways defines their cultural life in a specific manner. Within indigenous communities, as well as within religions in a later period in history, the creation legends lead the people of the community or religion to see the world in a particular way. Hence, it shapes 'world views', which include attitudes, values, and expectations concerning the world, and guide collective thoughts and actions.

Warli art

Warli art is an example of a cultural relationship between the creation legend and art forms.

Ranjit Hoskote (1996)[7] writes that Warli art is a sort of receptacle into which the community puts its effort and from which it draws its selfhood. The subtle connections between humanity and the cosmos, built through traditional insight, are continuously drawn. The drawings provide a sacramental order to the communal life, embedding it in the life of the universe and affirming its ties with the natural cycles of growth and rejuvenation.

He further notes that the forms and magical belief systems with which Warli paintings are associated are of Neolithic descent. The 'Neolithic' implies the phase of human society that developed the cultivation of crops (which we have discussed earlier as the foundation of tribal society). The Warli paintings have great similarities with the geometrical shapes and white-outlined rock paintings of Central India, as well as with those of the Hopi and the Navajo tribes of southern North America.

Warli art also depicts the *tarpa* dance. Dances like the *tarpa* involve everyone. There is no separation between performers and audience, and there is an overall ambience of harmony and joy.

Investigating the past

The migration of people from one place to another has historically shaped places, cultures, economies, and social relationships. Such processes have happened across the world.

How can we figure out what *probably* happened in the past? What are evidences? How do we search for them? And how do we *interpret* them? The two italicised words are of prime significance in the process of knowing about societies of the past time–space. Here are some examples of sources from which inferences can be made.

Oral traditions

Creation myths are examples of oral traditions that are passed on from generation to generation by word of mouth. These extend from times when there was no written word. Let us look at another example. 'Manganiyars' of Rajasthan are musicians and storytellers, mainly from Jaisalmer, Jodhpur, Bikaner, Barmer, and Jalor. Their songs and stories tell us of several happenings of the past. They can easily recall accounts of ten to fifteen generations of their own and other families. They used to provide musical services to people and receive camels, goats, cattle, and cash in exchange. Their stories are sources of happenings of the past. These are often different from what the rulers usually took care to record as written documents, which had more to do with the running of the states, battles, or the valour of kings.

> In your area, do you know of any oral traditions that give information on the past? Check folk artists in your area and, if you find anything that belongs to the oral traditions, you can record them, interview the persons, and write about the historic information that you can gather.

Written documents

Government documents, political declarations, letters, autobiographies, diaries, and so on are important sources of knowing about bygone time–space. In this category of sources, '**travelogues**' occupy a special position. People have travelled from one place to another for various reasons. They have then written about their travels, of places in which what we experience today is very different from how it was in the past.

From such records, we can interpret processes of continuity and change in society. Megasthenes, Hiuen Tsang, Marco Polo, and several others are well-known travellers whose travelogues are valuable documents of space–time. Many of them were eminent scholars like Al-Biruni, an Iranian scholar of astronomy, physics, mathematics, history, medicine, linguistics, and so on. His writings on eleventh-century India are considered to be remarkable.

Taking another example, we get information about Lakshadweep from the writings of Ibn-e-Batuta, who was a Moroccan scholar and had visited the islands in the twelfth century. People of Minicoy Island, he writes, were devout Muslims. These are records that show us how people had taken to Islam in much earlier times, about four centuries before people in the northern part of the subcontinent embraced Islam. In the times described by Batuta, trade as well as institutions of education in the Arab region extended the exchange of culture and knowledge in the Arabian Sea trade region.

> From other sources, find out about the writings of:
>
> - Megasthenes, who travelled to the Indian subcontinent from Greece in the 4 BCE.
> - Hiuen Tsang (or Xuanzang) from China in the 7 CE.
> - Marco Polo from Venice in the last decades of the 13 CE.
> - All these travellers had distinctly different interests in travelling. What were they?

CE and BCE are used as secular terms in place of AD and BC. AD stands for 'anno Domini', meaning 'in the year of the Lord', BC for 'before Christ', CE

Studying society 23

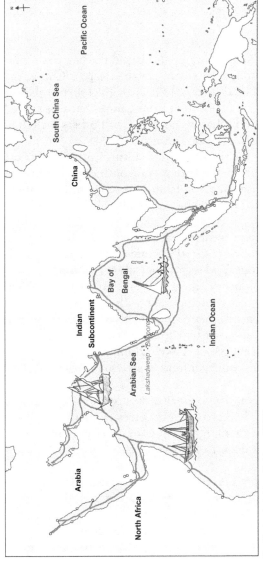

The ships shown in the sketch are called dhows. A dhow is a generic name given to traditional ships which has one or more masts with lateen or settee sails. These were commonly used in the Indian Ocean. Beypore (in North Kerala) still makes them from wood, which is considered the largest handicrafts in the world, and is called Uru in Malayalam. Traditionally they have been cargo ships. But the modern versions, that are bought by rich royal families of Arabian countries, are luxury yachts with bedrooms, kitchens and modern navigation systems.

FIGURE 1.2 A sketch of the Arabian Sea trade region (eleventh-to-twelfth century).

for 'common era', BCE for 'before CE' has become more widely used in the past forty to fifty years.

Marco Polo travelled along the 'Silk Road', a land-based trading route that emerged in the second century BCE and which stretched across China, the Indian subcontinent, Persia, Arabia, Greece, and Italy by the fourteenth century CE (see Figure 1.3). Silk was a major item from China that was traded in Europe. Silk was not the only item that was traded, with others including paper, gunpowder, tea, cotton, salt, copper, and iron.

The Silk Road paved the way for the mixing of cultures of Asia, Africa, and Europe. Buddhism spread from the Indian subcontinent to northern Asia, China, and Mongolia. Christianity and Islam spread from the Arabian and European regions to the east. These exchanges of ideas led to the enriching of literature and art.

The trade route created complex systems of interactions. including the spread of political ideas, religious and social customs, languages, agricultural practices, scientific knowledge, and technological innovations.[8]

Merchants began their long journey along the Silk Road from **Xi'an**. During the Han dynasty – which was contemporary with the Roman Empire – it was the site of the largest palace complex ever built anywhere in the world.

Chinese traders travelling westwards had to cross the enormous Gobi Desert. On its edge, along Crescent Moon Lake, **Dunhuang** was an oasis. This was a relief for travellers who could get food, water, and shelter on their travels.

Taxila, in modern day Pakistan, was a great centre of learning. Taxila's Buddhist monasteries and *stupas* had attracted devotees from all over Asia. The Mogao Caves nearby consist of a large number of caves cut out of rock by Buddhist monks over a period of 1,000 years. These are a UNESCO World Heritage Site.

Balkh (or **Bactra**) was the key centre of Zoroastrianism. It was later known as the place where the prophet Zoroaster had lived and died.

Samarkhand, in present-day Uzbekistan, is located at the centre of the Silk Road. Ibn Battuta, who visited Samarkand in 1333, remarked on the exquisite beauty of the city. In the modern-day city, the turquoise tiles of

Studying society 25

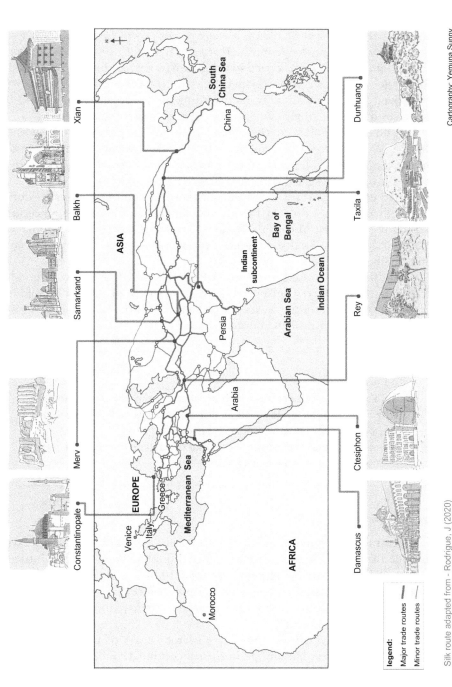

FIGURE 1.3 A sketch of the silk trade route (eleventh-to-twelfth century).

three exquisite *madrassas* give it a beautiful appearance through art in the centre of the city.

Merv, situated on an oasis, was known by several names – Alexandria, Antiochia, and Marw al-Shāhijān. It was a major city in Central Asia where human settlements existed from the third century BCE. Because of its central location, several empires tried to conquer Merv to control the silk trade.

Rey is located between the Caspian Sea and the Persian Gulf. It is a city that thrived as a result of caravans travelling along the silk trade route. It was a sacred place of Ahura Mazdā, the supreme Zoroastrian deity.

The Silk Road enhanced the spread of many religions of the world. At its peak, **Ctesiphon** was a metropolis of great diversity with people of Zoroastrian, Jewish, Nestorian Christian, and Manichaen religions living together. It lies in present-day Iraq.

Located at an important crossroads of two trade routes – a north-south route from Constantinople to Egypt, and an east-south route connecting Lebanon with the rest of the Silk Road – **Damascus** was a crucial point on the Silk Road. In the English language, the word 'damask' became a synonym for silk.

Constantinople represented the end of the Silk Road. The luxury goods of China and India were transported across the length of Asia to be sold in the markets of Constantinople. It is in present-day Turkey and had been the capital of the Eastern Roman empire.

From the sketch map and the note given along with it, find out:

- Cities and religious centres which developed along the trade route.
- The many shorter trade routes which operated as well – trade was not happening only between China and Europe.
- The architectural and artistic effects that can still be traced in the regions that were lying along the Silk Road.

Cave paintings

In the central part of India, in Madhya Pradesh, there are marvellous cave paintings in rock shelters in a place called Bhimbhetika. These paintings appear to have been made by people around 10,000 years ago. These are, therefore, from 'prehistoric' times, that is, times before human beings started to write. White and ochre colours can be seen in these paintings of animals, hunting scenes, and dances.

Such paintings, which are found in different parts of the country, are evidence of the earliest human life in the subcontinent. Similar paintings in rock shelters can be found in almost all the continents of the world, and they show much commonality in style and colours.

In the nineteenth century, Bhimbhetika was identified as a Buddhist site, but archaeological excavations, conducted in the late 1950s by the Archeological Survey of India (ASI), showed that there have been continuous settlements in the Bhimbhetika region till around the second century BCE.

The archaeological evidence shows us glimpses of human settlements in Bhimbhetika in the transitions from hunter–gatherers to cultivators. From this evidence, we can make more sense of the cave painters. The region, with more than 750 rock shelters, has been managed by the ASI since 1990. In 2003 it was declared a World Heritage Site by UNESCO.

Chakravarti (2003; 40)[9] writes that Bhimbhetika is a Mesolithic site where women are depicted as engaging in fruit gathering, as well as hunting small game using baskets and small nets. They also appear to have combined their role as mothers with their activities as gatherers. Paintings include those of a woman with a basket slung across her shoulders with two children in it, as well as an animal on her head; another one depicts a woman dragging a deer by its antlers, while a third depicts a woman engaged in trapping fish. Women carrying baskets are often depicted as pregnant, and there are group hunting scenes in which women too are present. Sometimes, they wear an elaborate headdress, and it is possible to argue that they had both a symbolic and an actual participation in ensuring the success of the hunt.

From this, it can be deduced that there were no sharp divisions of labour between men and women as developed in later times. Chakravarti (2003; 40) observe that the relative status of men and women can, at most, be characterised as 'separate but equal'.[10]

Find out from other sources:

- What is carbon dating? Is it possible to date any object through this method? Or are there limitations?
- In which places in the northeastern and southern regions of India have cave paintings been found?

- What is a Mesolithic site?
- Among tribal communities, we can still find social practices of erecting monoliths. Do you know of such practices in your community or elsewhere? Find out more about monoliths.

Megaliths

Just as in the case of cave paintings, megaliths are also found across different continents of the world. Megalithic stones, resembling dolmens, exist in all parts of India. These have been created in ancient times by placing a large horizontal capstone on top of two or more vertical stones that support the former. In the design, a chamber is created below, which is sometimes closed in on one or more sides. These have often been used as a burial chamber or tomb. These are the earliest surviving human-made monuments. These are mostly found across the Deccan Plateau, Kerala, and Goa, and in the northeastern parts of India.

These structures have been interpreted as being either grave markers or as memorials to the dead. They have a linkage to ancestor worship. There are examples of sites from which actual burial remains have been found; for instance, the mushroom-shaped burial chambers found in Kerala.

In many cases, they are constructions of roughly hewn large-sized stone slabs. In Meghalaya, where a large number of megaliths are seen,

FIGURE 1.4　A sketch of megaliths.

Source: Created by Vrushali Joshi.

the horizontal flat stones placed on the top are locally called 'moo kyn thai', meaning 'women', and the vertical stones are called 'moo shynrang', meaning 'men'. Haraniya (2018)[11] writes that the largest of these stones in Meghalaya are 8 metres high and 45 centimetres thick.

These constructions had been carried out across the world over a certain time period, perhaps, as in the case of cave paintings, signifying a comparable sort of evolution of human beings across the world. The time period of the Megalithic culture is observed as being from 2500 BCE to 200 CE.

Archaeology

We have already mentioned archaeological excavations in Bhimbhetika, and how the traces of the past obtained there brought new interpretations and understandings of the past in the region. The archaeological evidences obtained from Bhimbhetika were *artefacts*, *wares*, and *monoliths*.

Wares mostly refer to pottery and also to articles made of metals, glass, and so on. 'Artefacts' include a wide range of objects, including wares and tools, made by human beings for specific purposes like pots, metalware, jewellery, clothing, and weapons. A 'monolith' is used to describe a naturally formed single massive stone or rock. But here, we are referring to monoliths that are artefacts. 'They are like memorials meant for marking the place where the dead lay buried and later on these memorials were worshipped by the people related to the dead person'.[12] As you have gathered from the above, archaeology is a particular method of study of the human past based on material remains.

Archaeologists generally excavate or dig up the soil to unearth artefacts and other evidences. This is usually done in situations when there is a likelihood of obtaining very crucial information on the past. Only a small part of the site is usually excavated. Once an excavation is completed, archaeologists curate the collections of 'finds', analysing them, and making a research report available.

Archaeological methods are scientific and systematic. Initially, surface surveys are carried out to search for any evidence on the site. The exact location of the site and any evidence found are recorded through photography, notes, and drawings. The next step is to dig test pits. The soil is sifted to search for small artefacts.

Shovels, trowels, spades, brushes, sieves, and buckets are some of the tools that archaeologists use. Archaeologists have to be very careful not to damage any artefacts. That is why gentle tools, like brushes, are used. Once excavation has reached a certain level, the tools are changed, recordings are made, and photographs are taken. This is because further digging changes the site situation which would then not be available for anyone to see in that situation.

> Why is great care taken in dealing with evidences? How do scientific perspectives help?
>
> Find out from other sources:
>
> - Sometimes, we hear of political powers seeking the falsification of history. Why do you think that happens?
> - What is ethics in knowledge seeking? Why is it important for human society?

It is mainly through archaeological sources that we come to know of how the Indian subcontinent was peopled. There is evidence of migrations of people from one part of the globe to another from prehistoric times. Archaeology, as well as linguistic and ethnographic research, has been conducted to figure out how people moved in different times and regions. DNA procured from skeletons from burial grounds also give clues. In 2015, it was found that DNA from the petrous bone at the skull base could give very reliable information, compared with other bones of the human skeleton.

The Indian subcontinent was initially inhabited by migrants from Africa who reached it around 65,000 years ago. Africa is recognised as the cradle of human origins and culture, from where people migrated to other parts of the world. Historians like Irfan Habib and others point out the need to study the prehistory of India against the backdrop of India's geological formation and African prehistory.

> Find out from other sources:
>
> - What is DNA? How has the study of DNA hugely helped in analysing migrations of people in the past?
> - Find out about the petrous bone in the human body. Why is it able to give more reliable information from DNA than other bones?
> - Why is the understanding of geological formations important to examine the social changes across time–space?

Around 7000 to 3000 BCE, a prominent migration of people happened from Zagros, a region in Southwestern Iran. This is from where we get the first evidence of goat domestication. The people of Zagros were also agriculturists. They perhaps brought herders and cultivators to the Indian subcontinent. They mixed with the people who were already living there. It is thought that these people together went on to create the 'Harappan culture'.

The Indus Valley civilisation, or the Harappan culture, is the earliest known 'urban' civilisation in the Indian subcontinent. It is dated to have existed in the Bronze Age, the period from approximately 3300 to 1750 BCE. It comprised parts of some provinces of what are modern-day India and Pakistan. It was the largest of the four ancient civilisations, which also included Mesopotamia, Egypt, and China.

Harappa and Mohenjo-daro, two great cities, emerged around 2600 BCE in areas now located in the Sind and Punjab provinces of Pakistan, respectively. Archaeological data provide evidences of trade, art, architecture, planning, transportation, and writing. With Harappa being the first city to be excavated, the name 'Harappan culture' was coined. It had trade relations with Mesopotamia located in the area of modern-day Iraq, Kuwait, and parts of Syria. Texts written on clay and stone tablets show an independent script development, which linguists and archaeologists have not been able to decipher to date. The Mother goddess of fertility was worshipped, but there is no evidence of any religious rites or structures of worship like temples.

The Harappan culture is understood to have had an early, evolving phase (3200 to 2600 BCE approximately) and a later, mature phase. In the early phase, crop cultivation developed, with barley, wheat, peas, and lentils being the staple crops. At Kalibangan, there was a field that showed cross furrows implying intensive cultivation. Ratnagar[13] notes that writing, seals, weights with precise weight-values, possibly the spinning wheel and metallurgy are developments that identify the mature Harappan period. There was also evidence of defensive mechanisms and weapons of war:

> ...the Kalibangan cylinder ... shows two warriors with buns flanking a third person, probably a woman, with their arms raised, holding long-handled pointed weapons, probably swords or daggers...There are ballista

32 Society, state, and consciousness

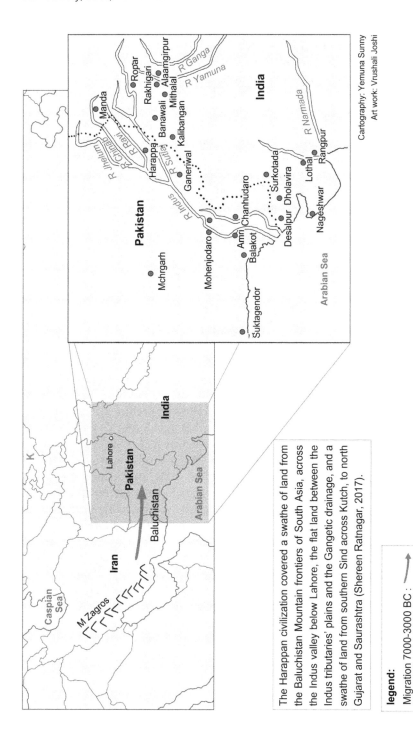

FIGURE 1.5 Migrations, mixing of people, and the Harappan culture.

The Harappan civilization covered a swathe of land from the Baluchistan Mountain frontiers of South Asia, across the Indus valley below Lahore, the flat land between the Indus tributaries' plains and the Gangetic drainage, and a swathe of land from southern Sind across Kutch, to north Gujarat and Saurashtra (Shereen Ratnagar, 2017).

legend:
Migration 7000-3000 BC : ⟶
Kazakhstan: K

or baked clay missiles (that could be thrown at the enemy from the inside of a fort) found ... on the parapet of the citadel wall of Mohenjo daro ... the elaborate gateway of that site (no enemy could rush in) where there are several turns in the entry ways.

> In the narrative above, identify the historic evidence. What are the different artefacts that are mentioned?

The second prominent migration – into the Indian subcontinent – happened after 2000 BCE. The Indo-Aryans, probably from the Kazakhstan region (Figure 1.5), migrated to the Indian subcontinent. They brought with them to the subcontinent an early version of Sanskrit and various rituals. These gradually evolved as the basis of early Vedic culture. Thapar[14] writes that the Indo-Aryan language gradually spread over northern India, incorporating some elements of Austro-Asiatic and Dravidian languages. The Indo-Aryan, she remarks, is a language label, indicating a speech group of the Indo-European family, and not a racial term. The reference is to an identity that involves language, social status, and associated rituals and customs.

The two major migrations mentioned above happened in the past 10,000 years. Several others also happened, like those from South East Asia, such as the speakers of Austro-Asiatic languages. The importance of the past 10,000 years is that it was from then on that a major change happened through the beginning of the cultivation and domestication of animals, and the emergence of the tribal society.

Historians have divided the past into such time periods, depending upon some happenings that have impacted deeply on the social life of the times that followed. For instance, the period from which writing started is the beginning of the 'ancient period'. Such categorisations of the past can be done in different ways. There is nothing standard or universal about that. Indian historians, for instance, divide the past depending on the happenings on the subcontinent. For example, the subcontinent experienced around four centuries of British colonialism. So, this can be called the 'colonial period'. This is different from the European division of time periods of history that is based on happenings in Europe. Their divisions are prehistory, classical, Middle Ages, early modern, and modern eras. There has to be some theme that distinguishes a certain time period from another. This cannot be religion, but something much more appropriate and based on real-life processes of different times-spaces. Thapar's[15] suggestion for the periodisation of Indian history is as follows:

1. Hunter–gatherers, pastoralists, and early farmers.
2. First urbanisation: the Indus Plain and Northwest India.
3. Megalithic settlements of the peninsula.
4. Chiefships and kingships, 1200–600 BCE.
5. Second urbanisation and state formation in the Ganges Plain, 600–400 BCE.
6. The Mauryan state, 400–200 BCE.
7. The rise of the mercantile community and cross-cultural contacts, 200 BCE–300 CE.
8. The creation of Sanskrit cultures.
9. Distributive political economies and regional cultures.
10. The assertion of regional identities.
11. The Mughal state and subsequent regional kingdoms.
12. British colonial rule and the Indian nationalist approach.

Conclusion

Studying society requires data, perspectives, and methodologies. Social science, as the study of society, searches for sources and evidence to examine and interpret social relations across time- space. There is a huge difference between making your own common-sense interpretations about the past (which implies the continuity into the present) and being able to examine and understand society scientifically. This is the crux of the dilemma of 'studying society' because the 'common-sense position' that you hold would be informed by your own class, caste, and gender positions. Social science as a modern discipline helps you to rise above those limitations to be able to grasp the social relationships that build society. It also throws light on the global relationships that influence your locations.

As the nature, structure and practices of society changed across time, there were spatial frictions between the earlier orders and the new one. If you try to map out the spatial dynamics of the tribal, feudal (or semi-feudal), and modern (capitalist) social formations on the Indian subcontinent, you would be able to infer their mutual relationships, which are socially, economically, and administratively perceived within a hierarchal order.

Notes

1 Sunny, Y (2022), *Sprout: A Story of Spaces and Geographia*, Eklavya Publication, Bhopal.
2 Engels, F (2010), *The Origin of the Family, Private Property, and the State*. Penguin Classics, London.
3 Karl Marx (1818–1883) and Friedrich Engels (1820–1895) were both German philosophers, political theorists. economists, historians, and social revolutionaries. Together, they wrote the famous 'Communist Manifesto'.

4 Vaswani, P (2021), 'Mythological trial of Manav Sangrahalaya: The Gond Origin Myth', http://www.dsource.in accessed 29 June 2021.
5 Long, Charles H, 'Creation myth'. *Encyclopaedia Britannica*, 20 October 2020, https://www.britannica.com/topic/creation-myth. Accessed 20 April 2021.
6 Singh, KS (ed.) (1995), *People of India: Mizoram* Vol XXXIII. Anthropological Survey of India, Seagull Books, Calcutta.
7 Hoskote, Ranjit (1996), 'Situation and symbol: A ritual identity and mode of expression under bourgeois cultural appropriation (with special reference to Warli art)', *The Indian Journal of Social Work*, Vol LVII No.1, Jan 1996, pp. 79–90.
8 Williams, Tim (2015), *Mapping the Silk Roads*: https://www.researchgate.net/publication/280096308 accessed 9 June 2021.
9 Chakravarti, Uma (2003), *Gendering Caste: Through a Feminist Lens*, Stree, an imprint of Bhatkal and Sen, Kolkata.
10 Uma Chakravarti taking from Gerda Lerner (1986), *The Creation of Patriarchy*, Oxford University Press, New York, p. 29.
11 Haraniya, K (2018), 'Meghalaya's ancient sentinels' https://www.livehistoryindia.com/story/eras/meghalayas-ancient-sentinels Accessed 20 April 2022.
12 Krishnamurthy, S and Tiwary, S Kr (2016) 'Origin, Development, and Decline of Monolithic Pillars and the Continuity of the Tradition in Polylithic, Non-Lithic, and Structural Forms'. *Ancient Asia*, 7: 1, pp. 1–14, http://dx.doi.org/10.5334/aa.78 accessed 12 June 2021.
13 Indus Valley Civilisation: Interview with Shereen Ratnagar, 27 March 2017, https://www.sahapedia.org/ accessed 15 April 2021.
14 Thapar, Romila (2002), *The Penguin History of Early India: From the Origins to AD 1300,* Penguin Books, London, p. xxiii.
15 Thapar, Romila (2002), *The Penguin History of Early India: From the Origins to AD 1300,* Penguin Books, London, pp. 30–32.

2
STATE FORMATION AND SOCIAL CONSCIOUSNESS

Introduction

The tribal structure of collectivity, and common ownership started to change with the formation of the state (kingdoms). Kingdoms tried to expand their territories and also protect them from the attacks of other kingdoms. For this purpose, some people were withdrawn from cultivation and other production areas to form armies. At the same time, royalty was defined and maintained through the luxurious ways of life of the ruling families. For all these purposes, the rulers collected tax from cultivators and other producers. These were some of the major changes happening in society as a result of state formation.

The expansion of kingdoms implied the conquest of other kingdoms as well as tribal territories. These conquests mostly happened through wars. People of the defeated kingdoms or tribal communities sometimes negotiated with the conquerors, but, often, people were made slaves by the conquerors. Sometimes, people managed to escape and sought shelter in forests away from the conquerors and the state. This is why we see numerous tribal communities living in forests and uplands. They could no longer continue their earlier practices of river valley cultivation. Instead, they gathered and hunted from the forests and also practiced small-scale cultivation.

State formation and social consciousness 37

Some kingdoms became very large through conquests of territories and became monarchies. In the Indian subcontinent, monarchies evolved along the valley of the Ganga River and its vicinity (see Figure 2.1)

What happened to the creation legends?

The tribal communities continued to keep alive the oral traditions of the creation legends, that were linked to day-to-day customs, rituals, and community practices. They also continued with a social structure that was more-or-less equal, with common ownership of land, in which they gathered, hunted, and cultivated. Their collective expressions of dance and art and nature worship, and practice of food production only at levels of community needs, characterised the tribal way of life.

In the states, new gods and religions evolved, making marked changes in the worldview. The new stories justified the emerging unequal relationships among people. 'Manusmriti', which must have been formulated in the first or second centuries, is an outstanding example that still holds an influence on social life in the Indian subcontinent. The creation legend in Manusmriti talks of 'Brahma' as the creator, who reveals the story to Manu, a sage, who, in turn, reveals it to other sages. Brahma creates the Brahman, Kshatriya, Vaisya, and Shudra castes of people through his mouth, arms, thighs, and feet, respectively. From this emerges a social system called *'chaturvarnya'* (from *'chatur'*, for 'four', and *'varna'*, for 'groups'), that is hierarchical, with the Brahman as the highest social class and the Shudra as the lowest, creating and legitimising a complicated and unequal society.

Manusmriti is in written form and is part of the ancient Vedic Sanatana Dharma, which is today called the Hindu religion. It is an instruction on how to organise society on the basis of social classes and gender. Hatcher (1996; 863)[1] in a review of Smith (1984)[2] notes how the author reminds us that classification is construction, and classification through *varna* amounts to the Brahman's attempt to 'naturalise' their view of reality. In other words, *varna* operates as an ideology, a view of the world purporting to be objective, while, at the same time, creating a society of different classes called castes.

38 Society, state, and consciousness

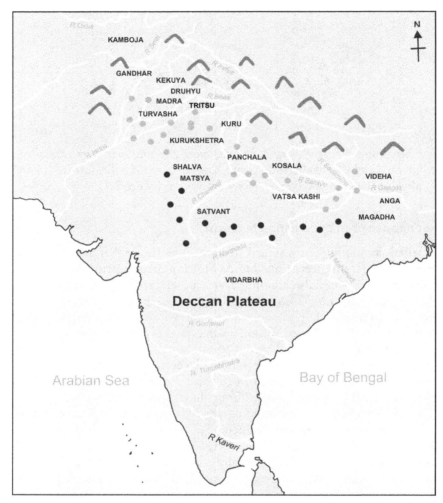

The sketch map is based on Thapar, R (2002)

Cartography: Yemuna Sunny
Art work: Vrushali Joshi

legend

Himalayas and Tibetan highlands : ⋀

The central plateaus : ●

Northern River Valleys/Plains : ◉

FIGURE 2.1   Monarchies in the North Indian River plains (1200–500 BCE).

The Kshatriya fought battles and ruled kingdoms and monarchies. Their role was legitimised by the Brahman through *yagyas*. The Brahman is the only caste who has direct contacts with the gods. For ceremonies, like weddings or death rites, the people had to depend on the Brahmans and pay them in kind (in more recent times, in cash) to live with the goodwill of the gods. The Vaishya caste conducted trade, whereas the Shudras did all the manual work. The Shudras laboured on all life-sustaining necessities like cultivation, pottery, weaving, carpentry, , leatherwork, and so on, yet they were perceived as 'untouchables'– or groups of people to be kept at bay by the so-called upper castes, lest the latter become 'impure'.

Whereas, in the tribal society, women were revered for their reproduction, in the caste society, they are considered impure at times like menstruation, particularly so in the so-called upper castes, where women could not worship or enter the kitchen at such times. The mobility and sexual choices of women were rigidly controlled. Manusmriti holds nuanced instructions on the control of the sexuality of women of all ages. It describes women as seducers who can lead men astray and make them slaves to desire and anger. The control of the sexuality of women is instrumental in maintaining the caste society.

In the tribe, there were matrilineal practices. You can still see some examples. (Urban (2011)[3] notes that '…the Khasis, Garos, Jaintias, and several other tribes of southern Assam and northern Meghalaya are matrilineal, with descent passed through the mother and property inherited by the youngest daughter'. Remnants of such practices can also be seen in Kerala and Lakshadweep.

- Examine the patriarchal practices in India and compare with matriliny. Why do women experience more confidence in the matrilineal system?
- Much of the popular literature in various Indian languages showcases the irony of the caste–gender experiences. Write about such literature in your own language that reflects the indignities and sufferings of people through this social system.
- Collect information on 'honour killings' in contemporary India. How would you analyse this as governed by a caste–gender society?

With a large majority of the people being poor, money lending was carried out by the rich and powerful castes. These dealings followed a pattern that deepened the poverty of the people in the lower rungs of the caste system. Manusmriti spelled out the different interest rates for the four varnas. While the interest on the loan was least for the brahman, it increased down the caste hierarchy, with the Shudra having to pay the maximum interest.

Today, with modern banking, money lending has seen a major decline as compared with the past. Modern banks do not treat people differently on the basis of caste. Even then, there are individual moneylending practices that often charge exorbitant interest rates.

Wealth could be produced only by the so-called upper castes. Caste and gender played the most important roles in ensuring unequal social relationships.

> Jyotirao Phule[4] in the nineteenth century coined the term *'shudradishudra'* to describe the most marginalised social group of people in Indian society. Can you find out more about the implications of the term?
> Find out from other sources how Jyotirao and Savitri Phule attempted to educate the *'shudradishudra'*?

The interfaces of the tribal and the brahmanical systems

Through the conquests of new territories, the new social order of the feudal state spread to more areas from the Ganga Plains. These processes did not bring the same outcomes as they did in the Ganga Valley. This was because the regions themselves were in different practices of relations with nature (production), social relations as well as religious beleifs. It was in such heterogenous lands that the brahmanical system attempted to incorporate and control new lands.

The *chaturvarnya* system, Rajeevan (1999)[5] writes, represents the division of labour of a production system that disrupted the primeval unity in the tribes. The new agricultural village system, depending upon the iron plough, the calendar, and the rainmaking rituals, was one in which the separation between mental and physical labour was complete. As territories expanded to new areas, this social system interfered with the tribal social forms in different parts of the subcontinent, which were in different forms of social development.

The emergence of the Rajputs in Rajasthan was historical processes of occupying the tribal settlements in the early medieval period. Areas that were inhabited by tribal communities became occupied by the setting up of markets by merchants, and the settling of brahmans and soldiers. The rulers who came to be known as Rajputs represented a mixed group of different origins who had succeeded in controlling land in such ways. There were many instances in this process when the tribal communities merged with the new system, like the Medas who are considered to have acquired Rajput status. So, the Rajput formation was a process of state formation.[6] Many emerging powerful clans came together, and consolidated power by making Rajput clans. The Hunas who had acquired sufficient political power became part of the Rajput clan list. Marriage of persons from different emerging powerful clans was a popular way of strengthening the relationships between the clans.

In the Deccan Peninsula, the Kaveri River delta (see Figure 2.2) was a fertile agricultural land, and well connected to various trade routes in the early centuries of the Common Era. The tribal formations of the Kaveri River delta was transitioning towards state formation and developing divisions of labour. The tribal heads had become kings, and some social classes had already developed on the basis of performing different types of work, but these were not 'castes', the functions of which were decided by birth. As the caste–gender system arrived in this region from the Ganga Plains, Rajeevan (1999) notes that it was relatively easily accommodated, compared with those geographies where the egalitarian tribal structure was strong. Some examples are given below.

In the southernmost part of the Deccan Peninsula, in the region that is present-day Kerala, as the *varna* system, must have reached in the first millennium CE. The tribal formation was very prevalent. Thapar (2002)[7] notes that brahman settlements that gradually occupied the various agriculturally rich areas were a source of support, for instance, to the Makotai kingdom in the Periyar Valley. These give us an idea of how the varna system transformed the regions, a process that is called 'sanskritisation'. It entailed local recruitments into brahman ranks , and adjustments or negotiations were made with the local kinship systems, for instance, the adjustments to matrilineal systems took the form of Nambudri brahman men and Nair women entering relationships of 'sambandhams.'[8] Rajeevan notes that the Kshatriya and the Shudra categories did not evolve in Kerala as they did in the Ganga Valley. Instead, these functions were conducted by the Nair caste, with Vaisya being totally absent.

In the regions lying far to the east of the Ganga Plain, along the Brahmaputra Valley, matrilineal tribal communities and practices were prevalent. Many Khasi and Garo folktales claim that the hill of Kamakhya temple was originally a site of their own tribal goddesses. Powerful mother goddesses were worshipped by many of the tribal communities, such as the Bodos, Chutiyas, Jaintias, Khasis, Lalungs, and Rabhas. Assam's kings,

42 Society, state, and consciousness

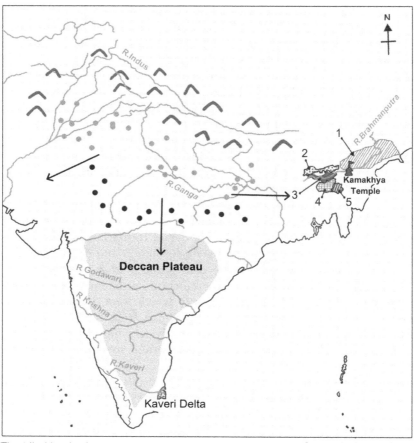

The tribal lands shown are only broad indications.

Cartography: Yemuna Sunny
Art work: Vrushali Joshi

legends :
Tribal Land
1: Chutia
2: Bodo
3: Rabhas
4: Khasi
5: Jaintias
Himalayas and tibetan highlands : ⋀
The central plateaus : •
Northern River Valleys/Plains : •

FIGURE 2.2 Interfaces of the tribal and the brahmanical systems: the north-eastern and southern regions.

from the fourth-century Varmans down to the eighteenth-century Ahoms, came from the local tribes that were only gradually 'sanskritised'.

Sanskritisation cannot be seen simply as the assimilation of the brahmanical order onto other geographies, but it involved also the absorption of tribal, non-brahmanical traditions into the brahmanical one. Urban (2011) notes how sanskritisation interacted with Kamarupa, the initial state formation in the Brahmaputra Valley located in the present-day Indian state of Assam. The complex negotiation between Sanskritic and tribal traditions can be seen in both the mythical and historical narratives of 'Kamarupa'.[9]

The mythical origin of Kamarupa is told in Kalikapurana, an important text from early Assam, dating to the tenth and eleventh centuries. is told It says that Kamarupa was conquered by King Naraka, the son of Vishnu and the Earth, who drove out the tribal hill peoples of the region and established Vedic worship in the land. But, significantly, the Kalikapurana suggests that even before the arrival of brahmanism, as implied by the arrival of Naraka in the region, Kamakhya, as 'the mother of the world', was worshipped in Assam. After his conquest of the region, Naraka was commanded by his father, Vishnu to continue worshipping the goddess.

The narrative, as Urban notes, suggests that Kamakhya was herself an indigenous goddess, who was then appropriated and absorbed into the brahmanic system that pursued the worship of the goddess in the same way as it was done before their arrival at Kamarupa.

The brahmanical gods thus play different roles as emerging in the negotiations and contestations in different locales. In some cases, the tribal communities expressed in their stories their resistance to the brahmanical conquests and the refashioning of the system which took away the egalitarianism of their prior system. Theyyam as an art form provides ample evidences of such resistance and reflections.

Theyyam

'*Theyyam*' is a ritual dance in North Kerala and South Karnataka, performed by tribal and *dalit* communities. There is a large variety of theyyam, with different folklores and stories around them. For instance, '*Devakoothu theyyam*' is performed by women. In '*kaliyattom*', the performer, who is a man, represents a legendary blind figure, capable of a deep vision through his inner eyes (Pereira, 2018)[10]. Two assistants hold his hands on either side as he walks over a bonfire, accompanied by drums and songs. The performer of theyyam wears an elaborate headgear and immediately s/he assumes a supreme power.

In '*Maari theyyam*', the narration is of a goddess returning on her wooden ship from a visit to Aryanadu, implying the northern part of the subcontinent. Two evil spirits of Aryanadu, called Maari and Mamaaya, boarded the wooden ship surreptitiously and reached the region where they spread calamity and made conquests. The desperate people called the magician Polla, a Pulaya[11] youth to drive away the evil ones by performing rituals.[12]

The story depicts the intrusion of the brahmanical order into the tribal system. Pereira (2018) notes that theyyam often plays themes of protests against the caste system and the unfair distribution of wealth. Anurag (2017)[13] observes that many versions of theyyam also portray martyred people of the so-called lower castes, who were killed for opposing the conventions of the caste system.

Theyyam is a ritual art form thousands of years old:

- How does it express resistance to the reorganising of their society through the state/brahmanism?
- The 'blind' theyyam performer has 'deep visions'. There is a certain importance in his being able to see what others cannot see. Do you think this implies social consciousness?
- How is the art form still being used for social resistance?
- What possible purposes could the mask be serving in some performances?

Changing polity and people's resistance and philosophy

The state and its practices that developed caste, class, and gender have been resisted across the Indian subcontinent.. One of the most outstanding examples is the ' '*lokayata*', meaning 'that which was prevalent among the people'. Chattopadhaya[14] (1992; xv), who had studied lokayata, perhaps most extensively, notes that it implies 'that which is essentially this worldly'. In its original form it must have been very ancient, though how very ancient, it is impossible to be precise about. It was pre-Buddhist and pre-Upanisadic. It eventually became a highly developed philosophical system and represented the strongest opposition to the earliest form of Indian idealism, namely the Vedanta.

As the original literature of Lokayata (also known as Charvakas) has been lost, sources available to us today are only their interpretations. These are the *shastras*, *Mahabharata* and *Ramayana*, documents of conversations with Buddha, and Jain literature. The writings on lokayata which are available are often biased against that tradition because they had taken a stand against the powerful social philosophy of brahmanism. They rejected ideas like reincarnation of birth, the journey of the soul to heaven/hell after death, religious rites, '*punya*' (good and holy deed), and destiny. They pointed out the insignificance of the *Vedas* and how those function only as a livelihood for priests. Chattopadhyaya (1992; 30) underlines the sufficiently strong grounds in favour of Lokayatikas being the first logicians of the country, in which the birth of Indian logic was linked up with the defense of popular interest against religious deceptions.

In contradistinction to the thoughts of Buddha and others, lokayatas were materialist, who did not reject worldly desires. Instead, they defined heaven as a country/place on earth where people can live without unnecessary control. The rule of a king, they remarked should be a function of justice, knowledge, and compassion. Charvakas had participated in the proceedings of the court of Emperor Akbar, where they recommended welfare activities for the people. So, it is inferred that they spread their influence not only among the people but also among the rulers. Chattopadhyaya (1992; Xxii) observes that so long as human consciousness retains its moorings in manual labour, it remains instinctively materialistic. The emergence of the idealistic in the human consciousness presupposes a separation of thought from action of mental labour from manual labour, along with a sense of degradation attached to the latter.

Nehru (1989; 97)[15] notes that "possibly much of the literature of materialism in India was destroyed by the priests and other believers in the orthodox religion during subsequent periods. The materialists attacked authority and all vested interests in thought, religion and theology. They denounced the Vedas and priestcraft and traditional beliefs, and proclaimed that belief must be free and must not depend on pre-suppositions or merely on the authority of the past. They inveighed against all forms of magic and superstition. Their general spirit was comparable in many ways to the modern materialistic approach; it wanted to rid itself of the chains and burden of the past, of speculation about matters which could not be perceived, of worship of imaginary gods."

Another example is the *Ajivaka* that was formed by Makkhali Ghosla in sixth-century BCE who pointed out the futility of the priestly rituals. He pointed out that material elements, like water, earth, air, and fire, were the core of life processes, and not the Brahman. The so-called upper castes condemned Ajivaka and described them as confusion-creating artisans. Ajivaka, as a group of thinkers, belonged to the labouring class and the so-called lower castes.

The consciousness that emerged from early Buddhism in the sixth-century BCE, also questioned the unequal society of the kingdoms and monarchies. Omvedt (2003)[16] points out the emergence of two major political formations – the stratified, but still 'tribal' *gana-sanghas*, and an emerging monarchy. The former was democratically and collectively governed, they were nevertheless incipient class societies themselves. Given time they may well have evolved in to 'citizen' based political societies like the Greek city states. But the material facts of geography were the major obstructions. In the Gangetic plain, the *gana-sanghas* were vulnerable and finally overwhelmed by the rising monarchies.

People entered the new society with no established moral-philosophical codes. Hence it can be said that Buddhism arose as an all-embracing solution to the human predicament in a world of transformation. The Buddha borrowed the term and probably the model of a collective society for his Bhikku Sangha or the order of monks came from the ganasanghas.

From seventh and eighth-century CE, the Bhakti movement emerged from the southern Indian peninsula. Its origins can be traced to Tamil devotional movement influenced by Vaishnavism and Shaivism. Thapar (2002, p. 351) notes that they were an expression of local sentiment questioning the attempts at homogenisation made by Vedic Brahmanism, with its insistence on orthodox practices and social inequality. There was an emphasis on personal devotion and reciprocity. Bhakti movements were broadly anti-Vedic or non-Vedic, and its origins could also be sought in the Tamil Shangam poems from which the poetry of love and devotion is said to have evolved. The deity as a lover could sometimes inspire the most powerful poetry on the interfaces of the sacred and the erotic.

The poems of Andal,[17] who lived in the ninth century and was one of the best-known women poets, were popularly sung in the Tamil region. In her poems, she sees Vishnu, not as a giver but as someone from whom she demands reciprocity. This is in contrast to Sanskrit traditions of reverence and obeisance. In place of status, privilege, and knowledge associated with the Vedic religion, here we see the focus on emotional and spiritual experiences. Andal belonged to a privileged caste. In her poems, she expresses sexual desires in union with Vishnu and she rejects the established path of marriage.

But, in later times, these traditions were reinterpreted within the framework of patriarchy, and Andal became considered a goddess. A couple of years back, there was a heated discussion as someone termed her the first feminist and she was also referred to as a *devadasi*. The discussion took on political turns, and the question was raised on whether it was right for brahmans, whose system is patriarchal, to invoke the legacy of Andal.

In the twelfth century, Basavanna, a minister in the Kannad region, became a proponent of Bhakti. In the same period, in the Warkari movement of Maharashtra, Tukaram, who belonged to a suppressed caste, had started to write on religion. He was strongly rejected by the powerful castes. Sects with teachers and poets propagating bhakti found expressions in North India in the fourteenth century. Thapar (2002, 485) notes that this was not a proselytising movement, but an expression of similar thoughts arising out of not dissimilar conditions. Bhakti evolved literature and songs in local languages like Tamil, Kannad, Marathi, Awadhi, Bhojpuri, Punjabi, Maithili, and so on.

Bhakti is comparable to Sufism, which originated in Arabia and spread to the Indian subcontinent. We can often see both these movements coming together, of which Kabir is a prominent example. In the fifteenth century, Kabir critiqued the hollowness of the religious practices of Hinduism and Islam. Bhakti and Sufism achieved a blooming of social values, art, culture, religion, and politics. Kabir had been threatened by both Hindus and Muslims for his views, which are well reflected in his couplets:

Saints I see the world is mad.
If I tell the truth they rush to
Beat me,
If I lie they trust me

(Kabir, Shabad-4)[18]

But ironically, when he died, both Hindus and Muslims claimed him as theirs.

In the sixteenth century Mira Bai in Merta of Rajasthan, who took to the Bhakti movement, considered Rabi Das of Varanasi as her guru. This caused immense upper-caste anger as Mira belonged to the Rajput princely circles and Rabi Das was from the caste of *chappal* makers.

In the seventeenth–eighteenth centuries Gurugovind Singh critiqued the caste system and attempted to bring together some basic premises of Bhakti and Sufism. Through this process, he established Sikhism.

Mira

In children's story books and films, Mira is known only as an ardent devotee of Krishna. This has created popular imageries that contradict her life as a bold woman who pushed aside caste, gender, and class and lived as a *fakir* among ordinary people, despite strong resistance from the upper castes.

Omvedt (2003; 36) points out that the social situations during the Bhakti movement have resulted in repression, and perhaps murder of radical bhaktas such as Tukaram, and the effort to totally wipe out the contributions of Dalit bhaktas such as Nandanar and Cokamela illustrates the dominance of brahmanism and the hardening of caste social structure in medieval India. Bhakti movement did not have a materialistic base. Thapar (2002; 444) mentions how there were a few instances of what have been interpreted as peasant uprisings, but the more widespread lack of these is partly attributed to the ideology of bhakti directing attention away from the impoverishment of material conditions.

- From the above narratives, identify different instances in which new thoughts opposed existing social practices. Which practices were each of them trying to critique and break?
- How would you reflect on the reinterpretations made by the dominant, patriarchal society on Andal and Mira?

Romila Thapar (2020; 5)[19] notes:

> When ... Buddhists, Jainas, Ajivikas questioned Vedic Brahmanism, there followed a long period of discussion about the ideas that came out of this questioning. This is reflected not only in the remarkable inscriptions of Ashoka Maurya but also in sections of the *Mahabharata* that were composed at this time.
>
> There was also more than a hint of it in the subsequent forms taken by Hinduism, as, for instance, by some of the bhakti *sants*. When the

bhakti poet Ravidas describes his vision of a utopia and speaks of a social equality that had no use for caste hierarchies, he is giving form to dissent. This tells us about the priorities of those that control society and those that question it. But these aspects don't often find a place in the teaching of social history – they remain religious texts whose implicit views about society are seldom commented upon analytically.

The history of dissent and protests has influenced the dominant practices to some measure. We have also seen above that the Vedic religion had changed some of its practices in tune with religious and social practices in different regions in the subcontinent.

> Find out from other sources about the inscriptions of Ashoka Maurya mentioned above. These and other evidences show you that there are crucial 'absences' of information on dissent, discussions, and shifts in ideas in our teaching/learning materials. What are your reflections on this?

Thapar (2020; 2) also points out that the Shaiva and Vaishnava sects of the Puranic religion did not agree with each other, just as the Barelvis and the Deobandis of the Quranic religion also disagreed with each other.

Joseph (2018)[20] remarks that Indians have created a long-lasting civilisation from a variety of heredities and histories. The genius of Indian civilisation during its best periods has made inclusion, not exclusion, the central theme of India's genetic makeup.

Religion and the state

Given below is a list of some of the ancient civilisations of the world:

Mesopotamian civilisation (3500–500 BCE). In present-day Iraq, Syria, and Turkey; several main gods and thousands of minor gods worshipped; astronomy, medicine; priests created rituals to honour the patron deity of the city-state.

Indus Valley civilisation (3300–1900 BCE). Banks of Indus River; in present-day Northeast Afghanistan to Pakistan and Northwest India; architecture, accuracy in measuring length, mass, and time; perhaps, priest-kings existed who controlled the economy.

Egyptian civilisation (3150–30 BCE). Banks of Nile River, in present-day Egypt; construction of pyramids; religion with a large number of deities; the state and religion were inseparable; the pharaoh was the head of state and seen as the representative of the gods on earth.

Greek civilisation (2700–479 BCE). In present-day Italy, Sicily, North Africa, and as far west as France; concept of democracy, the senate, the Olympics; they believed in gods who were involved in all aspects of human life, and there was no separation of religion and state.

Mayan civilisation (2600 BC–900 AD). Around present-day Yucatan, Mexico; complex understanding of astronomy; the kings sought the advice of the priests who had great influence on how the kings ruled; Mayans developed a hierarchical state ruled by kings and priests.

Chinese civilisation (1600–1046 BCE). Banks of the Yellow and Yangtze Rivers; invention of paper, silk, printing, compass; during the Han Dynasty, the emperor became clearly identified as the mediator between the gods and the people.

Persian civilisation (550–331 BCE). Present-day Iran; construction of the royal road; established regular routes of communication between Africa, Asia, and Europe; first Persian empire was closely connected to the religion Zoroastrianism.

Roman civilisation (550–465 BCE). Present-day Rome; in the tenth century, both the state and the church were expanding their powers; the Catholic church declared that the role of the state was primarily to defend the cause of the church.

Aztec civilisation (1345–1521 CE). Southcentral region of pre-Columbian Mexico; agriculturists, developed army; religion of Aztecs had several goddesses and gods, like god of rain and of war; their religion was controlled by high priests.

Incan civilisation (1438–1532 AD CE). Present-day Peru; large empire in South America; builders of fortresses; kings were considered the direct descendants of the sun god; high priest was the second most powerful person in the empire, after the king.

> From other sources find out more about the different early civilisations mentioned above. As state formation strengthened:
>
> 1. Was there an effort to bring people under a common religion?
> 2. Was there a trend of redefining the role and image of women, which was also sanctified by religion?
> 3. Did religion help the state to create a hierarchical society?

In taking people into the fold of the state, to be part of a system of not only production and labour, but also of socioeconomic control, religion played an important role. We can contrast this with the tribal and folk cultures. In the tribal formation, religion, or more correctly, spirituality, with a primary relationship with nature, the creator, and people, therefore did not have society bifurcated in to levels of privilege and of want. Let us examine this aspect a little more closely in order to understand the processes of the state vis-a-vis the geographies of tribal society.

Whenever states have attempted to capture tribal lands in the past, the tribal communities often fled to more secure places. So, geographically, there is a conglomeration of tribal spaces, culture, and religion, even as perpetually threatened, that attempt to live in the ethos of a stateless society. Even today, you can see the modern state displace tribal communities as forest lands are occupied by the state and corporates for developmental projects like mining and the building of dams.

Scott[21] calls attention to the relations between landscape and state formation. He notes that, in pre-modern Southeast Asia, the concentration of personpower was the key to political power. The creation of kingdoms was easiest where there was a substantial expanse of flat, fertile land, watered by perennial streams and rivers, and, better yet, not far from a navigable waterway.

Today, as these spaces fall within the territories of modern states, there are many aspects of these two systems that do not overlap, and the concept of religion is one of them. Modern states do not typically align with religion as feudal states did. But the modern state is a descendent of the feudal and holds institutional structures of religions. As with production, social stratifications, wealth production, and ownership, religion is also a matter of contestation, negotiation, or assertion happening between the state and the tribal communities.

Citing an example, the Census of India in its enumeration of population, has largely been recording tribal religion as 'Hindu'. In Jharkhand, in the 1990s people had demanded a change in this practice and in 2020, they protested and asserted that their religion is '*sarna*', the worship of nature. They insisted that the Census of 2021 should have a tribal religion code. The Jharkhand state assembly passed a resolution on the same.

You have seen that tribal communities across the subcontinent, in different and varying measures, were forced to replace or negotiate their gods with that of the brahmanical Hindu religion that spread and dominated the geographical, economic, and cultural spheres of the subcontinent. Some regions like the islands and hilly tracts had lesser contacts with these processes.

In these discussions, it is recalled that the different regions of the subcontinent had connections with other parts of the world. Travelling for information, trade, spiritual enquiry, and so on happened since ancient times. The differences in languages and customs did not become a hindrance for people to communicate and build relationships of various kinds.

> Find out from other sources about historic relationships between:
> - Mesopotamian and Harappan civilisations.
> - The coastal areas of the Indian subcontinent and China between the thirteenth and sixteenth centuries.

The early spread of Christianity and Islam in the southern parts of the subcontinent as well as in the islands of Lakshadweep bring forth such a process that ensued from interactions of people from different parts of the world.

Just as the state and the varna system of the Ganga Valley spread to other lands to its west, south and the northeast, and took with them the brahmanical religion, in a later period of time the Mughals, who came to India, brought with them their faith, Islam. They expanded their territory, as did all monarchies and kingdoms before them. They conquered, governed, contributed, and made an empire, as did other emperors and empires on the subcontinent.

With a history of large numbers of migrations and conquests across time–space, the inside/outside concept on the basis of religion, race, or language does not hold well. A major detour happened at a later period, with European 'colonialism' in many parts of the world like in Asia, Africa, the Americas, and so on. By creating 'colonies', the core idea was to extract resources. Unlike conquerors of earlier times who owned, inhabited, and became a part of the cultural ethos of the subcontinent, the colonialists transferred resources to Western Europe. This was a historic-geographic process of wealth accumulated on one region of the world through extractions from other regions of the world. This marked the beginning of a global process of economic transfer and change, and gave way to the rise of European capitalism.

The emergence of capitalism

You have read in Chapter 1 about the cave paintings of the hunter-gatherer society, and how the river valleys had emerged most prominently in the creation of surplus production, social stratifications, and the state, several contexts that, by being together in time and space, have created socioeconomic and cultural exchanges, as well as changes. Perhaps one of the most important tasks in the endeavour of studying society is to capture the contexts of socioeconomic changes..

Society after state formation is most broadly described as feudal. This implies the presence of feudal lords who were answerable to the ruler of the state (king/monarch). In Europe, feudalism emerged from a prior system of slave labour. In the Indian subcontinent and in many other regions, even as there was some slave labour, it cannot be described as a slave mode of production (it was the varna system). In spite of such contextual differences, the underlying aspect that describes feudalism is the emergence of a landlord class. Here, the basic premise is of a system in which wealth and status were rooted in the ownership of land and the surplus wealth extracted from the peasants who cultivated the land. The tribal, nomadic peoples and the urban tradesmen were outside this system in which the social hierarchies, economic derivations, and cultural manifestations were directly linked to production from the land.

Early systems of trade across land in caravans as well as through major riverways and the oceans developed in different parts of the world. You have read about the Silk Road and the Arabian Sea trade system in Chapter 1. Many of the goods traded were agricultural produces, but many were finished goods, like silk, ceramics, gunpowder, and others, the control over the production of which rested with another group of people who operated from urban centres, rather than from the spatially large expanses of the countryside.

The initial system of trade, which gradually gave way to the development of capitalism, is called 'protocapitalism'. This is a commodity economy which began on all the major continents of the world and continued for approximately three centuries. Chinese scholars call this the sprouting of capitalism.[22] Blaut (1989)[23] describes it as countless centres of incipient capitalism springing up across the Old World during the two or three centuries prior to 1492, when Europeans reached the Americas. He writes that there was no major evolutionary difference between Europe and other regions of the world until 1492[24]. Everywhere, on one margin of feudal society, lay classless society (meaning the tribal formations), while, on the other, lay centres of incipient capitalism, or protocapitalism. Even though some centres were larger than others, all of the larger centres were equal in rate, direction and level of development of proto-capitalism. More significantly, they were interconnected nodes of a single hemisphere-wide network.

> In an outline map of the world, mark the following places: Malacca, Calicut, Canon, Sofala, Cairo, Timbuktu, Venice, Antwerp. You can label the oceans. Now you have a map for which you can give a title 'Incipient capitalism prior to 1492'.
>
> You can make a small note on each of the places mentioned.

The map you have made represents the world that was not neatly defined by nation-states as we know them today. Your map indicates:

- A network of trade prior to 1492.
- These were also networks through which ideas, techniques, and people, other than goods, moved between different places.
- The diffusion of ideas also included the production of ships and technologies.
- The diversity of languages and religious beliefs did not become a barrier to the flows in the network.

In production, the change in the place of things made possible through transportation is as important as the change of the form of things. This is because both these processes increase the value of commodities.

In the fifteenth century, the ships sailing in the Indian, Pacific and Atlantic Oceans could have different designs, but the same levels of technology. 'In that period, Africans were sailing to India, Indians to Southeast Asia, Arabs to China, Chinese to Africa, and so on. Europeans were basically excluded from this trade by the location of their ports' (Blaut, 1989).[25] They later travelled through the already well-charted route around Africa. The above-mentioned scenario started to change with the conquest of America by the Europeans. Blaut attempts to contextualise the European navigations historically and geographically as follows:

1. The voyage made by Columbus was one of several long-distance exploratory voyages undertaken in other times and spaces: Chinese voyages to Africa, and an Indian voyage in 1420 around the Cape of Good Hope which was said to have gone some 2,000 miles out into the Atlantic before, finding no land, the seamen turned back.
2. In the Atlantic Ocean, the trade winds make the sailing easy from the Canaries to the West Indies, and, when returning via a more northerly route, one is pushed on by the Westerlies. So navigation becomes more favourable as compared with the Indian Ocean, with strong prevailing winds around the Cape of Good Hope. Similarly, the North Pacific is a zone of storminess and unhelpful winds. Therefore, even as technologies were similar, it is most unlikely that communities in the Indian or the Pacific Oceans would have reached the Western Hemisphere at the time the Europeans did.
3. Even as West Africa, too, was in a comparable location to Europe, it did not have major ports in that period. Instead, there was massive trade from West Africa to the rest of the hemisphere over land via the Sudanic, Saharan, and other inland routes. This was much more direct and much cheaper than movement by sea. The great cities of West Africa in this period were inland cities.
4. In the Americas, the early settlers had migrated from northeast Asia, from regions that were too cold for cultivation to develop. They had to invent agriculture, which occurred only some 7,000 years ago, perhaps 4,000 years later than it happened in the Eastern Hemisphere. In 1492, the Americans had almost caught up with people of the Eastern Hemisphere but were still well behind them in terms of military technology.
5. There had been no major biological contact between the Western and Eastern Hemisphere civilisations for millennia. Devastating pandemics began after the Europeans reached the Americas in 1492 and this

basically accounted for the inability of American civilisations to survive in the face of the European attacks.

The protocapitalism of Western Europe received a boost by the massive accumulation of capital made possible through the conquest of America and later the colonisation of African and Asian regions. The merchants, artisans, landlords, and others in Europe made huge capital that gradually made them economically more powerful than the traditional landlords.

There had been much discontent with the feudal system. Whereas, in other continents, that scenario got mixed up with colonialism by Europeans, in Europe the huge capital made through colonialism was used to overthrow feudalism. Hence, Western Europe saw the transition from feudalism to the development of capitalism. In the other continents, the struggles to gradually free themselves from European colonialism became the primary necessity.

Heller[26] examines how West European advance came directly at the expense of Eastern Europe and Asia, Africa, and Latin America. The process of Western European transition entailed turning other areas into dependent economies and colonies. Seizing resources from advanced areas and from colonised regions became an intrinsic feature of West European colonialism. This gave way to the emergence of capitalism in West Europe through a worldwide process of appropriation.

As one major impact of colonialism by the Europeans was its instrumental role in ushering in capitalism in Western Europe, another impact was that gradually this economic redesigning of the world created spatial hierarchies in the form of the developed, the developing, and the underdeveloped regions.

People who have protested and continue to protest against the capitalist system include peasants, workers, women, blacks, students, transgender, and so on. At the same time, tribal communities and others have been opposing the heavy onslaught of capitalism on nature. 'Deforestation, pollution of the air from coal burning, and of the water from industrial and human waste were already problematic in the sixteenth century' (Heller, 2011, p. 242). This model spread to all parts of the world, so that we are today placed in the ecological jeopardy of global warming and climate change.

> What should development mean?
>
> - Inclusive social and economic processes?
> - Regenerative ecology?
>
> Do you think that these two aspects are deeply connected? Please examine.
>
> - Do you think that learning about society can help us to contribute to shaping a better world?
> - How would you define a 'better' world?

Conclusions

The way in which religion has been utilised in the feudal state for the control of people, and how people have articulated and resisted in different forms and ways, is part of a fascinating history of social and cultural processes on the Indian subcontinent. These resistances tried to do away with the middlemen in the institution of religion, through which caste–gender-class-based exploitations operated.

The people's formulations in the changing polity are usually represented in dominant texts and articulations as a substratum. But their vibrant role, for instance, in the arena of religion is stated by Thapar (2002; 351) as that which operated in the plain of interplays, accommodations, contestations, and experimentations. The essentials of religion that lay in the articulations of such groups tend to be overlooked by those who see religion solely through a series of texts.

Similarly, as Chattopadhyaya (1992; xiii) points out, the degree of economic development attained by a given people or during a given epoch form the foundation upon which the state institutions, the legal conceptions, the art, and even the religious ideas of people concerned have been evolved, and in the light of these things, must therefore be explained, instead of vice versa, as had hitherto been the case.

The role of the state and the critical role played by the collective consciousness of people represent a dialectical[27] relationship. This entails tensions and negotiations, influencing the ways in which every aspect of socio-economic relationship is shaped, like nature/land, politics, distribution of wealth, culture, trade, war, and peace.

Notes

1 Hatcher, B A (1996), Reviewed Work: *Classifying the Universe: The Ancient Indian Varṇa System and the Origins of Caste* by Smith, B K (1994) Review:. Hatcher, B.A, *Journal of the American Academy of Religion*, 64 (4), Thematic Issue on "Religion and American Popular Culture" (Winter, 1996), 863–866,

Oxford University Press, Oxford, https://www.jstor.org/stable/1465626, accessed 1 July 2021.
2. Smith, B K (1984), Classifying the universe: The Ancient Indian varna system and the origins of caste, Oxford University Press
3. Urban, Hugh B (2011), 'The Womb of Tantra: goddesses, tribals and kings in Assam', *The Journal of Hindu Studies* 2011; 4:231–247, https://www.researchgate.net/publication/270529066, accessed 20 January 2020, 234 pp.
4. Deshpande, G P, ed. (2002): *Selected Writings of Jotirao Phule*, Left Word Books, New Delhi.
5. Rajeevan, B (1999), 'Cultural Formation of Kerala' in Dr. P J Cherian (ed) *Essays on the Cultural Formation of Kerala: Literature, Art, Architecture, Music, Theatre, Cinema* http://www. keralahistory ac.in/publication htm.
6. Sunny, Yemuna (2022), *Sprout: A Story of Spaces and Geographia*, Eklavya Publication, Bhopal, pp. 88
7. Thapar, R (2002), *The Penguin History of Early India: From the Origins to AD 1300,* Penguin Books, London, 332 pp.
8. Only the first son in Namboodiri brahman families married women of their caste, while others had relationships known as 'sambandhams' with Nair women in the latter's house/premises and the offsprings were located socially in a hierarchy higher than the Nairs and lower than the brahmans. This way the properties of the brahman families remained consolidated.
9. First kingdom of Brahmaputra Valley that existed between 350 and 1140 CE.
10. Pereira, Filipe (2018), 'Theyyam: The Dancing Gods', *Journal of Anthropological Films*, May 2018, 2(1):1369.
11. Pulaya is one of the so-called lower castes in Kerala
12. Vijisha, P and Raja, E K G V (2016), 'Existence of untouchability towards Maari Theyyam – A traditional art form of Kerala'. *Open Journal of Social Sciences*, 4, 260–263. http://dx.doi.org/10.4236/jss.2016.43032, accessed 22 April 2021.
13. Anurag, N T (2017), 'Influence of brahminic hegemony on folk art theyyam: Historical analysis of theyyam myths and socio-cultural events in North Kerala', *International Journal of English Research*, 3 (4), July 2017, 38-42.
14. Chattopadhyaya, D P (1992), *A Study of Ancient Indian Materialism*, People's Publishing House, New Delhi.
15. Nehru, Jawaharlal (1989), *The Discovery of India (Centenary edition),* Oxford University Press, New York.
16. Omvedt, G (2003), *Buddhism in India: Challenging Brahmanism and Caste*, Sage Publications, New Delhi, 2003, 28-30 pp.
17. Rangarajan, U, '(2020), The legacy of Andal: Exploring the impact of Andal's poetry on the identity of the modern Tamil woman, Confluence-'*Journal of Interdisciplinary Studies*, 4, https://cjids.in/vol accessed 5 July 2021.
18. Hess, Linda, Singh, Sukhdev (2002), *The Bijak of Kabir*, Oxford University Press, p. 4.
19. Thapar (2020), Interview by Venkataramakrishnan, R, Romila Thapar on the history of dissent and how it shaped Hinduism and India, Scroll.in Oct 31, 2020, https://scroll.in/article/977026/interview-romila-thapar, accessed 5 June 2021.
20. Joseph, T (2018), 'How ancient DNA may rewrite prehistory in India, 30 Dec 2018, BBC News, https://www.bbc.com>world-asia-india-46616574 accessed 29 May 2021.
21. Scott, J M (2009), *The Art of Not Being Governed: An Anarchist History of Upland Southeast Asia,* Yale University Press, https://www.jstor.org/stable/j.ctt1njkkx.

22 A large number of studies can be seen that deal with this issue, like Hung, Ho-fung. 'Imperial China and capitalist Europe in the eighteenth-century global economy." *Review (Fernand Braudel Center)*, 24, (4), 2001, pp. 473–513. *JSTOR*, www.jstor.org/stable/40241528. Accessed 23 July 2021.
23 Blaut, J M (1989), 'Colonialism and the rise of capitalism', *Science and Society*, 53, (3), Fall 1989, pp. 260–296, http://www.jstor.org/stable/40404472, Accessed: 29 July 2013, pp. 276–77.
24 Christopher Colombus was sponsored by Isabella and Ferdinand, the rulers of Spain, to find a western ocean route to China and India in search of gold and spices. Instead of these lands, he reached Cuba and Hispaniola in 1492 and thought these to be China and Japan. In some of his later journeys, he reached Mexico and the American mainland. Over the next century, the riches of these lands made Spain the wealthiest and most powerful nation. Vigorous colonial activity in the Americas led to economic prosperity in and imperialism of Spain and other European countries, while the Native American people underwent huge deprivations, death, and suppression. The year 1492 marks the beginnings of European extraction of wealth and resources from other parts of the world, as well as of people in the form of slaves, and their transportation to Europe.
25 Blaut, J M (1989), 'Colonialism and the rise of capitalism', *Science and Society*, 53, (3), Fall 1989, pp. 260–296, http://www.jstor.org/stable/40404472, accessed: 29 July 2013, pp. 276–77.
26 Heller, Henry (2011), The Birth of Capitalism: A Twenty-first-century Perspective, The Future of World Capitalism, Pluto Press, London, http://library.oapen.org/handle/20.500.12657/3077, accessed 20 March 2021, pp. 33–34.
27 The conflict of opposites which evolves historical processes of change.

3
THE MODERN STATE AND CITIZENSHIP EDUCATION

Introduction

In the modern state, the people are 'citizens', who voted for the government for a certain period of time. Hence electoral 'democracy' is defined as the rule of the people through their elected representatives. Abraham Lincoln in 1863, in his speech at Gettysburg, articulated 'the government for the people, by the people, and of the people'. These words are expressed across the world as the idea of democracy in the modern state. Political parties that compete in elections negotiate the relationships between the modern state and the citizens.

Democracy is not limited to elections only. A number of aspects can build democracy in everyday lives. What are these and how are they to be spelled out and worked out? Modern states have formulated Constitutions which are national documents on democratic relationships between the people and the state. 'The Constitution of India' spells out the fundamental political code, structure, procedures, powers, and duties of government institutions and fundamental rights, directive principles, and duties of the citizens.

The promise of democracy requires extensive journeys from being a mere concept to being a praxis.[1] Without a praxis that can change the practices of feudalism and colonialism, the unequal power relationships continue. That is why India, despite having changed a lot through the modern state, holds large remnants of feudal and colonial legacies within its modern institutions. How can the people's collective agency change the relationships towards democracy? Let us look at some narratives from the ground:

'Some stories I heard, and some that my eyes saw'[2]

(Bhatnagar, 2021)

DOI: 10.4324/9781003449348-5

In the nineteen eighties and nineties, while working in Khedut Mazdoor Chetna Sangath in the Alirajpur district of West Madhya Pradesh, and living among the *adivasi* people, I got a chance to know and understand their life deeply. This story is of Namla (name changed), who was a member of the organisation. The account is based on what I heard from Namla and what I myself saw.

Namla's father, Phool Singh, was a native of Puvasa village where farming was negligible. Phool Singh went to Chhoti Gendra and became the *Gohri* of the village. The work of the Gohri was to feed the animals of some houses of the village and to take them back in the evening. Someone from the Gohri's house would then go to all these houses with a basket and *handi* in which they got *roti*, *ghat*, *dal*, or whatever else for their food.

Namla was a very young child then. Gradually, Namla and his siblings grew up in the Patel Phalia of Chhoti Gendra by eating such food earned by grazing goats, bulls, and cows. The hut in which Namla and his four siblings grew up would be about eight arms wide and ten to twelve arms long. The full height of the hut was ten feet and the walls were only five feet high. There was only a small space in the hut, near the middle wall, where one could stand upright. The roof was covered with flattened tiles and teak leaves.

After Namla got married and had two children, he built a house on the slope of the hill. To build a house, he had to serve the *nakedar* some chicken and also give him four to five hundred rupees. Namla also knew some people who, on the strength of the organisation, had built houses without paying money to the nakedars. But Namla was very poor and very scared. Moreover, he did not originally belong to that village. He tried to get a little upward mobility through the goodwill of the *Patel* and some wealthy Assamese persons who lived there. The adivasi people could get any work done only by asking, or rather pleading, with the nakedar. The main thing was that Namla did not have enough power to voice any opinion. He said that he wanted to build a house, and then did whatever the Patel and others asked him to do.

Anyway… somehow or the other, Namla has now built a house, on the way to Aadi Khudi. Once, while we were going to Aadi Khudi, we met Rawal Seth on the way. After the initial 'Hello' and so on, we came to know that he is coming from Namla's house. Behind him, an assistant was bringing along a bull. Later, on probing Namla, we realised that the bull had been Namla's.

The rest of the story is very simple, and not particularly spicy.

The sorghum that Namla and his family farmed was enough to feed them for only three or four months of the year. So, once Namla had borrowed forty kg of *jowar* from Rawal Seth. It had been many years ago, so the interest on the loan had increased. Namla had paid back some money, but some still remained. By handing over the bull, the account was settled.

In the meantime, Sega came out from the hearth, wiping his mouth with the edge of his *dhoti* and Namla's wife brought him a plate. Wiping his long thin moustache with his hand, he sat beside the fire. Namla made him a *beedi*. Sega was called in to talk to the Seth. Maybe he would help to reduce some of the interest on the loan. But nothing like this happened. Sega only helped finish the chicken and the drink.

Namla narrated these happenings very simply. We also understood that he did not want to tell the whole story, being afraid that we'll create some ruckus. Namla didn't want to get caught up in all this. But we were also compelled by habit. The whole thing had to be figured out. After enquiry, one tea, two, three Kachra and Kakri, we came to find out that it had been about eight or nine years since the sorghum grains were borrowed. In return, Namla has given him twenty kilos of maize, some groundnuts for a year, lentils for a year, and about six hundred rupees. The Seth had come and eaten chicken about eight to ten times. Even after giving all these, the account was not closed, so Rawal Seth untied the bull and took it away.

While telling us all this, Namla could not hide the disappointment and frustration in his mind. All I had to say was that this *jowar* has cost you more than a hundred rupees a kilo. And the dam of emotions within Namla burst. He narrated his sorrow and kept cursing the times. Even if the farm gives a good yield, how can people like Namla prosper? They will earn and pay the loan. But the interest of the loan will only continue to grow.

Nakedar means 'forest guard' who is an employee of the modern state. His relations with Adivasi people, as seen in the above story, is one small example of the state–citizen relationship. How do you evaluate this relationship?

- As Amit Bhatnagar notes about Namla, 'The main thing was that Namla did not have enough power to voice any opinion'. Do you think this is a crucial point that needs change in a democracy?
- Do you think that the relationship that Rawal Seth exerts on Namla is a continuation of feudal practices? Why?
- How can such real-life stories change so that people like Namla can live democratically?

Schooling in the modern state

The state controls all these relationships. The modern school emerges from within these complex relationships. Would people like Namla through modern schooling reclaim their voices that had seen historic subjugation (detailed in Chapters 1 and 2)? The question of schooling is of being able to examine social relationships, and have a voice and opinions through democratic praxis.

In the modern state, literacy and numeracy play enhancing roles for the voting citizen, the industrial labourer, and the consumer in the modern market. But where schooling produces only such peripheral roles in the modern state and the market, it does not engage with the democratic possibilities and the rights of the citizens. Predominantly, schools get students to rote learn. Memorising is not thinking, and this is what Paulo Freire (1972) had called the 'banking education'.[3] Freire, who had grown up in Brazil in contexts of poverty and struggle, had clearly recognised the lacunae of such learning.

In the 1940s, when literacy was a requisite in Brazil for voting in Presidential elections, Freire had begun to work with the illiterate and poor people to develop an educational praxis. In 1962, he got the opportunity to try these out on a large scale. He worked with three hundred sugarcane harvesters of Brazil, who learnt to read and write in just forty-five days. The Brazilian government encouraged the expansion of the work across the country. He developed learning materials that were not only concrete but also developed through the participation of the learners themselves. He used folk traditions and helped to create knowledge through a collective process.[4]

The relationships of the school with the state emerge in multiple ways. In addition to the aspect of citizenship, there is a context of people as labour with which schooling has a deep linkage. Machines in industries were created from earlier ingenuities of skills and innovations that had been done by hand. The machines run by electric power produce goods on a large scale, and the role of labour is to assist the machines. The labourers have to align their minds and bodies with the machines that move with a pre-set plan. The thinking, innovative handloom weaver, the shoemaker, and so on were replaced in this way through industrial production. The modern labour needed training, and we can see a replication of the school bells that announced class periods, lunch times, and play times in the sirens in the factories that indicated the work time.

To move according to a pre-set timetable is of great importance in the functioning of schools. Disciplined behaviour synchronises with the relations between the machines and the minds and bodies of labourers. Rote learning gels with this ambience of the system where unthinking and mechanical reproduction by labour was the key to industrial production.

The other important aspect, touched upon earlier, was the training for being good citizens in the modern state. The social studies were most dominantly attuned to meet this requirement. But, even as industrial labour and citizenship were the basic premises of schooling, what happened on the ground paved the way for possibilities that could reinvent democracy in multiple ways:

(1) Socialisation – One main spatial aspect that evolved was that the school became a site that brought together students from all walks of society. This paved the way for socialisation that could untangle traditional constraints bound by class, caste, and gender. In principle, the school and the classrooms declared equal space for all students, where they could know each other's experiences.

The school is a site where subaltern people can access literacy and formal knowledge from which they were excluded in feudal society. But such re-imagination through the school was resisted by the powerful strata of society. For instance, Jotirao and Savitri Phule had set up schools for '*shudradishudra*' in the eighteenth century. There was powerful backlash from the so-called upper castes.

(2) Access to knowledge – The thrusts of social reforms in the nineteenth and early twentieth centuries were initiated by several persons like Ayyankali, Fatima Sheikh, Sree Narayana Guru, Ramabai Ranade, Raja Ram Mohan Roy, Tarabai Shinde, and several others, who emphasised schooling for changing the socioeconomic and cultural traditions of caste–gender–class. Prior to the emergence of modern schools, knowledge in the Indian subcontinent in a formal sense was largely limited to upper-caste men, and this had the ideological backing of religious texts which we had discussed in Chapter 2.

(3) Critical Knowledge – Jotirao and Savitri Phule had rejected traditional knowledge such as the Manusmriti, which advocated subhuman lives for *dalits* and women. What emerges is a struggle for and against 'knowledge' by marginalised sections of society through a critical examination of dominant knowledge.

In 1952, E.V. ('Periyar') Ramasamy formed the 'Self-respect Movement' that listed one of its main objectives as the diffusion of useful political education. He gave much importance to the role of reasoning that can help people to live in freedom rather than in the slavery of the caste system, its superstitions, and meaningless ceremonies. These are examples in which the thinking mind is sought to be awakened for changing an unjust social system. He pointed out that education could help women to reclaim their legitimate position in society and become rightful citizens of the country.

M.K. Gandhi tried to reconstruct knowledge for schooling by including the life skills of the so-called lower castes in schooling.

> Indeed, I hold that, as the larger part of our time is devoted to labour for earning our bread, our children must, from their infancy, be taught the dignity of such labour. Our children should not be so taught as to despise labour.
>
> *(Gandhi, 1966)*[5]

As Kumar (2005) points out, this involves great political potential of the direct conflict of the school curriculum with the indigenous traditions on which the so-called low-caste groups had a monopoly. But Gandhi's vision of basic education did not bear fruit anywhere in the country. Given the deep roots of caste and gender, the connotations of social prestige were clearly a function of not doing manual labour (Sunny, 2014, pp. 32–35).

(4) Social relationships within the school – B.R. Ambedkar, born in the last decade of the nineteenth century, went to school but on the site of the school the traditional and feudal caste inequalities continued to operate.

> I knew that I was an untouchable and that untouchables were subjected to certain indignities and discriminations. For instance, I knew that in the school I could not sit in the midst of my class students according to my rank but that I was to sit in a corner by myself. I knew that in the school I was to have a separate piece of gunny cloth for me to squat on in the classroom and the servant employed to clean the school would not touch the gunny cloth used by me. I was required to carry the gunny cloth home in the evening and bring it back the next day. While in the school, I knew that children of the touchable classes, when they felt thirsty, could go out to the water tap, open it and quench their thirst. All that was necessary was the permission of the teacher. But my position was separate. I could not touch the tap, and unless it was opened by a touchable person, it was not possible for me to quench my thirst. In my case the permission of the teacher was not enough. The presence of the school peon was necessary, for he was the only person whom the class teacher could use for such a purpose. If the peon was not available, I had to go without water.
>
> *(Ravikumar & Anand, 2007, p. 11)*[6]

In independent India, the government schools played an important role as they provided access to students within the act of the Constitution of India for 'free and compulsory education up to the age of 14'.[7] But the reproduction of the socioeconomic inequalities within the school continues to be contested

(5) Common education for all – One of the most dynamic education recommendations in independent India has been that of the Kothari Commission[8] in 1968 which upheld the need for common education for all, meaning the same type of education for all children in the country

The demand for common schooling is something that has been voiced in many parts of the world. It was put forth by Antonio Gramsci in Italy during the regime of Benito Mussolini. Gramsci was born in 1860 and had suffered much poverty and ill health in his lifetime. Mussolini was the Prime Minister of Italy from 1922 to 1943. He founded the fascist movement that opposed the concept of social equality.

There was a spurt in specialised vocational schools in Italy during the rule of Mussolini. Gramsci noted that this encouraged the future activity of students along traditional lines of vocation. Instead, he put forward the need for a common basic education, which would strike 'the right balance between development of the capacity for working manually (technically, industrially) and development of the capacities required for intellectual work' (Hoare & Smith, 2009, p. 27).

(6) Schools can function as both oppressive and potentially liberating spaces. Schooling becomes a part of the structure and practices of society. As with democracy and linked with it, there is a tussle on how formal institutional knowledge should function. There is a potential in schooling through which it can be turned for the benefit of all people. Sarup (1982) explains this as follows:

> The educational system is a site of struggle, exemplifying the tension between those who wish to transform it as a part of a revolutionary process and those for whom the school is largely an agency of social reproduction and control. Let me put this in another way: there is the struggle of the working class to secure opportunities and benefits for itself through education, but underlying this there is also the continuing struggle by capital to ensure the reproduction of the necessary social relations.
> *(Sarup, 1982, p. 73)*[9]

Hence, we experience modern school as a site of contradictions. Sarup writes that this is not surprising because there is a real contradiction in that schools are both oppressive and potentially liberating.

The social science

In modern times, specialisations of knowledge like social science, science, mathematics, and languages are encouraged. It is not as though such knowledge emerged in the modern times, as these disciplines have been evolving over space and time in human history. But modern institutions tried to shape specialisations of knowledge through institutional structures. Research was defined through standardisations of scientific methods and methodologies.

In social science, we study social processes in which we are ourselves deeply located and embedded. The objective distancing from the object/process of study that physical science traditionally aspires to does not in the same way become the premises for the study of social processes. So, there has been and continues to be debates on blending perspectives of objectivity and subjectivity in the methodology of social science. Quantitative methodology involves the collection of information that can be quantified. These are then examined for patterns and causal relationships that can be subjected to statistical analyses and inferences. Qualitative information is based on conversations, interviews, and discussions. These capture the emotions, the lived experiences, and perspectives of people and give insights into the reasoning and motivations that reflect social relationships.

Until the eighteenth century, conventions on social science were on articulating how societies should be, with a dominant input of philosophy. The popular statement by Rousseau (1762)[10] makes the point: 'I seek right and reason and do not argue about facts'. The scientific thrust in the eighteenth century brought forth the need to study how society is, rather than how it should be. This was emphasised by August Comte[11] and many others, as what is called the 'positivist' approach. It described a scientific approach to looking rationally in to how societies are and how they operate. But this always led to questions of how societies should be, and what sort of changes one should aspire to. So, philosophical and political thrusts could not be kept out for long.

The placing of social science on an objective basis was one of the major contributions of Marx[12] as he pointed out that the whole anatomy of society was based on the relationships of the forces of production. This gave way to the fact that society cannot be explained only by the opinions of people in society, but there are very real causes of this that the participants may not be aware of. Another significant point that emerged is that Marxism was the first attempt to explain things as a complete system, in which all social phenomena were linked. This could take social science to a wider audience, as noted by Duverger (1964; 19):[13] 'no other system developed since has been as complete, and no other has had an audience beyond a small group of specialists'.

As the modern state, shaped by industrial production and electoral democracy, changed societies the world over, there were questions emerging on the responsibilities of the modern state towards the people. The people vest their powers on the government through elections, and, in response to that, the government needs to fulfil their responsibilities towards the people. Emerging from France, a cultural revolution in Europe. called the Renaissance, evolved a vision of a government which is responsible for all aspects of human society. It was the cultural revolution that addressed the social problems emerging from the Industrial Revolution. It upheld the responsibility of the modern state towards the people in the new situations.

The power desired of the state, as described above, to fulfil social requirements, is called sovereignty. This and other ideas gave way to the specialised development of political science as a discipline. Economics had already been specialising in the industrial phase. The nineteenth century saw the emergence of many disciplines of knowledge. The navigation of Europeans to other parts of the world had given way to a utilitarian thrust in the development to the discipline of geography. The Europeans were also engaged in studying small societies in different parts of the world, through anthropology. Comte had coined the word 'sociology' to describe the science of humanity. The realities of society cannot exist outside history, and one of the fundamental principles of Marxism is a full-fledged interpretation of history in the study of society. Social statistics developed as a subject. Social geography emerged, examining the spatial aspects of society. Thus, specialisations were increasing in the social sciences, along with the trend to unify the social sciences.

In most parts of the world, where the transition from feudalism in the eighteenth century was not to a well-defined rise of capitalism, as in Europe, the process of knowledge and disciplines has gone through different trajectories. In the neocolonial modern states, there is a thrust to liberate knowledge from the dominant perspectives of feudalism and colonialism. The critical grounding of knowledge creations in these contexts makes it distinct from Eurocentric knowledge.

Knowledge reinterpretations

Let us look at some concrete examples of reinterpretations in neocolonial contexts:

(1) Critical examination of India's social history
The European perspective on India's past fell largely into two categories – one that romanticised the oriental, and the other that looked down on it as being inferior to European history. On the other hand, nationalist historians in India had become defensive and glorified the Indian

past. But none of these perspectives could help to enhance the process of the critical examination of India's past and the role played by its social structures. This problem was addressed by historians like D. D. Kosambi, who made sharp detours from the earlier trajectories of history writing. The path was of reinterpretation, led by a passion that was not dogmatic, dismissive, or chauvinistic, and 'could take a stand and tell a story from the point of view of those who laboured, but did not count in a history detailing achievements'.

(Chakravarti, 2006, p. xix)

R. S. Sharma, D. R. Chanana, R Thapar, V. V. Jha, U Chakravarti, and others further contributed to shape reinterpretation of history of the Indian subcontinent. They utilised historic sources that were in the common people's languages, like Prakrit and Pali. These sources helped them to infer on the lives of the common people, and on social relationships, which was not possible through the sole use of Sanskrit sources. Social changes across time were reinterpreted by linking them to the modes of production. Feminist and subaltern history writing brought in new perspectives of reinterpretation. As Thapar (2002)[14] notes, 'Historiographical change incorporates new evidence and new ways of looking at existing evidence'. These new practices of writing history evolved critical interpretations which brought to life inclusive histories of social relationships.

(2) Decolonising knowledge

Recently, a new institution of higher education[15] in Africa, located in Mauritius, stated that its central idea of work is decoloniality. It sets out to start from scratch and evolved from the context of the South African students' movement to decolonise their universities, the 'Black Lives Matters' protests in the USA, and the much deeper history of national re-imagination in Africa and in other parts of the world. The faculty, along with their students, are working towards a decolonial social science curriculum. This, they hope, would 'shift educational discourse in a more equitable and representative direction' (Auerbach, 2017).[16] Some of the key aspects include the usage of language beyond English, open sources of knowledge, student exchange ratios of 1:1 (African and European students), going beyond texts, collaborations with a wide range of people, and promotion of ethical standards.

(3) Countermapping

Decolonising knowledge has been interpreted in a wide array of ways across the neocolonial world. For example, 'counter-mapping' is largely being done by indigenous communities and by migrants from the neocolonial worlds to USA and Europe. 'Decolonising' implies not only moving outside the ambit of European colonialism, but also outside the exploitative national neocolonial processes that have been detrimental to tribal communities. It maps the continuity of exploitation of the neocolonial world by the erstwhile colonies through a circuit of labour flows. Countermapping defines itself as mapping against dominant power structures and aims to move towards progressive goals. It also becomes a tool for documenting the changes happening on lands through climate change.

> 'Whose woods are these? Countermapping forest territories in Kalimantan, Indonesia' by Peluso (1995) points out how forest mapping by government forestry planners allocates rights of resource use and land access according to forest types and economic objectives. But they barely recognise the occupancy rights of the indigenous communities and local people. Maps and official plans ignore, or even criminalise, traditional rights to forest, forest products, and forest land for temporary conversion to shifting agriculture. Indigenous activists redefine traditional forest rights by sketching maps to reclaim territories.
>
> - How does countermapping give priority and representation to customs and claims on the land usually ignored by modern states?
> - Can you link the above to the idea of democracy and citizenship?

It can be derived that decolonising is a critical recognition of the processes of exploitation of the people by various dominant powers. It seeks to create knowledge that can enhance the subaltern people.

(4) The writing of 'people's history' of the USA in 1980 by Zinn is a historic narration of mass movements and of immigrants.

> You can read about the writing of people's history and examine:
>
> 1. Why is it called 'history from below'?
> 2. Why should societies be examined from subaltern locations?

Decolonising knowledge vis-à-vis traditional knowledge

In contradistinction to the above-mentioned examples, the term 'decolonising knowledge' is sometimes, as in contemporary India, articulated by some political forces as the reestablishment of 'traditional knowledge'.

In traditional Indian society, the labouring people had developed skills required for basic necessities of everyday life, such as farming, cooking, animal rearing, pottery, carpentry, shoemaking, and clothmaking, and so on.

Traditional knowledge also involved medicine, astrology, architecture, martial arts, warfare, and astronomy. Classical art forms occupied a distinct elite space that stood apart from popular art forms. Above all these forms of knowledge stood the ideological sources of knowledge extended by religious texts that were interpreted (by the brahmans in India) to retain the hierarchies of the social system. In India, caste and gender had decided what each person would do in life – the nature of knowledge and how it was to be acquired were pre-decided (Sunny, 2014).[17]

It is these varied knowledge systems, created through a power structure of hierarchy, that have been questioned and rewritten through a collection of social science writings in India rich in critical examinations of the traditional structures and practices. Some examples are given below.

In 'History of Doing', Radha Kumar (1993)[18] explains why the women's movement in India is not an unnecessary import from the West, as some people describe it. She notes how, in the nineteenth century, the Indian subcontinent saw a large number of reforms that sought to make changes in the internal structure and practices of society. These included the banning of child marriage and *sati*, as well as lifting the ban on the remarriage of widows. After independence, women played an important role in changing the gender equations in different parts of India. The 1970s saw women's protests against the sale of alcohol at village levels and larger campaigns against dowry deaths, rape, and sati.

Habib[19] has written a series of books entitled *People's History of India*, that focus on themes such as prehistory, Indus civilisation, the Vedic age, ecological history, medieval India, and agrarian structure. Habib's research and writings, like those of several historians mentioned earlier, bring to us the importance of 'historiography' – meaning, the way in which history is written. This marks a sharp change from the traditional writings on history that glorified kings, their wars, and valour. The history of social and economic relationships brings together holistic processes of time–space.

In the book *Turning the Pot, Tilling the Land: Dignity of Labour in Our Times*, Ilaiah[20] writes on the art, skill, and science of the labouring people in traditional Indian society. These include the *adivasis*, cattle-rearers, potters, weavers, farmers, leatherworkers, *dhobis*, and barbers. Their labour fulfilled the basic necessities of everyday life, but Indian tradition categorises the people into castes, through which the labouring castes are despised as 'lowly' and 'backward'.

Decolonising knowledge is not confined to liberating knowledge only from colonial dominance. It equally seeks liberation from traditional power structures like class, caste, and gender, which are legitimised by religion and family, and continue to exert influence on contemporary institutions.

Anchoring citizenship education

Let us look at some concrete examples from the country to grasp the nature of the above-mentioned relationship.

In the nineteenth century, there had been a number of social reforms in India. The Arya Samaj had emerged as an active supporter of women's education. But it discouraged women from higher education:

The Hindu girl has functions of a very different nature to perform from those of a Hindu boy ... [We do] not encourage any system which could deprive her of her national traits of character. The education we give our girls should not unsex them.

(Kumar, 1993, p. 29).

In the early twentieth century, social reformers, philanthropists, and the government pointed out that the education of women was crucial for the healthy upbringing of children, and therefore of a healthy race. But, in later part of the century, women had become more active in sociopolitical movements across the country. They resisted the above-mentioned perspectives on education that sought to strengthen the traditional roles of women. They articulated the problems faced by women and, as Kumar (1990) notes, the Indian feminist movement has particularly looked into issues of tradition and modernity.

The interactions of traditions and modernity were surely paving the way for change. Often, schooling, which helped readership, further helped to build perspectives for social and political struggles. Phule was very much influenced by Thomas Paine's *Rights of Man*, which he read in 1847. Gandhi was influenced by the writings of Leo Tolstoy. Similarly, Marxist writings and praxis influenced peasant movements and trade unions in the country. These were largely the implications of reading, as well as interactions that helped people across the world to learn from each other. Readers could know of different sorts of perspectives and struggles in different spaces and times.

Whereas, in feudal states, religion had played an important role (as you have read in the previous chapters) in legitimising the state, in the modern state, this was replaced by new sources of legitimacy, such as science and technology, as well as liberating ideas such as equality and justice. Science and technology were crucial for industrial production and innovations in transport and communication. The factory created new forms of drudgery for the working class, but it also served as a space to crack open the deep roots of caste–gender sanctioned by religions. A large number of social reform movements evolved that also sought the accessibility of the marginalised social sections to modern schools.

Given below is an excerpt from a field-based study done in Tamil Nadu by Chinnakutty (2009):[21]

Many social activists shared the following during my interviews with them: 'In some schools, students clean their classrooms. Mostly girl students are doing this and the teacher selects them from the Dalit community'.

Children do some work in school, like cleaning and helping teachers, and it is good that children do this because, even in their homes, children do some work. But the bad thing is that it is based on gender and caste as it is in society. Here is an example to illustrate this from my interview with two students:

Me: Apart from studies, what do you do in the classroom?
Boy student (BS): We clean the classroom.
Me: "We" means?
BS: "Ivakka" (he shows a girl), they clean.
Me: You do not clean?
BS: No, no... we arrange bench/table.
Me: Why do they clean? And why do you arrange the bench/table?
BS: They can't carry the bench/table.
Me: How do you know that they can't?
BS: (very silent) Illa (No), the teacher says that.
Me: (I ask a girl student) Can you carry bench/table?
Girl student (GS): Yes, we can.
Me: Then why do you do the cleaning?
GS: Teacher says that I should clean the classroom.

Girl children are always expected to do cleaning work by teachers. It is seen that boys get the idea that girls should do the cleaning. The teachers assume the important role of reproducing the social stratification by telling children what to do and who should do it. Thus, a hidden curriculum works in school that is clearly a brahmanical idea. In our society, cleaning and physical work are considered low and dirty. So those who do them like women and dalits are consider low. This includes upper-caste women too. This way, women are low in all communities and all social institutions.

Such experiences throw light on those issues that are taught to and learnt by students in informal ways. These, termed the hidden curriculum, are often the ways through which the social practices and biases get reproduced in the classroom. Teachers and the school system, along with the values that children themselves carry from their homes and society, play important roles.

- Imagine that you teach in the school described above by Chinnakutty. How would you act to make schooling a means of changing society towards equality and fairness?
- From other sources find out what is meant by 'cultural capital'. How does this operate in schools?
- How can teachers become critically conscious of the operations of cultural capital?

Social studies as citizenship education

The foregrounding of the relationships between the modern school and society in day-to-day practices can further be linked to the role played by the curriculum and the content of schooling.

Ilaih (2002)[22] narrates the concrete experiences of alienation that keep happening as food habits, the gods, the language expressions (even while using the same language), the stories and epics, the poetry, and the gender roles of the brahmanical system dominates the school.

Does the subject social studies help to reorient the traditional social relationships that are being reproduced in the classroom?

'Social science' is involved with the social life of human societies. 'Social studies' mean the study of humanities and social science, designed to promote citizenship education. Social science feeds in to social studies as school subjects, but the major thrust is on the concept of citizenry of the modern state. It becomes a medium through which knowledge and skills deemed desirable for citizenry is built. It includes commitment to democratic values, duties and rights of citizens, their participation, and so on. Let us look at three of the most common subjects of social studies in school education – history, geography, and civics. What are their foci?

The contents of the textbooks are taught in certain ways, and that is called 'pedagogy'. The content and pedagogy together create the teaching/learning process in classrooms. Textbooks contain information and facts, which are usually read out and explained by teachers. There are questions at the end of chapters, the answers to which are written out by students in notebooks and memorised to fulfil the requirements of the examinations.

This is often the state view, or a dominant view only, whereas students and teachers experience a multitude of other processes in their lives. The people's side of the story is usually absent.

Efforts have been made by several organisations to change these situations. Learning materials, pedagogy, learning from concrete observations, creative skill developments, and so on have been some of the basic concerns of alternative efforts in education. Special focus has been on those sections of the society that have been deprived of education through traditional practices of exclusion. These include adivasi, dalit, fishing and nomadic communities, and women/girls.

National Curriculum Framework (NCF) 2005 marked a watershed in the national curriculum perspective of citizenship education. This was notable also because of the textbooks of NCERT (National Council of Educational Research and Training), New Delhi and of some states of India that were written after that, in a changed perspective of citizenship. The language was much more engaging, the methods and insights from social sciences were much more enriching, and the issue of citizenship education was critically addressed.

A striking change that came about through these processes was a critical intervention into the subject called 'civics':

> 3.1.4. It is suggested that there is a need to bring about a change in nomenclature, from civics to political science. This change is sought on the following grounds. Civics as a subject had appeared in the Indian school curriculum during the colonial period against the background of increasing 'disloyalty' among Indians towards the Raj. An analysis of the first textbook of civics, *The Citizen of India,* authored by Lee Warner, shows that civics was intimately linked to the colonial project of rule, cultural assimilation, and establishment of British hegemony (Jain, 1999).

Emphasis on the obedience and loyalty of citizens – the colonial ethos of order, improvement, and rationality; the discourse of the shortcomings of the personality of the natives and Indian society; the projection of the state as an agent of change within the native; and the creation of civil society according to the universal values of progress – these were the key features of colonial civics (ibid).

Conventionally, Civics is the subject that most directly deals with citizenship education. From the above passage, you can see a critique of how civics became an orientation for students to be loyal 'subjects' or citizens for the running of a colonial state. Decolonisation can take place only through democratic relationships of the state with the people.

Can you look for examples of democratic and authoritarian practices in contemporary India? Give reasons to support your examples.

Conclusion

In this concluding chapter of the first part of the book, 'Society, state and consciousness', the readers could reflect upon the contemporary experiences of neoliberalism. We experience sharp changes from an earlier equation of state and national capital vis-a-vis labour. The move towards privatisation have shrunk public enterprises, institutions, and employment, forcing people to be controlled more by corporate practices on labour and on resource extraction. The shifts in the political and economic sphere brings in changes on what is taught (the legitimised knowledge) and which socioeconomic segments of the society are enhanced by schooling.[23] The curriculum, pedagogies, and textbooks go through transitions. Censorship is executed by the content of the syllabus to be taught in schools and colleges.[24] Legitimised knowledge becomes further alienated from the rights of the citizens to knowledge in a modern democracy and from the Constitution of India- the torch bearer between the state and the people.

Economic restructuring induces restructuring of social relations in which inroads of communalisation of education can also be traced. The already-existing biases of society come in handy at such times and some people get labelled as 'outsiders'. The Muslims and, to some extent, the Christians in India, immigrants in Europe, and Blacks in America are examples of such exclusions. The capitalist crisis, therefore, is both an economic and a social crisis. Sarup (1982, p. 112) observes that, just as the character of nationalised industries changes during a crisis of capital, the character of schools also changes. Capital attempts to re-establish its dominance, which includes domination over education. Sarup points out the example of the reduction in autonomy of teachers, the question being 'How are these agents (teachers) to be controlled to ensure that they reproduce the necessary bourgeois relations?' (Ibid: 74).

Notes

1 Praxis – practical application of a theory.
2 Bhatnagar, A (2021), https://yuvaniya.in/2021/09/15/tribal-of-alirajpur-exploited-by-the-upper-caste-groups/ accessed 19 December 2021.
3 Freire, Paulo (1972), *Pedagogy of the Oppressed* (translated by Myra Bergman Ramos), Harmondsworth, Eng. Penguin.
4 In 1964, the President of Brazil was overthrown by members of the Brazilian armed forces, supported by the government of the USA. The military junta did not approve of the educational programmes of Freire, and they put an end to it. Freire was imprisoned as a traitor. Later, he worked from Chile. In 1967, he published his first book, *Education as the Practice of Freedom*. His most popular book, *Pedagogy of the Oppressed*, was published in 1968.
5 Gandhi, M K (1966), Collected Works of Mahatma Gandhi, Vol 21, 1966, The Publications Division, Ministry of Information and Broadcasting, Government of India: 38 pp.
6 Ravikumar, D and S Anand (2007), *Ambedkar: Autobiographical Notes*, Pondicherry: Navayana Publishing.
7 Article 45 in the Constitution of India was set up as an Act: The State shall endeavour to provide, within a period of ten years from the commencement of this Constitution, for free and compulsory education for all children until they complete the age of fourteen years.
8 Government of India, Ministry of Education (1966), Report of the Education Commission, 1964–66 (Chairman D S Kothari), Govt. of India, New Delhi.
9 Sarup, M (1982), *Education, State, and Crisis*, Routledge and Kegan Paul, London, pp. 73.
10 In Duverger, M (1964), *Introduction to Social Sciences*, George Allen and Unwin, London, pp 15.
11 August Comte, French philosopher of the nineteenth century, known as the founder of positivism.
12 Karl Marx was a German philosopher, critic of political economy, economist, historian, sociologist, political theorist, journalist, and so on in the nineteenth century. His writings focussed on power relationships between capitalists and workers, and the struggle and conflict between them, which has a worldwide impact through 'Marxism'.
13 Duverger, M (1964), *Introduction to Social Sciences*, George Allen and Unwin, London.

14 Thapar, R (2002), *The Penguin History of Early India: From the Origins to AD 1300*, Penguin Books, pp xix.
15 African Leadership University, with operations in both Mauritius and Rwanda.
16 Jess Auerbach (2017), 'What a new university in Africa is doing to decolonise social sciences', *The Conversation*, May 13, 2017, Creative Commons, accessed 5 January 2021
17 Sunny, Y (2014), 'Knowledge and the politics of education', *Economic and Political Weekly*, December 27, 2014 vol xlix no 52, pp. 32–35.
18 Radha Kumar (1993), *The History of Doing: An Illustrated Account of Movements for Women's Rights and Feminism in India, 1800–1990*, Kali for Women, New Delhi.
19 Habib, I, the general editor of the series, has authored six volumes and co-authored two volumes. These have been published by Tulika books from 2001 onwards.
20 Kancha Ilaiah (2007), with illustrations by Durgabai Vyam, *Turning the Pot, Tilling the Land: Dignity of Labour in our Times*, Navayana Publishing House, New Delhi.
21 Chinnakutty, M (2009) 'Brahmanical Thoughts Affecting Teaching Profession', Unpublished study of field assignment in TISS, Mumbai, for the course MAEE.
22 Ilaiah, Kancha (2005), *Why I am not a Hindu: A Sudra Critique of Hindutva Philosophy, Culture, and Political Economy*, Samya, Calcutta.
23 See Sunny, Y (2020), 'National Education Policy 2020: Realigning the Bhadralok', *Economic and Political Weekly*, Mar 6, 2021, pp. 17-20.
24 Examples of censorship include the changes made in 2019 in NCERT textbooks like deletion of almost 70 pages that includes the chapter, Clothing: A Social History, that examines how social movements influence how we dressed; a second chapter, on history and sport, on the history of cricket in India and its connections to the politics of caste, region, and community; and a third chapter, Peasants and Farmers, which focusses on the growth of capitalism and how colonialism altered the lives of peasants and farmers (*Financial Express*, 18.3.2019). A chapter entitled Novels, Society and History was also deleted which examined the rise in popularity of novels and its impact on social reforms and ideas of womanhood in the West and in India (*Wire* 8 April 2019). The deletion of various valuable lessons from the Delhi University's college syllabus was also witnessed. The essay 'Three hundred Ramayanas', by the late scholar and linguist, A K Ramanujan, which formed part of the BA History (Honours) course was scrapped. It had attracted the ire of Hindutva activists (The Hindu, 15 September 2011).

PART 2
Democracy, education, technology
Intentions and implications

As we have seen in previous chapters, human societies evolved gradually through different phases.

For humans, the social nature of living is an innate need for more than one reason. Over a period of time, through phases of evolution, the need for living collectively has led to complex and myriad ways of organizing societies. Consciousness is the basis of the relationship among humans and with the non-human world. In everyday terms, it means values and frames of ethics that form the core of social organization; of these, some are continuous and some are transient. Social organization and consciousness are linked with how power is held and distributed, giving societies particular sociopolitical characters.

Societies have changed from less hierarchical to highly stratified social organisations, in which control and manipulation of knowledge and technological know-how have played a crucial role. The changes in social organisation reflect contestations in principles and ideologies. These contestations are not linear, reflecting something 'less progressive' to 'more progressive'. It is in this context that we need to see the idea of democracy as a mode of social organisation. Is it exclusively modern? Is it linked exclusively with the Industrial Age and European 'Enlightenment'? If we look at the long stretch of human history over different time periods and, most importantly, in different parts of the world, we find evidence of societies and groups organised around democratic principles, but not necessarily identified or labeled as democracies. They represent more fluid, less hierarchical power-sharing among members of the groups and, most importantly, stake representation in collective decision-making.

DOI: 10.4324/9781003449348-6

Democracy as an ideological identifier, as a way of governance, emerged in the process of transitioning from feudalism to industrial capitalism, from a monarchy sanctioned by established religion to electing a collective of people's representatives where all adults can cast their vote. Rationality, recognition of individual rights, and private property are some of the universal features of modern democracies. These have existed in a complex mix of colonialism, concentration of capital, and exploitation of labour and resources during the eighteenth and nineteenth centuries. The phase of colonialism culminated in the two World Wars unleashing unforeseen devastation. Fascist holocaust of innocents in Germany and the horror of nuclear weapons dropped on Hiroshima and Nagasaki by the USA, brought up fundamental questions about justice, power, development trajectory, and relationship with nature. This ushered in the period of freedom from colonialism and imperialism in Asia and Africa. Representative democracy became the chosen form of governance in the newly decolonized nation-states. Post WWII and the founding of the UN meant readjusting power equations which had been taken for granted for centuries. Inequalities of power, race, colour, gender, caste, and class – everything needed revisiting. Thus, in the twentieth century, democracy emerged as both a natural choice of governance as well as an ethical option.

Since the nineteenth century, the system of mass education emerged as a need of industrialising societies and, from the end of the century, the dimension of 'citizenship education' became pronounced. In the home countries for the colonial regimes, teaching for democracy became a stated rationale; in the colonies, citizenship education was aimed at not challenging but accepting colonial rule. At the same time, in all societies, including the newly decolonized ones, despite the stated equality and universal franchise, ideas of defining certain groups as full, natural citizens and others with differential status have always existed. With mass school education becoming a universal norm and recognized by the UN as being essential for peace and justice, citizenship education foregrounded teaching for democracy. Democracy as a way of governance exists in different forms in different countries but the principles underlying different democracies often vary. While democracy is the preferred form of governance in reality the political elite use electoral mandate in favour of market forces – this is particularly evident from mid-1980s. Democracy is seen merely instrument of governance by seeking the mandate for rule by the powerful, with traditionally oppressive structures of gender, race, caste, still intact. Public thinkers, political scientists, and educationists have raised critiques about these issues, often drawing attention to the fundamental flaws, perpetuation of inequalities, widening fissures, and alienation of citizens. Some others, instead of critiquing this reality, have justified hierarchy as being 'natural'. These debates are mirrored in citizenship education. These differences not only reflect what is selected for teaching but how it is taught. The 'approaches' to teaching are therefore embedded in the worldview and purpose of teaching.

Post WWII we see the re-emergence of greed and desire for absolute power, particularly evident in the 'Cold War' period. It is from this phase that digital, satellite-based technology began growing, seen as a trump card! Today, digital technology has made inroads into the private and public spheres of our life. Development and use of such technology has not taken place in a vacuum, but is nestled in ideologies that see democratic governance as a mere tool to validate power. Knowledge needs to be seen as both a generator and an outcome of these processes of dominance. Despite these constraints, those who strive for justice also embrace technology. These debates need to be taken on board while looking at technology in education, in continuation of the reflections about what is the form of democracy we strive for and what kind of citizenship is nurtured through education. The purpose, intentions, or vision about democracy define the character of education. Similarly, technology in education needs to be seen in terms of these debates. Chapters 4 and 5 throw light on these issues.

Chapter 4 unravels the debates about society and education. It situates social science education in our conception of democracy. The manner in which we approach the teaching of social sciences is not merely limited to the pedagogical strategies, but is about the histories and contexts from which the different approaches have emerged, carrying with them specific intentions, pointing at certain implications.

Chapter 5 looks at the way digital technology took shape and the context in which it grew to encompass all aspects of our lives today. We look at the impact digital technology has had in education, on knowledge generation and social structures. In this chapter we look at ways in which social science educators have integrated technology in their practice for nurturing democratic citizenship.

4
APPROACHES TO TEACHING SOCIAL SCIENCES

Why, what, and how?

Introduction

How Mumtaz has organized her classes for the day

Mumtaz teaches history in a school. Today, she has Class VIII in the morning and Class VI later in the afternoon. She has prepared her 'lesson plans' and organized the material for both classes.

The Class VI history syllabus is mainly about the life and times of the iconic local king, celebrated in popular culture. He is regarded as a protector of the dominant culture against 'outside invaders'. Riots often break out and minorities are attacked, if anyone challenges these claims. For today's class, Mumtaz is doing part of the chapter 'The great King and his war strategies'. She is doing the section on how the king and his close confidants planned a guerrilla attack on the camp of a mighty opponent who had surrounded his fortress, by joining a wedding procession passing by the enemy camp. She has asked the students to bring in garments easily available at home and mock weapons, to enact different roles as the wedding party and the opponent's soldiers. She is carrying a few extra things and has written a short, simple, drama script.

For Class VIII, the chapter Mumtaz is teaching today is 'Our past – How do we know about it?' It is about the various methods and tools used for investigating and interpreting what happened in the historical past. She is using the same celebrated local king as in Class VI, to use as an example about the process of historical investigation. Mumtaz has decided to divide the class in two groups and has organised two sets of material:

DOI: 10.4324/9781003449348-7

For group 'A', she has sourced copies of photographs like coins minted by the king and the seal of his kingdom, with his motto that says 'Our rule in our place'; there is also an edict to the army that, while travelling, they are not to destroy crops standing in any farmer's fields and never to demand free food or services from people either in his kingdom or any other place and an illustration of a dagger the king used to kill one of his enemies by deception. For group 'B', the material consists of a map of the spread of his kingdom and a timeline to show when he expanded it to capture new regions, a letter written by a feudal lord who served another ruler about the imminent attack and capture of their lands by the king, and a folk-song from one of the regions he captured about the attack by the king's army describing their terror and might. Each group is supposed to present their idea regarding the reign of the king, i.e., his character sketch.

Think

- What do you think about the way Mumtaz has organized her lesson plans for the two classes?
- What may her reasoning be behind developing the two lesson plans? What kind of learners are imagined in each of the lesson plans?
- While the chapters appear on the same subject, what discrete features mark their distinctiveness?
- What, according to you, may be the rationale underlying the selection of content and organization of chapters in the textbook?
- Do you think there is a close relationship between selection/organization of textbook content, pedagogical choices, and larger societal, national goals? In what way?

The way Mumtaz has conceived her lessons for the two classes and the type of learning expected in her planning as a teacher seems to have some obvious reasoning and the answers to this question are woven throughout the chapter. We can start looking at the questions here by going into the reasoning behind the approaches Mumtaz has adopted for her lessons in the two classes and the kind of learning expected in her planning as a teacher. However, additionally, instead of merely looking at what Mumtaz has done and why she has done it, we need to imagine not one but many teachers like Mumtaz and thus we need to look at the vision behind selection and organization of content in the textbooks that usually forms the basis for teaching/learning. This is possible only when we seek clarification regarding the place and purpose of social science in school education and understand how these are tied to the larger societal and national goals. It is only natural, then, that while scrutinizing the role of social sciences in a certain society, it is imperative that we investigate them in the context of the goals a society defines for itself.

Let us try to identify the two main issues here

The reasoning behind the way Mumtaz has organized her classes rests on the concept of Pedagogical Content Knowledge (PCK) (Shulman, 1986)[1] which is a complex intermix of her theoretical understanding of the subject and knowledge of the concepts, pedagogical skills specific to the content to be taught, knowledge of how learning takes place, and a deep understanding of the age-group and contexts of children in her class. The textbooks Mumtaz has may or may not have clear indications about the desired pedagogies and Mumtaz may have planned her lessons based on her own experience and understanding developed over time. These issues are in relation to the first two questions we have posed above. We will develop our understanding and perspective about these by looking at them in more detail in Chapter 5.

What we will focus on in this chapter is a deeper look at the latter two questions which will help us locate the main issue of the rationale behind selection/organization of content/construction of textbooks used by teachers like Mumtaz and how a choice of a certain approach to teaching/learning is related to the larger societal, national goals. For this exercise, we will draw on understanding developed from Chapter 3.[2]

Part I

Social sciences and the social order: Transmission or transformation?

So, let us reiterate the key questions: What is the place and purpose of social sciences in a society? How does the choice of a certain 'approach to teaching' social sciences flow from a certain societal vision and in turn can it impact the shaping of certain kinds of citizen? In short, why, what, how, or the purpose of teaching and content pedagogy are inseparable.

There are ongoing debates about the role education plays in modern democracies. On a global scale, the UN recognizes it as an important human right that enables securing other rights: it is part of the Convention on the Rights of the Child (1989). In India it is a fundamental right under Article 21 of the Indian Constitution to be provided for by the State, inalienable from the right to life. It is seen as a leverage against historical conditions of inequality, like caste, gender, regional, and racial discrimination. More than anything else, it is seen as an equalizer, not merely in economic terms, but affecting social status. Although education is seen as an essential condition of modern democracies, there are conflicting views about the role it plays in shaping society. One view interprets it as an instrument of socialisation in the hands of the State and the powerful elite, thereby constraining democracy. This view advocates fundamentally changing the nature of education system in all its aspects, the structure, outreach, content pedagogy, and mechanisms of delivery. This view hopes to unleash the transformative potential of education for radical social change as against the popular view that sees it as a slow process as a socioeconomic leveler. Both these positions co-exist in real life.

From the phase of industrialisation, complex modern states require their citizens to be formally educated to serve the needs of the industrial (and now post-industrial) society, to produce labour that has specific skills and dispositions. We have seen in Chapter 3 the intertwined relationship between the modern state and economic capital. Since it is the State mechanism that facilitates (and controls) education, it ensures that such a system produces the required 'human resources', in the form of people with certain types of knowledge, skills, and dispositions, who will unquestioningly perform the given functions. Whereas in policy documents, the state may use the language of 'human rights and social betterment', the reality reveals an unequal, multilayered system with different socioeconomic groups gaining differential amounts and quality of education and thereby reproducing inequalities, ensuring a hierarchically divided 'human resource'. People passively absorb what is 'transmitted' to perform roles required of them by the state and the capitalist class. Such a society, for example, will produce a limited number of technocrats, scientists, and academics, doing pathbreaking research and inventions or increasing economic productivity, but the common masses are caught in uninspiring clerical or arduous physical labour for mere survival. It is this reality that is questioned and critiqued, demanding not only equal access to quality education for the purpose of parity but also for critically examining the age-old system. This view is 'critical of the dominant social order and motivated by a desire to ensure both political and economic democracy' (Stanley, 2005).

The character of society and the role of social sciences

The social sciences play a pivotal role in defining the character of education in society; its content pedagogy facilitates criticality, thereby revealing the nature of the relationship between society and knowledge. It seeks to unravel its core character, does it act as a vehicle of unquestioningly passing-on the dominant order or does it encourage critical analysis and act as a change-agent, as a 'transformative' force. With the help of an essay by W.B. Stanley,[3] a well-known educationist, we will explore the ongoing debates about democracy, education, and the role of social sciences.

Stanley asks: 'Should social science educators transmit or transform the social order?' In this context, we attempt to understand whether and how 'approaches' to teaching address the issues in relation to how power and privilege are distributed in a society. It is ironic that how and, indeed, why the social sciences are taught leave room for both – to not acknowledge or rationalize power imbalance in favour of the dominant few or to build capacities to analyse of how, why our society is iniquitously structured and to kindle motivation for working towards a fair, equal one. On the spectrum between these two positions, there also exist other views and preferences, leading to debates and disputes.

Debates about the role of social science education are ongoing and draw upon what has taken place in the past from global as well as specific cultural contexts. In Chapters 2 and 3, we saw how modern democratic societies have emerged as a byproduct of paradigmatic shift in cultural, philosophical, and social-scientific thinking. We have also seen how the forces of dominance and power have been intertwined with the growth of modern democracies in the West and how formal education has been a channel for the construction of a certain kind of citizenship in preserving the status quo, consolidating, and transmitting the dominant order. Democracy requires recognition and fulfillment of individual and collective rights in an equitable way, provisioning to rectify historic wrongs, by providing special privileges, reducing the gap between the socioeconomically powerful and the weak so that all have a comparable starting point. It means all, irrespective of their social and economic positions, have an equal voice in a nation's decision-making. But reality reveals that this is rarely the case. As a result, it is often argued that the current economic and political systems that carry the label of democracy require fundamental transformation, and changing the way we educate the young is an important starting point.

Despite its shortcomings, democracy remains a valued, aspirational societal ideal. But, within a democratic state, fulfillment of one's democratic rights is often selective – tied to privileges of birth and class (for example, access and quality of education for a girl child from a poor, Dalit family against a girl from an educated, upper-caste family). At the same time, the notional equal access to systems or institutions like universal adult franchise, law, public transport, education, employment, entertainment, etc., act as strong motivators and reference points for pursuing the project of democracy. In reality, although the social dynamics favour majoritarian values, allowing cultural dominance by certain religious and caste groups, there is a general atmosphere supporting equal rights or freedoms in a selective manner. (For example, although one often sees demands to ban telecast or screenings of a particular film, claiming it hurts the sentiments of a certain group, the elected representatives do not take a stand for fear of upsetting the concerned group and the police do nothing when theatres showing the film are vandalized. But, if the matter reaches the court of law, the judiciary usually rules in favour of the filmmaker's freedom of expression and the public's right to information.) That there are varied conceptions of democracy need to worry us as contestation is an essential part of democracy. What we need to worry about is whether contestation is among equals or is imbalanced in terms of the power held by the opposing parties. For democracy to really work, a society must provide for the weaker to gain strength, for minority to feel safe and on par with majority; for example by providing for legal remedies such as instruments of positive discrimination for the traditionally disadvantaged. We see that applying these principles in practice is never an easy task; the powerful and the majority do not willingly cede power and contestations take the form of discord threatening the very existence of democracy. Despite these shortcomings today democracy as a political structure is preferred over all other forms of governance. By and large, democracy is seen as a process, not a product, as a way of life, as a 'work in progress'. Our everyday lived experiences fall on a spectrum of denial or constraining of rights on one hand and relative equality on the other.

Although democracy existed in the ancient Greek city states,[4] and in less complex social structures of tribal societies or in movements for religious reform as a political philosophy (Protestantism, Bhakti),[5] in the modern world, this political thought emerged relatively later as a byproduct of 'industrial capitalism' and is seen as a preferred rule on a global scale. As said earlier, it called for a paradigmatic change in the value systems, in the notions of power and justice. It is assumed that democratic thinking and behaviour (citizenship) must be learned, and schools are sites where the young are exposed to this formal training of citizenship. 'Democracy is something we are always trying simultaneously to maintain *and* reconstruct, and education is essential to this process' (Stanley, 2005). Within an education system, it is the social sciences that carry the mantle of citizenship education. Given that there are many conceptions about democracy, there is also a plethora of ideas about 'citizenship education for democracy' and these viewpoints impact what happens in our classrooms. The debates about 'citizenship and democracy' will perhaps never cease and 'no single formulation will triumph' (Westheimer and Kahne, 2004). Different perspectives about democracy and 'citizenship education' will continue because 'the stakes are too high' – because perspectives about 'good citizenship' are linked with perspectives about 'good society' (Westheimer and Kahne, 2004). We will look at three main conceptions that have directly or indirectly influenced the construction of democratic citizenship, primarily drawn from Stanley (2005). Stanley's ideas are located in the context of the US, where the emergence of the subject of 'social studies' played a major role in debates about the nature of education and the nature of a democratic nation-state. Knowledge branches of social sciences were dovetailed in the form of 'social studies' – education for citizenship. The impact of these debates has been felt across the world. In connection with these ideas, we will draw parallels with the Indian context, with the help of examples given in the exercises. In the context of Indian school education social sciences have different nomenclature in different states. In some states they are recognised as branches of social sciences, i.e. History, Geography, etc. In some other states they go by the lable 'Social Studies'.

Democracy and education

'Building a new order'

As democracy became a widely accepted and desired political option, as it progressed beyond merely a political thought, as it became an entrenched political system in large parts of the world; it was only natural that it began being evaluated in terms of its conceptions, its promises. Democracy is tied to the notion of a 'welfare state' responsible for ensuring fulfillment of basic needs to lead a dignified life, like ensuring quality education for all citizens as an essential way for achieving equity. But, in Chapter 3, we have seen how education has been an instrument of social control either through religious codification or race-gender segregation. In modern societies, democracy and industrialisation have gone hand-in-hand. Industrialisation ushered in reorganisation of the 'production process' to control capital, resources, and labour and the democratic state apparatus provided philosophical rationale for '*laissez-faire*' economics. Both the diversion of democratic ideals as well as education aimed at producing specific types of human resources gave way to much rethinking, the foremost being the 'progressive movement in education'[6] in the USA. John Dewey can said to be its principal figure.

It can be said that much interest in educational research about children's learning was placed in the boundaries of psychology and cognitive development, not taking into account the contribution of the unique social context to children's learning. This meant understanding learning not as a one-way process of learners 'receiving' but 'constructing' knowledge located within a particular social milieu. Dewey influenced policy makers, educationists, academics, philosophers, and activists; among these was George Counts (educationist, activist, teacher union leader). As a post-graduate student of education, Counts steered away from the much-charted path of interpreting learning in the framework of psychology, preferring to explore it in terms of the 'sociology of knowledge' (the enquiry into social conditions and their relationship to knowledge), to study educational practice and problems. Counts saw in sociology the opportunity to examine and reshape schools by considering the impact of social forces and varied political and social interests on educational practice.

As the 'Great Depression' (1929–39)[7] exposed the gap between the better-off and the poor, Counts became a vocal critic of the 'progressive movement' for its lack of critical assessment of the prevailing system and absence of direction about the potential of schools to contribute to 'social reform'. Counts' educational philosophy was deeply influenced by John Dewey. Both looked at education as a vehicle for larger societal wellbeing, with schools as part of community life, as a 'social experience' with all its complexities, rather than insulated from sociopolitical forces. Where they differed was in terms of what should one do with such 'progressive' education. Counts felt it was necessary to clearly articulate a 'plan of action in the use for schools to fashion a new social order', to take a sharp political position, and not remain neutral. 'Dare Progressive Education be Progressive?', in his speech to the Progressive Education Association (PEA), and later the pamphlet 'Dare the School Build a New Social Order?' (1932), he extolled teachers to go beyond abstract, philosophical conceptions of democracy and confront the issues of power and injustice unambiguously through education, to expose the limitations of the prevalent economic model of progress that placed profit and individual success at the cost of others. Counts' curriculum for 'social reconstruction'[8] was aimed at a model of 'participatory democracy', where citizens actively engage in questioning decision-making to reduce disparities of income, wealth, and power through 'Social Reconstruction'. As such democracy was not to be taken for granted, it was not to be seen merely as a political mechanism of governance. Democracy had to be earned, maintained, by engaging collectively to pressurise the powerful and to assure justice for all. Education in general, and social sciences in particular, hold the responsibility to develop ways of facilitating this project.

Counts was clearly aware that his ideas about education would essentially be seen as 'imposition of a political agenda'. He underlined that, at its best, we should be aware of the reality that 'all education contains a large element of imposition', or 'indoctrination' – the question is what the motives behind indoctrination are – self-preserving individualism or equity and justice?

While Counts did not impact educational thinking as much as Dewey, his ideas remain a strong reference in the motivations for 're-structuring' society through education in the educational philosophy of 'Critical Education'.

'Indoctrination' vs 'reflection'

Dewey, while being the forerunner in acknowledging the social nature of learning and social purpose of education, was not in favour of explicitly proposing a stated plan for 're-construction'. Dewey wrote,[9] that;

> Those supporting indoctrination rest their adherence to the theory, in part, upon the fact that there is a great deal of indoctrination now going on in the schools, especially with reference to narrow nationalism under

the name of patriotism, and with reference to the dominant economic regime. These facts, unfortunately, *are* facts. But they do not prove that the right course is to seize upon the method of indoctrination and reverse its object.

(Dewey, 1937)[10]

As a 'Pragmatist'[11] Dewey's inherent belief in democratic means of education necessitated trusting in the power of learners to make sensitive, intelligent decisions. He perceived Count's proposal as short-circuiting democratic education, replacing the prevalent teacher-centred, standardised, mechanistic form of education by another preconceived prototype advocated by well-meaning adults. Democracy for him meant trusting learners to use their intellect to reflect on the complex reality around them, to sift between various choices, and collectively make decisions. Relevance to life, immersing in meaningful activity, examining and applying things within their context to verify what was taught, were integral to education.

The primary aim of education is 'to prepare individuals to take part intelligently in the management of conditions under which they will live, to bring them to an understanding of the forces which are moving, and to equip them with the intellectual and practical tools by which they can themselves enter into the direction of these forces.

(Dewey, 1933)[12]

Dewey did not see any conflict in actively advocating the 'pragmatic method of intelligence'[13] and education for democracy. That is why education had to be linked with everyday life by reducing the separation of experiences of community outside the school to the community inside the school.

Do you agree with Dewey's views about Counts's call for 'reconstruction'?

Think

For Dewey, 'pragmatic' education was expected to prepare individuals to take part intelligently in the management of conditions under which they will live, to bring them to an understanding of the forces which are moving, and to equip them with the intellectual and practical tools by which they can themselves enter into the direction of these forces.

Both Dewey and Counts were deeply committed to a justice-oriented democratic society and sought to design educational programmes to facilitate it. Counts felt the urgency to spell out clearly what such a programme was meant to do but Dewey rejected the idea and saw it as 'indoctrination'. Despite

Dewey's reservations about 'replacing one adult-initiated model by another'. But issues raised by Counts remain unaddressed:

- Who or what will play the role to 'prepare individuals to take part intelligently in the management of conditions under which they live'?
- What indeed are the 'forces' Dewey expected to bring an understanding of, in order that 'the individuals enter into the direction of these forces'?
- How can one hope to transform society without clearly discussing the factors that led to injustices, particularly if it had to go beyond small experiments?

The debate between Counts and Dewey never saw its conclusion, but these concerns remained and generated possibilities many decades later in other lands.

> Paulo Freire (1970) followed in these tracks in Brazil where democracy as a political institution of governance was constrained and later taken over by a military dictatorship. Freire's work organically enmeshed the urgency of Counts for directing vision of social change towards social transformation and Dewey's faith in methods of intelligence. His schools outside the formal structure were aimed at empowering the community of labourers through the process of self-examination of their conditions, by engaging in reflective, critical pedagogy.
>
> > The fewer the democratic experiences which lead through concrete participation in reality to critical consciousness of it, the more a group tends to perceive and to confront that reality naively ... The less critical capacity a group possesses, the more ingenuously it treats problems and the more superficially discusses subjects.
> >
> > *(Freire,1974)*

Thinking – a prerogative of the chosen few

Whereas Counts' and Dewey's examples reveal two different ideas of 'deliberative democracy'[14] to actively engage in society for an equitable vision through education, there are contrary views that need to be recognized. These take us back to the initial phase of mass education where passing on selective, subject-based standardised knowledge became the norm and Dewey's or Counts' ideas emerged as a reaction to these. But we see it drawing to a full circle. Ideas like 'democratic realism' ('individualism' and 'free-market') have directly or indirectly influenced theory-making in education in general and social sciences in particular.

The early 1900s witnessed a consolidation of industrial colonialism, the resultant wars in Europe and the curtailment or elimination of justice for large sections of society, leading to acknowledgement of the limitations of democracy simply as a method of governance. The growth of mass media and its presence in everyday life, instead of creating an informed citizenry, generated consumerism and manipulation. In this context, Walter Lippmann (progressive socialist thinker, celebrated American journalist, political commentator, and often called the father of modern journalism), raised questions about the nature of modern democracy and the average citizen's role in eco-political policy-making. Lippmann's ideas represent the position of 'democratic realism', which presuppose the limitations of the practical aspects of democracy and extend to his views about the purpose of education. Lippmann wrote on the topic in his newspaper columns, countering the propositions of Dewey about 'intellectualising' education and the reliance on 'reflective practice' in particular.

Lippmann (1922)[15] argued that industrialisation and urbanisation had led to drastic changes in the lives of small rural communities, where personal contact made it possible to develop an intuitive sense about socio-political realities in an immediate sense. In the transitioned urban, industrial cultures, powerful members of the elite and politicians mediated the mass media for their self-interests, manipulating 'public opinion'. Even within the arena of education, specialisation and expansion of information made knowledge the prerogative of the few intellectual elite. As a result, ordinary citizens remained alienated from knowing or grasping economic-political processes where the faceless state mechanism took vital decisions on their behalf. With the pressure to keep up with changed ideas of progress, citizens remained primarily occupied with their everyday survival or events that directly concerned their lives. Thus, Lippmann argued that, in such a scenario, 'deliberative democracy' was just an ideal and engaged, reflective education only a pedagogic model.

Lippmann's disputes with Dewey's (or Counts') ideas of democracy and education need not be seen as opposition to their political, moral principles or their attempts to work for an education system built on compassion, reason, fairness, and justice. Instead, he was exposing the serious road blocks, the challenges in synthesising education and democracy in realizing these goals. While commenting on the impact of industrialisation, Lippmann was not uncritical of what hyper-industrialisation and -urbanization had done to social relations – alienation, loss of agency in political decision-making, mass media fostering consumerism and manipulating public opinion. At the same time, it is essential to further analyse Lipman's 'democratic realism' in terms of placing trust in innate human drive for seeking a balanced society, to break the binaries between good and evil. It is essential to understand that self-interest and altruism, greed and compassion, rationality and nescience are not permanently at war with each other. Just as the oppressed are capable of finding ways to change their condition, the oppressors are capable of confronting the irrationality of repression. To give-up hope and agency is to collapse into blind faith, cynicism, and self-perpetuating stagnation. It is not that Dewey and Counts were not aware of the challenges of hyper-industarialisation and market control over knowledge that Lipman so accurately makes us confront. But it is equally necessary to acknowledge the possibilities of intervening in education to meet and overcome those challenges.

As we move forward in context of these three perspectives on democracy and education, we need to step backwards understand the ideologies that nurtured and legitimised social inequities of the industrial age which stand in clear contrast to Dewey, Counts, and Lipmann, the creed of 'social efficiency' applied to education by David Snedden a well-known contemporary.

David Snedden was one of the most prominent advocates of 'social efficiency' in the USA. Snedden worked in the Teacher's College, Columbia University, as a professor of educational sociology during 1916–1935 (during Dewey's tenure). Snedden was influenced by Benjamin Kidd, a British sociologist. Darwin's 'On The Origin of Species' (1859) impacted not only biological sciences but also social sciences and indeed social attitude, giving voice to the ideology of 'social Darwinism' that gained traction from the 1870s. Selectively applying the relationships between species, this ideology looks at competition as a primary principle between different groups (race and classes, for example) where the supposedly 'strong', and thus 'superior', have a natural right to dominate. In such a conception, the age-old inequities borne from exploitation by powerful groups and traditionally bestowed sociohistoric privileges of 'cultural capital' are overlooked. Snedden was inspired by Kidd and Herbert Spencer, (a foremost British biologist and sociologist). Spencer one the earliest to endorse 'Social Darwinism', popularised the phrase 'survival of the fittest'. Snedden designed educational programmes to tune education as a supply mechanism to fulfil the demands of the industrial capitalist society by arguing that children should be given only a specific type of education or vocational 'training as per their capabilities or interests'. He justified these as inborn traits of children of a particular class. He argued that the industrial society required only a few theoretically inclined students to engage in research and knowledge-creation to become decision-makers, inventors, industrialists, and wealth creators, while the majority could be trained in practical skills fitting their aptitude, to work in factories, farms, or as subordinates. He maintained that this approach was, in fact, more democratic, providing 'equality of opportunity' by giving 'education as per capacities' rather than creating redundancy by teaching the same theoretically oriented courses to those who had no use for such knowledge. He propagated industrial education and practical project work with inputs about 'character building' for poorer children, to join the workforce, providing early opportunities in the competitive industrial society.

Sneddon selectively borrowed ideas from 'progressive education' that opposed information-load and bookish learning, but criticised emphasis on self-reflection, expression, creativity, or self-realisation. Instead, he propagated the concept of 'scientific management' (proposed by Fredrick Taylor and adopted to school education by Franklin Bobbit) to boost industrial productivity. In his book *Educational Sociology* (1922), he explained his ideas that teaching in school had to be oriented to 'social efficiency' and had to meet the criteria of usefulness. A good democratic society had to be efficient like a 'team' in which there had to be leaders, who were above average, and others following them. As such, for a successful democracy, education had to train different social groups into the roles best suited to them to fulfil their niche jobs.[16]

At the turn of the twentieth century, the US economy was at its peak, realising the industrial dream with the products, services, and consumer gadgets making life easier for the middle class. Despite the exploitation of workers and the deepening inequalities of race, class, and gender, a large and vocal section of society was proud of the technological and economic advances of the USA. The 'social efficiency' advocates argued for a society that had democracy as a political system but was not morally bound by its principles, such as those supported by Dewey or Counts or others. Instead, they argued for a 'well-managed' society, based on efficiency, as its ideal. An ideal society for them was like a successful enterprise that operated by reducing costs to ensure efficiency, optimising the use of resources, preventing waste (either by acquiring cheap goods based on exploitative practices, like cotton grown by slave labour of African-Americans or by paying minimal wages to the poor and migrants, with policies of 'hire-and fire', preventing trade unions). Epitomising the assembly-line model developed by Henry Ford in the early part of the twentieth century, with profit maximisation as the mantra, the proponents of social efficiency saw the 'factory model' as an ideal of efficiency where nothing was wasted. For such a society, critical reflection, raising questions about the realities of life, was an obvious threat and the kind of education its proponents rooted for is where 'experts' would decide on what was to be taught, how, how much, and to whom, the teachers implementing the given curriculum 'like cogs in the wheel' without questioning, churning out students with specific abilities. School education represented a syphoning mechanism (Figure 4.1) for a society that needs people doing different kinds of jobs, performing required tasks, having differential status, to select a few for higher education and the others for so-called unimportant

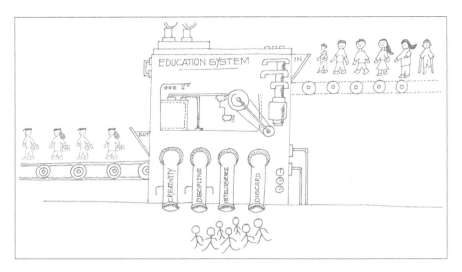

FIGURE 4.1   Factory model of education.

jobs. Social sciences, thus, would be taught only to the university-bound but seen as 'wasteful' or irrelevant for those selected for manual tasks.

This concept of a competitive, market-based, profit-oriented society, with its stratified education, is not new, nor restricted to industrialised USA or any one country. Most complex agricultural societies have had it in some form or the other – the Indian caste system or pre-WWII Germany displaying its technological might are some classic examples of this. Despite the post-WWII changes in redefining sociopolitical, ethical codes based on universal peace and egalitarianism, this ideology dominates or subtly permeates in all cultures. Even today, under the justification of building a strong, efficient nation, it is common to pay lip-service to Deweyan progressive ideals but uphold the alluring logic of merit in policy.

We have looked at the ideas of Counts, Dewey, and Lippmann representing differences in thought process on a continuum about the role of social sciences in democratic societies. There are others, like Snedden, representing the 'social efficiency' ideology, reflecting 'individualism' and 'critical thinking' as being either redundant or problematic. In reality, in most of the classroom practices, these thoughts do not reveal themselves as water-tight compartments.

Dewey's influence runs deep on educational thought and policy across the world but it is more often viewed from the lens of 'child centred pedagogy', rather than his ideas about democracy, purpose of education, 'social nature of learning', 'method of intelligence', or 'reflection on reality'. Count's ideas that education could not be 'neutral' and that the power imbalance in society needs to be dealt with by having a clear educational agenda have been acknowledged by 'critical theorists', justice-oriented education, philosophically, pedagogically sharpened by Paulo Freire, Michael Apple, and Henry Giroux, among others. Lippmann's views about 'democratic realism' emerged as political commentary, not directly acknowledged in education practice. But his concerns about the role of mass media in 'manufacturing public opinion', the loss of agency of average citizens to influence policy are an everyday reality resulting in 'individualism', and tightening the grip of market forces on all aspects of our lives. The ideology of 'social efficiency' has left a deep mark on education and on our conceptions of a successful society, and is increasingly becoming stronger (we will see this more clearly in Chapter 5).

The discussion so far will certainly offer insights into understanding and analysing the 'approaches to teaching social sciences' but not necessarily in a clear-cut, mechanical format. They can best be represented as strands and nodes in a complex web for understanding the relationship between society, education, power, and the role social sciences play in constructing, unravelling, and re-structuring our values, thoughts, and practices.

'Dare social studies educators try to build a new social order?' Stanley reminds us of this question raised by Counts by presenting some key debates. We know these debates continue today; they are reflected in our classroom practices. Dewey trusted reason, an inborn ability in all of us but not 'dry reason' without compassion, empathy, the ability for 'reasoning', for discerning judgement, an allegiance to a cause of democracy larger than achieving personal growth. Democracy as institutionalised political rule was born out of the geographic-economic process of the world coming closer and triumphing into capitalistic colonialism. But democracy is also an idea that challenges these designs of dominance. In this light, the choice of approaches in teaching social sciences plays a direct role in the choices we wish to offer to the young generations. History tells us the ideal of individual growth is possible for a few privileged, whosoever they may be in only temporary terms. There is a cause to be pursued, as well as perused, in its promises and disillusionments, it reminds us that the idea of democracy is a worthwhile one, and starting early to critically engage with what everyday life brings is essential.

With this understanding as the basis, let's proceed to look at the different 'approaches to teaching of social sciences', as acknowledged by academics and practitioners.

Exercise: Illustration of WEB/mind-map: Democracy and education

Based on the ideas explored above, here is a sample of the 'mind-map'. You too can make your own.

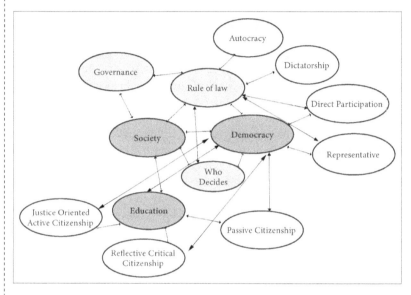

FIGURE 4.2 Web-map democracy and education

Part II

Defining the 'good citizen': Social sciences bear the mantle

The arena of school social sciences embraces ideologies that are both in convergence with and contestation against each other. The disciplines of history, geography, political science, and economics carry distinct knowledge traditions but are often intertwined. The knowledge, abilities, values, and dispositions expected to be nurtured by each of these subjects are impacted by the overt and covert ideologies of society, placed in the context of learners' developmental stage, social context, beliefs, and the capacities of teachers. The range of what is selected for teaching represents 'the study of all human enterprise over time and space' (Stanley and Nelson, 1994).

In the domain of school education, there has always been an ongoing tussle to define the purpose of teaching social sciences. More often than not, school social sciences represent an assortment of content pedagogies, symbolising the diversities and discords in real life. Thus, ironically, although

> **Social Studies**
>
> **HISTORY**
>
> I Ancient India 1
>
> 1. Villages and Towns 2
> 2. Trade and Commerce 7
> 3. Culture, Language, Arts, Crafts, Medicine 11
> 4. Everyday Life 17
> 5. Wars 22
>
> II Medieval Period 26
>
> 6. India in 11th Century 28
> 7. Mughal Empire 31
> 8. Emperor Akbar 37
> 9. Trade and Commerce 42
> 10. Culture and Innovation 48
> 11. Trade, Commerce, Exchange 53
> 12. Law and Governance 57
> 13. Villages, Towns Cities 61
>
> **CIVICS**
>
> 1. Constitution 65
> 2. Democracy 70
> 3. Central Administration 73
> 4. Our Role as Citizens 77
>
> **GEOGRAPHY**
>
> 1. Temperature (Part 3) 81
> 2. Varied Climatic Zones 87
> 3. Natural Disasters (Part 2) 92
> 4. India and Its Neighbors 97

FIGURE 4.3 Disciplinary approach textbook index

social sciences are largely seen as 'non-utility' subjects, they are the subjects where most sociopolitical interests and ideologies seek representation and dominance. As a result, right from their entry into formal education, different forces like the 'life adjustment movement', 'progressive education', 'social reconstructionism', and nationalistic history have held sway at various times. The debate over the nature, purpose, and content of the social studies curriculum continues today, with competing groups variously arguing for a 'social issues approach', the 'disciplinary study of history and geography', or 'action for social justice' as the most appropriate framework for the social studies curriculum. The space each force tries to claim is the geographically defined and socially imagined modern democratic nation-state. within which formal education and social sciences play a pivotal role in constructing a 'good citizen'. As we saw earlier, there are competing conceptions of democracy and of 'good citizenship', the task expected of social sciences education.

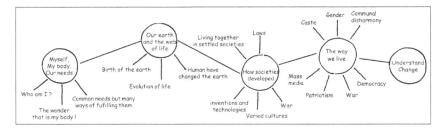

FIGURE 4.4 Integrated approach example 1
Avehi Abacus Project

Social science education – contestations and semblances

School Social Sciences are a combination of content pedagogy that tend to be both static and moribund, as well as reflecting changes impacting the society at a given time. The state-appointed bodies, acting under the influence of political dispensation of the day, re-define or clarify the purpose of social science education reflecting values preferred by them to be transferred to the citizens of the nation-state. Different political dispensations uphold ideas of democracy and citizenship education reflective of specific sociopolitical beliefs, about the nature of society. These are projected in education policies defining the purpose, selection of content, and advocating pedagogical practices. Such diverse and contending viewpoints have been studied by scholars to identify them into broader categories. The most prominent of these are in the context of the American 'social studies' curriculum but carry their influence in the Indian and South Asian context. Barr, Barth, and Shermis's (1977) *'Defining the Social Studies'* identifies three themes: 'cultural transmission', 'social science', and 'reflective inquiry'. This set the ground for others (Skeel, 1995;[17] Vinson, 1998)[18]. Martorella (1996)[19] extended the work of Barr, Barth, and Shermis, to include 'social studies education' as: (1) citizenship transmission, (2) social science, (3) reflective inquiry, (4) informed social criticism, and (5) personal development. Drawing on a summarisation of these perspectives by Ross, Mathison, and Vinson (2014)[20], let's look at the categories of approaches about citizenship education.

Social sciences as cultural transmission

Here, the objective is to pass on or transmit a set of values, dispositions, skills, and information that are seen as important to the hegemonic nation-state or to the culturally dominant groups. It is expected that students uncritically receive the pre-packaged pieces of 'knowledge' as being desirable and essential to becoming 'good citizens'. State-appointed bodies of 'experts' select what is to be taught, how, at what stage, and decide what has to be omitted. The kind of things selected for teaching usually remain unchanged or inert, unless a political dispensation bearing a less culturally dominant ideology takes charge. The running narrative is woven around the birth of the nation (usually about retaining or reclaiming its great past), and while unity of all despite diversity is proclaimed as a norm; differences, discrimination, and discords are brushed under the carpet. Addressing sociocultural, politicoeconomic differences in real life is seen as 'undesirable'. Social sciences are introduced at a crucial stage of developmental change, when children enter adolescence, changing physically and socioemotionally. Their experiences, perceptions, and ideas widen and sharpen as they interact with daily realities. However, standardised ideas of 'good citizenship' actively try to insulate the students against the realities of life, arguing that 'bringing real life into classrooms will vitiate the young minds', negatively impacting society. This perspective dominates despite evidence about the teaching of social sciences or how learning happens. All social science subjects carry the narrative of the successful nation-state but, while geography and political science ('civics') remain relatively static, the subject of history is most vulnerable to these forces and is often manipulated to suit the dominant narrative.

How social science knowledge is constructed

In the context of the USA, the mid-fifties were a political and cultural watershed. Politically, the 'Cold War' between USA and the USSR had begun as America dropped nuclear bombs on Hiroshima and Nagasaki, establishing its technological might, formally ending WWII, and turning the former allies into foes. In addition to indirect political involvement in far-off, relatively later-decolonised nations in Arabic regions, Asia, Africa, and Latin America, and by waging proxy wars led by the USA on one hand and USSR on the other, both sides also entered the space race. Economically and socially, the USA had settled to the 'American Dream' of plenty. The 'Great Depression' of the 1930s and later WWII had been years of stress and uncertainty. For the average American middle-class, automated consumer products and services offering a comfortable life had become the norm. Rapid mobility – both physical and social – was seeming accessible.

Culturally, there was rebellion brewing against old values of conformity, expressed in popular music. There was also the push for a less unequal society, particularly through the 'Civil Rights movement', demanding racial equality in all spheres. In 1954, the Brown vs Board of Education Topeka judgement of the Supreme Court made racial segregation (in educational institutions) unconstitutional. In 1955, Rosa Parks refused to give up her seat on the bus to whites. The ferment led to the passing of the Civil Rights

Act, 1957. Raising questions against conventions and dominance had found a voice. The same year, the USSR launched the first space satellite – Sputnik. The USSR had won the war of perception. Although the USA was not that far behind the USSR in space-age technology, middle-class Americans saw Sputnik as a challenge. It was felt that the obsession with consumerism had diverted the nation from its real technological advancement. 'In spite of evidence to the contrary, many Americans claimed the United States school system as a main cause for losing the technological race with the Soviets and blamed the popular progressive educational philosophy for this supposed defeat'.[21]

It is in this complex context that a new tradition of social sciences evolved in America. 'The post-Sputnik effort of social scientists to have a say in the design, development, and implementation of the social studies curriculum'[22] influenced particularly by the ground-breaking work of cognitive psychologist Jerome Bruner (1969, 1977).[23] Until then, the 'social studies' curriculum was mainly an assortment of information from the fields of social sciences with an emphasis on content or what was to be taught, having a general pedagogical approach to 'learning by doing'. The changes during 1950–60s saw a review of what was taught and the 'social studies' curriculum came under attack from different sections (from the nationalists for 'lacking in the spirit of nationalism', from subject specialists as 'lacking in appropriate content about specific themes', and from the pedagogues, for its inability to build conceptual knowledge). In 1960, in Woods Hole, Massachusetts, prominent scholars in the fields of different social sciences and practitioners of 'social studies' worked jointly in subject-based groups to attempt a reinvention of the social studies curriculum. Bruner's work influenced the evolution of 'social studies' into a curriculum, 'new social studies', mainly steered by Edwin Fenton (1966).[24]

This approach emphasised not merely *what was taught* but *how knowledge in each subject was 'constructed'* by professional practitioners in their respective fields. It stressed cognition rather than isolated information, arguing that the students' learning of subjects of political science, history, economics, and geography should take place in terms of the particular subject's distinct structure – its 'modes of empirical inquiry'. This meant exposing them to fundamental theoretical and conceptual frameworks, forming hypothesise, collecting, organising or discarding information, drawing conclusions with help of evidence, and theorising just the way a professional in the field would. Rather than merely learning given content in the subject, it pointed to the rationale behind the concepts, the ways of discovering that knowledge: to 'think like a social scientist'. This is what Mumtaz was attempting with her history class VIII, for the chapter 'Our Past – How do we know about it?', using different kinds of resources or 'evidence' to unravel the concepts and processes in historical sense-making as an example of this approach. She will, of course, need to use guiding questions or probes to 'scaffold' their investigation. She is helping her students to experience how 'historical knowledge is constructed' just as historians piece together found evidence to create a narrative of the past. She is trying to make her students aware of the fact that the narrative may change if the same historian uses different sources or another historian looks at the same evidence. She is making the students aware that historical knowledge construction is about making 'judgement calls' and in this process to accept that historical material about an event or a person reveals that there are often 'different pasts, not a singular one'!

In terms of this perspective, successful citizenship is seen as having mastery over social-scientific knowledge and procedures, to understand the specific 'structure of discipline'. Citizenship education is the proficiency in acquiring of social science concepts, generalizations, and processes of knowledge formation as foundational step for higher education enabling knowledge creation and thereby active participation in society. The citizens' ability to analyse social phenomena and processes in their sociocultural, historical context is seen essential for developing an understanding of society.

In the Indian context, although these ideas arrived on the academic scene without any delay, they matured and saw fruition in school education policy with the National Curriculum Framework 2005.

Reflective inquiry and social sciences

In the discussion earlier on democracy and education, we looked at John Dewey's idea of reflective inquiry (1933). The post-WWII statis, followed by ferment in American society, surged the need to reorganise education for realigning society. As a school subject the 'social studies' faced the brunt; the curriculum was viewed as being 'tentative' in nature, lacking specific orientation. In addition to general dissatisfaction about the subject from different sectors, its reliance on content (or lack of it) brought a Deweyan perspective of 'pragmatism' back to the centre along with the one discussed above. Two psychologists, Maurice Hunt and Lawrence Metcalf (1968),[25] recentred the focus on social education, adopting Dewey's socio-cognitive approach with an emphasis on citizenship for democracy. Hunt and Metcalf argued against the curriculum restricting focus on individual social science subjects (oriented to American society) and instead argued in favour of focusing it on 'closed areas of society' or 'taboo topics' that are either touched on superficially or omitted entirely from curriculum (like racism, economic disparities, homophobia, teenage pregnancy, a critical look at nationalism, etc.). They pointed that avoiding discussions on these areas would compromise the very essence of democracy, giving rise to ignorance, stereotyping, prejudice, and a lack of empathy. They pleaded for education embracing the reflective process, supporting values, skills, knowledge, and dispositions based on the principles and theories from different branches of social sciences, oriented to critical thinking and sensitive decision-making.[26]

As visualised by Dewey, life in schools must be closely linked with real life, 'the essential relationship between human knowledge and social experience'.[27] A democratic society was possible when schools supported students in being capable of the identification of problems by collecting evidence, organising their findings, analysing data, evaluating, and then making reasoned decisions about situations in real life. The growing nationalistic fever for a strong nation in the context of the 'Cold War', saw the elite pitching for orienting social sciences towards 'citizenship transmission' (an uncritical acceptance of selective values and content), or discipline-based social science teaching (for a technocratic society). Instead, reflective inquiry means building capacities for problem-solving, discerning decision-making not by abstract ideation but developing understanding with reference to specific sociopolitical contexts, related with the realities experienced by students and teachers. This process reflects the experience of 'creative democracy' (Dewey, 1939)[28]; including its challenges, making moral and ethical decisions based on mutual trust and respect – there are no simple solutions here, or one 'correct answer'. The 'problems frequently require decisions between several perceived good solutions and/or several perceived bad solutions' (Ross, Mathison, Vinson, 2014).

Right from the outset of his career, Dewey (1897)[29] clearly argued that teaching/learning in classrooms cannot be separated from everyday life and social issues confronting us. Indeed, it is only by creating awareness and curiosity about everyday problems that one can creatively think about certain option for resolutions and seek alternatives. Dewey saw school as a community reflecting a microcosm of society in its challenges, strengthens, ugliness, and beauty. Education meant the ability to process not only the validated given knowledge but also the everyday experiences by the process of reflection (Dewey, 1910), based on evidence and insights gained inside and outside school.

Other scholars like Alan F. Griffin, H. Gordon Hullfish, Paulo Freire, and Michael W. Apple followed and expanded or deepened Dewey's ideas.

Social sciences as informed social criticism

This framework is a continuation of and rooted in the work of the 'social reconstructionist' vision of democracy and education by Counts that was revived in the 1950s USA, with reference to Brameld (1956),[30]. It resurged and found strength by the contribution of Paulo Freire in the later 1970s, in the work of critical pedagogy theorists (Engle and Ochoa, 1988). The focal point of this perspective is to use the content and methods of social sciences to challenge the status quo and resist discrimination, to transform society into a less unequal and less exploitative one. Students are to be supported by clear tasks to critically analyse real-life situations and cultivate abilities for problem-solving, based on the values of justice and equality (Stanley and Nelson, 1986).[31] The discipline-based knowledge in social sciences is to be examined from the standpoint of justice. Along with the accepted methods of social sciences it is also to be examined in relation to the knowledge/traditions of less-empowered, marginalised sections of society (races, genders, classes, cultures, regions, etc.). 'Positivism' or 'objective facts' are to be placed in specific social contexts to stand the test of contextual accuracy. These pedagogical principles rest on using the social sciences as a floorboard, but goes beyond 'teaching of objective facts'. It calls for critical, evidence-based examination of ideas or given texts applied to people's contexts. It invokes personalised knowledge, experiences, and insights of learners and teachers by engaging in 'reflective thinking' and 'dialogical method' (Shor and Freire, 1987). Learning is seen as a by-product of democratic dialogue, listening to others, communicating one's ideas, including 'deconstruction' (Cherryholmes, 1980, 1982). The ultimate aim is not merely learning for individual self-improvement or education for personal gain, but a drive for social action oriented towards justice. In this sense, the very purpose of social sciences is to bring social transformation and to resist the tendencies of 'social reproduction' (Ross, Mathison, Vinson, 2014), i.e. those processes that strengthen and retain social institutions, mores, values, and traditions that are based on inequality and discrimination (like caste or gender). This includes questioning our iniquitous education system with private better-served schools for the elite, middle range for the middle class, and poorly served government ones lacking even school completion for the marginalised, resulting in only the higher and middle classes' entry to higher education and socioeconomic mobility.

At the core of this framework is education for social justice, which is a highly contested concept. We have already seen this in relation to Dewey's views that such position is instrumentalist, that it means an attempt to indoctrination, rather than democratisation. There are more shades besides Dewey's views. One position views it as investigating the reasons and articulating the expression of power dynamics amongst different social groups. The other position may not go into these complexities but may leave it at the level of being fair and just to all. In a sense 'Social justice teaching represents the essence of social studies' role in fostering democratic ideals in society' (Jorgensen, 2014)[32]. Adoption of his approach is riddled with impediments. In policy level it is opposed by entrenched social interests and by powerful social elite. During direct implementation it is resisted on grounds of prioritising completion of vast curricula, high-stakes testing on one hand and direct resistance by teachers having opposite ideology or due to inadequate teacher preparation.

Social sciences as an exploration

This approach is also influenced by Deweyan ideas of giving primacy to the learners' preferences and experiences, creating space and opportunity for them to explore and build their knowledge. Pre-selected textbook knowledge has only notional relationship with this method. By referring to broad thematic areas information relevant to the selected theme/s is developed into a comprehensive 'project'. William Kilpatrick, a student and later colleague of Dewey's, is considered the pioneer and advocate of the 'project method'. Influenced by 'progressive education' and later with personal contact with Dewey, Kilpatrick devoted himself to refining and disseminating his ideas. This approach views teachers in the role of a 'guide' and students' choice about selection and development of content is given importance, based on their needs, curiosity, and disposition. Children's are encouraged to take initiative, steering their interests to explore the environment through all their senses rather than information passed on by an authoritative figure of a teacher.

Historically, this concept has been said to have reference to 'projects' done by students of applied fields like architecture, engineering, and agriculture, and modified by Kilpatrick. Kilpatrick's work has been critiqued, for lacking a clear theoretical basis, for 'vocationalising' education, and that 'project method' can be best viewed as one of the pedagogic strategies instead of a theoretical framework. The reason underlying this can be the fact that, whereas Kilpatrick himself professed 'progressivism', his ideas did not clearly spell out an ideological position with regards to the larger issues surrounding citizenship education and notions of democracy. Today, with the exception of some schools, it is adopted as work to be done outside class or taken up a few times in the year to produce three-dimensional artefacts and not as a consistent 'approach to teaching/learning'. (You may instantly recall 'additional activities and projects' suggested at the end of a textbook chapter or making 'models' to display during annual events or school competitions.)

We have tried to understand the different ways of approaching social science education. As we can see these only broadly indicate pedagogical ideas. By outlining these different approaches, we have tried to unravel the societal vision they represent and the way they visalise the role of social sciences in society. One also needs to underscore that, in reality, one sees the interspersing of these 'approaches' as pedagogical choices. More often than not, this happens without understanding the ideological or historical contexts they are set in. The effort here has been to unfurl the very underpinnings behind the pedagogical choices suggested in syllabus documents and textbooks with a hope to steer school social sciences to build a culture of discerning, humane democracy.

Part III

Perspectives and policy – classroom realties

We conclude this discussion by understanding the different frameworks influencing the approaches for teaching of social sciences. We need to place this understanding in terms of how these conceptions have influenced citizenship education in Indian context. Here, we need to look at what the defined policy expects of schools in terms of social science teaching. At the national level, there are a variety of policy documents; the various education commission reports, the 'National Education Policies', and the 'National Curriculum Frameworks' that impact syllabus, textbooks, assessment, teacher development, etc. All these are (notionally) bound by the Constitution of India. Given the federal structure of the country education is a joint responsibility of the States and the centre. Thus we have regional variations in the curriculum, syllabus, textbooks. These have evolved owing to historical factors specific to the states, the sociocultural context of the regions, aspirations of different groups within the State or the ideological dynamics between the political parties. We will look at the national level policies as an example and specifically refer to the 'National Curriculum Frameworks (NCFs)(s), having overarching influence on the *why, what, and how* of content pedagogy-assessment of social sciences. While doing this, we will also place the NCFs in the context of, the political dispensation at the centre that facilitated the particular NCF, the then sociopolitical climate, and also sometimes refer to expression of public opinion in mass media, to illustrate the larger impact or public debate. This exercise will help us locate the ideas we explored about concepts of democracy and the different approaches with regards to citizenship education in schools.

Since independence and post framing of the Constitution, India so far has introduced four NCFs: NCF-1975, NCF-1988, NCF-2000, and NCF-2005. We will present here a few key excerpts from these documents, with a focus on social science education and the brief context in which these NCFs were introduced.

Note –'about the context': You can take a clue from these events and find out more information, probably of varied perspectives, from different sources. The differences may be due to the sources you use, the people you speak with, the region you live in, and your own perspectives and ideologies.

The context	The NCFs and conception of democracy and ideas about teaching of social sciences
The NCF 1975: (Literacy rate: 34.45%; male 45.96%, female 21.97%). • Prior to this period, different education commissions (the Higher Education Commission 1952/56, the Kothari Commission 1966, and bi-lateral educational events like the UN Conference 1952) guided the framing of the school curriculum. • The centre and most states ruled by the Indian National Congress from 1947. In 1966, Mrs. Indira Gandhi is chosen as the Prime Minister. • During 1947-1977, India fights four wars with its neighbours (three against Pakistan 1947 and 1965, with the 1971 war resulting in separation of East Pakistan and the formation of Bangladesh; in 1962 war with China). • 1974, India conducts its first nuclear test supposedly 'for peaceful purposes'. • 1967 Naxalbari Movement: peasant and youth uprising starting from West Bengal's Naxalbari block, radical youth influenced by Maoist ideology propose take-over of government by peoples' power, by resorting to armed revolution, it is suppressed by the government by force and violence. • Brewing turmoil in society over unfulfilled promises, growing social inequality, unemployment, and resultant unrest particularly in the rural communities and educated youth. This led to the declaration of an 'emergency' by Mrs. Gandhi in 1975 supposedly to protect national interests, (curtailing personal and political freedoms). This lasted for about 18 months, Mrs. Gandhi declared general elections and the Congress Party, and Mrs. Gandhi, lost the elections. • While other multi-party governments took charge, they were short lived and Mrs. Gandhi became the Prime Minster again in 1980. She was assassinated in 1984 by her bodyguards to avenge the Army take-over of sacred site of the Golden Temple from Khalistani militants and killings inside the temple. This leads to an anti-Sikh pogram, the 'Delhi riots 84' killing and displacing Sikh community.	**The social sciences in NCF 1975:** The major objective of the study of the social sciences is to acquaint the child with his past and present geographical and social environment. An effective programme of teaching of the social sciences in schools should help the public to take a keen interest in the ways people live and function through various socioeconomic and political institutions. It should also help children to develop an insight into human relationships, social values and attitudes. These are essential to enable the growing citizen of tomorrow to participate effectively in the affairs of the community, the state, the country, and the world at large. The teaching of the social sciences should enable children to appreciate India's rich cultural heritage and to recognize and get rid of what is undesirable and antiquated, especially in the context of social change. The schools should see that narrow parochial, chauvinistic, and obscurantist tendencies are not allowed to grow in our pupils. The schools should endeavour to develop the will and ability in every pupil to participate in the most important task of the construction of our society and economy with a sense of social commitment. Children should also develop a faith in the destiny of our nation in terms of promoting a spirit of tolerance and assimilation, and peace and harmony among the peoples of the world. Thus, instruction in the social sciences should promote the values and ideals of humanism, secularism, socialism, and democracy. It should inculcate attitudes and impart the knowledge necessary for the achievement of the principal values of a just world order, maximisation of economic and social welfare, minimization of violence and maximization of ecological stability'. (The Curriculum for the 10-Year School 1975, page 14, Subject-wise Instructional Objectives and Content.)

Approaches to teaching social sciences 111

The context	The NCFs and conception of democracy and ideas about teaching of social sciences
The NCF 1988: (Literacy rate 43.57%; male 56.38%, female 29.76%). India at the cusp of key changes in different fields. https://ncert.nic.in/pdf/focus-group/NCESE_1988.pdf • 1984: Mr. Rajiv Gandhi, the eldest son of Mrs. Gandhi, takes over as the Prime Minister. • 1984: The Supreme Court (SC) of India rules in favour of Shah Bano, an elderly Muslim woman, granting her the right to alimony, legalising rights to alimony to all divorced Muslim women, superseding the Muslim Personal Laws. Sections of the Muslim population see this as an attack on their religious rights guaranteed by the Constitution. • 1985: The Ministry of Education is renamed 'The Human Resource Development Ministry' • The National Education Policy (NEP) 1986, takes into account the sorry state of education in India and announces the programme 'Operation Black Board', revising the norms for teacher appointment, duration of elementary schooling of eight years, improvement in infrastructure, etc., in public schools. • The BJP supposedly representing Hindu interests begins a campaign to claim rights over a mosque, as the birth place of Lord Ram, in the holy city of Ayodhya. • 1986: the Rajiv Gandhi Government passes the Muslim Women (Protection on Divorce Act), overturning the SC judgement in the Shah Bano case.	**The social sciences in NCF 1988:** The study of social sciences as a component of general education is of critical importance in facilitating the learner's growth into a well-informed and responsible citizen. It should aim at developing in him/her an understanding of his/her physical and social environment, both immediate and remote, in terms of time and space, and an appreciation of the cultural heritage of India and various cultures of the world. Organisation of curriculum: Physical and social environment should help him/her of developing an understanding of the interaction of man with his physical and social environment and with the institutions – social, economic, and political – through which human beings inter-relate with one another and function in society. The study of social sciences should also aim at enabling him to see the present in the perspective of past developments. Similar to the study of the physical and natural environments in science education, the study of social environment in social sciences should have three aspects, namely, learning *about* the social environment, learning *through* the social environment, and learning *for* the social environment. This would mean that pupil will learn, for example, about the social customs, cultural heritage, history of society, etc., through observation, exploration, and scientific study of social phenomena and events, and will thereby develop a genuine interest in, and urge for preservation of what is good in our culture and improvement of the existing socioeconomic set-up.

The context	The NCFs and conception of democracy and ideas about teaching of social sciences
- To quell the perception of 'Muslim appeasement' in overturning the Shah Bano judgement, the government allows access to Hindus at the disputed site in the Babri mosque and the campaign for Ram Janmabhoomi gets traction. - 1990: BJP leader Mr. Lal Krishna Advani takes a 'Rath Yatra' to Ayodhya mobilising lakhs of Hindus to demand pulling down of the Babri Masjid, to make room for a Lord Rama temple (claimed by the BJP as Lord Rama's birthplace). The Masjid is damaged. - 1991: Rajiv Gandhi assassinated in Tamil Nadu, by 'Tamil Tigers', a militant group fighting for a separate Tamil state and rights in Sri Lanka. - 1991: a non-Congress led government is elected. Prime Minister, V.P. Singh, announces intent to implement recommendations of the 1973 Mandal Commission Report extending 'reservations' in higher education and employment in government colleges/jobs. The ABVP (student organisation affiliated with RSS-BJP) stages violent nationwide protests in opposition. In 1992, the SC in a related case challenging the Mandal Report recommendations, rules in favour of its implementation.	Social sciences is perhaps the singular curricular area which can prove to be the most effective tool for providing education in the context of the core components indicated in the NEP-86. Special care should, hence, be taken in designing the curriculum in social sciences so as not to overlook any of the core components (National Curriculum for Elementary and Secondary Education – A framework (Revised Version) NCERT, 1988, 26–27)

Approaches to teaching social sciences **113**

The context	The NCFs and conception of democracy and ideas about teaching of social sciences
• 1990, the 'Education for All' conference funded by IMF, WB, and UN agencies is held in Jomtin, Thailand. Period of elementary schooling declared as five years instead of the eight years recommended by the National Education Policy,1986. • 1991: India officially adopts 'economic liberalisation', reducing State role and investments in public sector (education, health, agriculture, transport, fuel, etc.), allowing increased investment by Indian and foreign private business. • 1992: India revises the 1986 NEP and introduces the 'Programme of Action' (POA, 1992). Period of elementary schooling reduced from eight to five years. • Norms about schooling diluted; instead of full-time formal education in schools, 2-3 hours of 'non-formal education' (NFE) classes outside schools taught by 'volunteers', aimed at the socioeconomically marginalised, mushroom throughout the country.	

The context	The NCFs and conception of democracy and ideas about teaching of social sciences
- 1992-93: the District Primary Education Programme (DPEP) introduced in some districts for the first time, partially funded by external agencies (WB, DIFID, UNICEF) - 1992: Yash Pal Report – 'Learning Without Burden' – critical of meaningless cognitive load, alienating education, proposes 'learning by doing', learning to construct knowledge in learners' context. - 1992: The second attempt to destroy the Babri mosque, it is finally brought down, and violent riots and pogroms against Muslims erupt in parts of India and against Hindus in parts of Pakistan and Bangladesh. - 1993: Series of bomb blasts in Mumbai (then Bombay) by clandestine Muslim extremists supposedly to avenge the killing of Muslims in response to the Babri violence. Innocents of all faiths and classes die. - 1993: The Unnikrishnan Judgement: Concern over lack of legal means for making education a fundamental right. Interprets Right to Education as part of Article 21 (Right to Life) of the Constitution – education inalienable from right to life with dignity. - 1995: The World Trade Organization (WTO), an organisation facilitating and regulating intergovernmental international trade, is formed. **The NCF 2000:** (Literacy rate: 64.83%; male 75.26%, female 53.67%): https://ncert.nic.in/pdf/focus-group/NCF_2000_Eng.pdf - The National Democratic Alliance of parties under the leadership of BJP is in power under the Prime Ministership of Mr. Atal Bihari Vajpayee (1997 onwards): - 1998: India conducts its second nuclear test. Pakistan responds by conducting six more tests.	**The social Sciences in NCF 2000:** Social sciences is integral to the general education up to the secondary level. It helps the learners in understanding the human environment in its totality and in developing a broader perspective and an empirical, reasonable, and humane outlook. It also helps learners grow into well-informed and responsible citizens with valuable attributes/skills so that they could participate and contribute effectively to the process of development and nation-building.

The context	The NCFs and conception of democracy and ideas about teaching of social sciences
• 1999: the 'Kargil war' between India and Pakistan breaks-out in retaliation to Kashmiri militants backed by Pakistan crossing the 'line of control'. India wins the war. • The NDA government led by the BJP deletes portions from textbooks 'not favourable to Hindus'. • The NCF 2000 introduces astronomy as a subject of study, gives primacy to Sanskrit, links 'moral development' with religion; the much-criticised concept of 'Minimum Levels of Learning' (MLL) is reintroduced. • 2000: 86th Parliament makes Constitutional amendment to acknowledge Right to Education as a fundamental right, but the age-group is limited to 6–14 years instead of 0–14 years disregarding Article 45. • 2000: Sarva Shiksha Abhiyan ('Education for all' campaign) becomes a flagship programme to universalise elementary education. • 2002: Gujrat, Mr. Narendra Modi is the Chief Minister. A compartment of a train from Ayodhya is set on fire in Muslim-dominated town of Godhra. A violent pogrom against thousands of Muslims ensues for nearly a month, with lives, property, livelihoods lost. • The BJP lead NDA government increases role of private sector and adopts economic liberalisation policies under the programme of 'India Shining'. • 2004: the NDA government loses the general elections and the United Progressive Alliance led by Congress takes power at the centre, backed by Communist parties.	The social sciences curriculum in schools will draw its content mainly from geography, history, civics, and economics. It may also include some elements of sociology. Together, social sciences provide different approaches to studying the human society – over space and time and in relation to each other. They help learners in understanding contemporary society better. Social science education aims at providing students with essential knowledge, skills, and attitude necessary for self-development and also for becoming an effective and contributing member of society. In order to make social sciences education meaningful, relevant, and effective, the concerns and issues of the contemporary world need to be kept to the forefront. To this end, the quantum of history may have to be substantially reduced. Past developments could be studied as a backdrop for understanding the present. As such, the needs and challenges of today must be responded to appropriately. Globalisation and liberalisation on the one hand and localisation on the other are going to have tremendous impacts on the future society. These have also brought in their wake many economic and social challenges and opportunities which need to be addressed effectively to build a strong, cohesive Indian Society. It also calls for developing emotionally intelligent learners, who are prepared to face new challenges and adjust to unfamiliar situations (National Curriculum Framework-2000, NCERT, p. 38). 'Teaching of social sciences ought to promote a humane and national perspective, and inculcate a sense of pride in the country and in being an Indian. It needs to strengthen the national identity and develop an appreciation for cultural heritage. It should promote communal harmony and social cohesion. Its teaching must be objective and free from all kinds of stereotyped images, biases, and prejudices' (National Curriculum Framework-2000, NCERT, p. 40).

The context	The NCFs and conception of democracy and ideas about teaching of social sciences
The NCF 2005: (Literacy rate: aprox. 70%; male 80%, female 60%): https://ncert.nic.in/pdf/nc-framework/nf2005-english.pdf • Dr. Manmohan Singh is the Prime Minister of the UPA government. • The concept of 'Constructivism' is introduced, but there are concerns expressed from the academics and civil society about its lack of clarity, the modified version places it in the context of 'critical pedagogy' • Acts passed, such as Right to Information (2005), Right to Education (2009), key pro-poor measures; the 'Mahatma Gandhi National Rural Employment Guarantee Act (MGNREGA), reservations in medical colleges etc. (next step of Mandal commission reforms providing reservations to OBCs), protests by Akhil Bhartiya Vidyarthi Parishad (BJP's youth wing). At the same time, measures are introduced expanding the role of the private sector. • Pakistani terror attack 2008 in Mumbai, Amendments in Unlawful Activities (Prevention) Act, (amended 2008, bringing stringent mechanisms against those who are seen as a threat to state authority), introduction of Aadhaar- Unique Identification Authority of India (2009) for mandatory registration of biometric data of citizens, Government loses elections in 2014 rocked by allegations of economic scam. • The BJP lead NDA government with massive BJP strength takes over. Mr. Modi becomes the Prime Minister of India. Privatization of the economy gets a boost, diluting many fundamental rights including RTE and RTI passed by the UPA government.	**The social sciences in NCF 2005:** The social sciences encompass diverse concerns of society and include a wide range of content drawn from the disciplines of history, geography, political science, economics, sociology and anthropology. Social science perspectives and knowledge are indispensable in building the knowledge base for a just and peaceful society. The content should aim at raising students' awareness through critically exploring and questioning of familiar social reality. The possibilities of including new dimensions and concerns, especially in view of the student's own life experiences, are considerable. Selecting and organising material into a meaningful curriculum, one that will enable students to develop a critical understanding of society, is therefore a challenging task. Because the social sciences tend to be considered non-utility subjects and are given less importance than the natural sciences, it is necessary to emphasise that they provide the social, cultural, and analytical skills required to adjust to an increasingly interdependent world, and to deal with political and economic realities. It is believed that the social sciences merely transmit information and are text centred. Therefore, the content needs to focus on a conceptual understanding, rather lining up facts to be memorised for examinations. Reiterating the recommendations of 'Learning Without Burden (1993), emphasis has to be laid on developing concepts and the ability to analyse sociopolitical realities rather than on the mere retention of information without comprehension.

The context	The NCFs and conception of democracy and ideas about teaching of social sciences
	It is also necessary to recognise that the social sciences lend themselves to scientific inquiry just as much as the natural and physical sciences do, as well as to indicate ways in which the methods employed by the social sciences are distinct from (but in no way inferior to) those of the natural and physical sciences.
The social sciences carry a normative responsibility for creating a strong sense of human values, namely freedom, trust, mutual respect, and respect for diversity. Social science teaching should aim at generating in students a critical moral and mental energy, making them alert to the social forces that threaten these values.
The disciplines that make up the social sciences, namely history, geography, political science, and economics, have distinct methodologies that often justify the retaining of boundaries. At the same time, cross-disciplinary approaches that are possible should also be indicated. For an enabling curriculum, certain themes that facilitate interdisciplinary thinking need to be incorporated (National Curriculum Framework, 2005, NCERT, pp. 50–51).

Exercise

Carefully read the events in the left column and the excerpts from the NCFs given in the right column. Compare the 'context' and the various 'NCF's conception of democracy and ideas about teaching of social sciences'. You may also read more details by accessing the documents with the help of the links given above. Additionally refer to news items, watch documentaries, to widen your understanding of the sociopolitical context during which these documents were introduced. Reflect on the relationship between the two by discussing with your peers, educators. Based on the discussion in this chapter and the inputs given here, write a brief note with reference to the following points:

- What kind of conception/s of democracy do these particular NCF documents reflect?
- What do you think is the preferred suggested framework/s for teaching social sciences as indicated in a particular NCF?
- Do you think the context in which these documents were framed has impacted the nature of the NCF? If so, in what way?
- Is the relationship between the context and the prominent ideas in the NCFs always have a direct causal relationship or is it more complex?
- Do you think the space of education in general and social sciences in particular is used by different ideological, political dispensations sometimes in combative and some other times as a conversational course-correction in relation to the larger economic, political policies? Try to identify such spaces.

Conclusion

We close the discussion here about the approaches to teaching social sciences. We began with Mumtaz organising her classes and, with the help of the questions, you would have noted some of the reasons behind her planning the two classes in a certain way (age appropriateness, the nature of subject matter given in the textbook chapters, etc.). For class V, she chose the simple narrative style of the given chapter and helped the young children understand and remember the king and his reign by using 'drama' or 'role-play' as a strategy. But, for class VIII, despite the fact that the subject matter had nothing to do with the king, she used the children's prior knowledge to allow them the experience insights and reasoning behind the way historians work with found evidence, how the nature of evidence may change their interpretation about the past, etc. The concept of PCK briefly described earlier helps us to understand how her professional development and her experience as a teacher has enriched her 'teacher knowledge'.

Closely looking at her planning particularly for class VIII, we understand that Mumtaz has a wider view of the purpose of education. She needn't have chosen the same king as an example and collected diverse type of evidence about his reign; she could have used other strategies like using a PowerPoint presentation or showing a short documentary or photos about the work of archaeologists and historians, etc. Her choices reflect her concerns to deal with real life because the king is used as an icon of a dominant culture, that he is projected as being opposed to another sub-culture, he is given 'divine' status in popular culture, and thus views, perspectives challenging this narrative are opposed, to the point of physical threats. Mumtaz chose to confront these tensions, instead of avoiding them, by creatively weaving the assorted types of evidence to unravel the process of professional history writing, to demonstrate how 'past' is not uniform, that it is often full of contradictions. Thus, with this example, Mumtaz encouraged her students to think like professional historians who are open about looking at the past from multiple angles, rather than to deify and blindly emulate any historical figure or phenomenon, or see them in a unipolar way. Her pedagogy attempts to communicate that one needs to appreciate history to be multi-dimensional and essentially contested. She is not just concerned that children understand, retain, and recall the given information but that they should grow up as rational citizens, willing to engage with real-life challenges.

The discussion about 'democracy and education' helped create a platform to make us aware that democracy as a concept is understood differently, and thus the perspectives to look at the role education plays/ought to play in democratic societies are varied. We briefly touched upon the historical contexts in which some of these ideas emerged. From here, we looked at the main 'approaches or frameworks' identified by scholars for the teaching of social sciences. Recollecting Mumtaz's class planning, we complete the circle here.

Finally, this diversity and contestations in these frameworks or 'approaches to teaching social sciences' reflect differences and contestations about the perspectives to look at the interlinkages between democracy and education. These ideas directly or subtly impact what happens in our classrooms. It is essential for us to be aware that by preferring or underplaying a particular approach to teaching social sciences, we make choices that have larger consequences for the kind of democracy we envision, 'because the stakes are too high'.[33]

> Exercise
>
> - Interview at least one social science teacher/teacher educator or student teacher about what they understand by the concept and institution of democracy. For this task, you will need to develop a few questions along the line of points suggested here: Regarding the relationship between education and democracy, the role played by education in general, and social science education in particular in shaping a certain kind of democratic society; what, according to her/him, are the three most important characteristics which social science curriculum/education should have in shaping democratic citizenship, what is their understanding of our current society in terms of its democratic character, and do they think the kind of education system and the position of social sciences within it have anything to do with the kind of society we are?
> - After this interview you will need to do two things: 1. Summarize the responses of the teacher; and 2. Write a reflective piece on the theme 'Social sciences and the social order: Transmission or transformation?

Disciplinary and integrated[34]

We have tried to look at the 'approaches and frameworks' in light of our discussions about democracy and education. Across these frameworks, and irrespective of the arguments in favour or against any of these, one may see multiple practices operating in reality. Within these are two debates in favour of pedagogical perspectives to teaching/learning – 'disciplinary-based' and 'integrated'. There is a common misconception about the disciplinary approach being constraining, with it's stress on rote learning, whereas integration is seen as desirable and more pedagogically advanced. So, it is necessary to keep in mind that both 'approaches' have distinct features and neither is necessarily superior to the other. It is the context of learners, principles rooted in teaching, and purpose underlying education (advocated in State policies) that decides their merit.

BOX 4.1 THE DISCIPLINARY APPROACH

In formal education, disciplines are indispensable. Disciplines are nothing but those accumulative insights and historically refined processes through which we understand the world around us. Very intense and vigorous critical reflections and inquiries within as well as across the disciplines have always been the source of development and refinement of the disciplinary perspectives. Changes in society have impacted the way the disciplines have developed, enriching them, and widening perspectives and practices.

However, often the teachings of disciplines/subjects in schools do not seem to reflect the histories and features discussed above. They often seem to be confined only to the contents/facts. They seem to fail in inculcating those accumulative insights and multiple perspectives as well as abilities which are very distinctive to the particular disciplines that help its students to understand and explore the phenomenon or object of the study. Consequently, such teaching/learning processes reduce the students to passive and dependent-for-ever-receiver of the information. They never initiate a process of independent learning by acquiring those mechanisms and processes which help them to construct the legitimate and plausible understanding of the subject of the study at present as well as in future.

Therefore, discipline teaching needs to expose students to that process of knowledge building through which various concepts and theories emerge. However, such teaching is only possible when a teacher himself understands those processes of knowledge construction and the histories of each discipline, distinct processes that are very specific to each discipline.

There is a strong relation between the understanding the histories of how the discipline came about, developed, and changed and the epistemological structure of disciplines along with teachers' conceptions of teaching, their approaches to teaching, their beliefs about the purposes of education, and their reflections on planning teaching.

An understanding of epistemological structure of the discipline and its historical connotations helps teachers to identify the epistemological differences or similarities across the disciplines/subjects they teach in their schools. The identification of this difference is of great importance for school teachers. How is social science knowledge different from scientific or mathematical knowledge? Do we construct social science knowledge, mathematical knowledge, or scientific knowledge through the same methods, or are there some differences among them? Do social sciences encompass a particular kind of knowledge or a variety of knowledge? Such understanding helps teachers to devise their pedagogy which suits the content they transact in school.

This entire epistemological understanding has very serious implications for subject teachers. If we talk about a social science teacher here, she can now easily visualise which social science knowledge will help her to accomplish the selected aims of education. She will also be able to set criteria based on the epistemological structure of social science to devise her teaching methods, adjudging and developing the TLM, and eventually the methods and objectives of the evaluation.

Such epistemological structures are unique to each school discipline, which a teacher needs to understand in detail.

BOX 4.2 INTEGRATING THE CURRICULUM

Since some of the frameworks we discussed indicate going beyond the 'conventional' discipline-centred approach to teaching, there is an direct or indirect inclination towards integration. In this context it is useful to understand the concept of integration more specifically. Here is a summary of points concerning the issue of curriculum integration based on 'Integrating the Curriculum', Pring, R. (1976). *Knowledge and Schooling*. Well: Open Books.

Curriculum integration: What it is and what it is not

The meaning of 'integrated curriculum' depends on the nature of problems it aims to meet.

'Integrated curriculum' is an imprecise term covering a range of curriculum responses to the difficulties of conventional subject-based curricula. Underlying the proposals to integrate are principles of organisational and educational rationale. 'Integrated curriculum' has different meanings as well as being diverse in its organisation. It's important to ask – *What, Why, How* integration is sought to be integrated.

- **What** – all subject matter or only some?
- **How** – is it being integrated (through a particular theme/topic, a central subject, or the pupil's own inquiry)?
- **Why** – the need to integrate (to provide a flexible arrangement or a deep-seated belief about the unity of knowledge)?

These principles reflect *important differences in theory about the nature of knowledge*.

Integration in co-relating distinct subject matters

- An 'integrated curriculum' should link some themes/concepts/periods/geographies across 'main subjects', while maintaining subject boundaries. This involves tricky questions: '... not simply organizational questions, but logical questions about the relation of one subject matter to another'.
- Behind this notion of integration is the belief that there are logically distinct subject matters, and that these restrictions need to be respected in planning a curriculum.
- There is also the realisation that certain kinds of knowledge presuppose others of a certain kind and it is necessary to find the complementarity across subjects.

Integrating through themes/topics/ideas

- Themes/topics/ideas – explored in an interdisciplinary manner and in exploration the disciplinary differences become blurred, possibly unrecognizable.

When the basis of the curriculum is an idea that is supra-subject, and which governs the relationship between subjects, a number of consequences may follow. The subject is no longer dominant, but subordinate to the idea which governs a particular form of integration.

- Bernstein (1967)
- Organise learning to co-relate distinct disciplines, explore large and complex human issues, personal concerns of learners

But themes in supplanting the notion of distinct disciplines sometimes presuppose them.

Or they are seen as alternative ways of structuring by exploring overarching ideas, not confined within boundaries of any subject, but crucial structuring elements in our thinking.

And while only integration can achieve a certain perspective, looking at different issues, it cannot be ignored that there is a distinct kind of subject matter and different kinds of knowledge which the pupil must draw upon.

Also, the curriculum planner/teacher has to decide on selection of themes and organising knowledge in an integrated manner, without trivialising it

Theme-based curriculum – an alternative way of organising the curriculum

But:
- It should be evident how, by mastering the central idea of the theme, the pupils would be able to think in a *distinctive way of structuring* their *thinking*, aiding *developing minds in a certain way* and be made *more effective*.
- In order that this is possible, it is essential that there be *publicly developed modes of awareness*

Else: *it may lead to trivialisation*
   Integrated approach will thus need *public scrutiny, acceptability, commonality of practice* (not merely 'randomised words', 'false idea of integration').

A word or concept cannot by itself structure or integrate the child's thinking

- Words make sense only within a 'language'.
- Concepts have meaning only within a way of 'characterised thinking' by a range of concepts, a trajectory, testing the 'truth' of what is said.
- To link them backwards to logically distinct subject matters.
- What is being studied, what is to be enquired into depends not on a title but upon the questions being asked about the selected words/themes/concepts.

These questions/modes of enquiry are expected to locate:

- The enquiry in different subject areas.
- Because of their interdisciplinary nature, they require the understandings and skills developed within more than one subject area
- These set of questions/problems/modes of enquiry are what provide structure, not the title.
- The topic/idea.

Integration in practical thinking

- This may not mean integration of the whole curriculum.
- Some areas of 'practical thinking' escape traditional subject areas.

Approaches to teaching social sciences **125**

Avehi Abacus Project

Essential features of this curriculum programme are:

- Multi-disciplinary.
- Enquiry-based.
- Probing important, 'controversial' issues.
- On the basis of evidence.
- In areas of practical living.

The practical resolution of issues by each pupil is the integrating element

Integrative role = practical thinking = values and factual issues

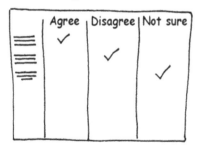

Write the following questions on the board as you say them aloud:

- What is the change that has occurred?
- Who is benefiting from it? Who or what is being harmed by it?
- Who has decided to make this change?
- What does the change hope to achieve? Are there any other ways of achieving that?
- What other information do we need before we decide whether to welcome or oppose the change?

Avehi Abacus Project

- Decisions about moral behaviour require a complex evaluation, putting out general principals of conduct, ordinary matters of fact, and theoretical understandings of the situation.
- Educating pupils about their personal concerns – more intelligently, imaginatively, with personal engagement and agency.

It is not usually possible to accommodate these processes in water-tight timetables and in one subject area

Integration in the learner's own interested enquiry

- Enquiry – a very general term, including a wide range of activities.
- Task of a subject-specialist – to teach the methods of enquiry appropriate to a subject matter
- All enquiry is basically of same kind (those powers of mind, habits of thinking, skills) which are common to all intellectual pursuits an give unity to thinking, irrespective of the conventional distinctions thrown-up by subject boundaries
- The personal enquiry of each pupil is the integrating element

Teachers must help, encourage, and further that.

An integrated curriculum means different things to different people

It reflects the constraints and difficulties found in dealing with subject-based curriculum (timetable, water-tight organisation, lack of relevance, practical concerns, etc.).

The integrated curriculum represents different educational rationales, rooted often in philosophical views about the nature of knowledge.

Here, Pring deals with four;

- Logical interconnections between different kinds of knowledge.
- The structuring of knowledge around themes.
- The integration of knowledge in practical thinking.
- The integration in enquiry.

A curriculum seeks to provide a meeting place between the already-active, thus educable, minds of the pupils and teachers which represent living traditions of thought that are relevant to the pupil's concerns and interests.

But in order to do this, different kinds of preparation, planning, resource, and cooperation between persons are required:

- Different foci of curriculum organisation (despite valuing distinctive disciplinary traditions).
- There are good educational reasons for alternatives for organisation within the same curriculum (interdisciplinary areas like 'practical living' and individual interests and enquiries that the pupil wishes to pursue).
- Such foci of curriculum structure make particular organisational demands – greater flexibility, timetabling, block-spacing, more collaborative planning, teaching, and reflection – resource centres with easy access, links with the local community, tutorial arrangements, teacher capacity building, and creating a culture of acceptance in larger society for such a programme

Avehi Abacus Project

Notes

1 Shulman, Lee S (1986), 'Those who understand: Knowledge growth in teaching', *Educational Researcher*, 15, 4–14. https://doi.org/10.3102/0013189X015002004
2 In Chapter 3, we tried to understand how social sciences have been part of the project to further historical/geopolitical processes, like global colonialism, intertwined with the formation of modern states. We have seen how social sciences have been key contributors to the construction of certain kinds of citizenship. This theme will also be integral to our discussion in parts of this chapter as we seek clarity about issues at hand.
3 Stanley, W B (2005), 'Social studies and the social order: Transmission or transformation?', *Social Education*, 69(5), 282–286. Retrieved on 12 July 2021from Google Scholar.
4 Greek city states: In ancient Greece city-states, a form of democracy existed. Unlike modern democracies, where all citizens of a nation get basic equal rights, most crucially universal adult franchise, allowing them to indirectly participate in law-making by casting their vote to represent someone to rule on their behalf in Greek states, only the privileged and educated males were citizens; women,

the poor and slaves were not deemed citizens. Thus a 'citizen was both ruler and ruled' (Aristotle), making as well as following laws.
5 Religious reform as a political philosophy (Protestantism, Bhakti): Patriarchal monarchies supported by strong institutionalised religion controlled most parts of the world for more than the first millennium AD. Social inequality was a norm and codified religion-sanctioned economic, gender exploitation – for example, caste in Indian subcontinent and tenets of the Roman Church in Europe. In these contexts, some sections of society, usually those outside the ring of power, challenged the rationale of established religion mainly by asking questions to priestly classes who posed as custodians/interpreters on behalf of the divine. The Bhakti movement in the Indian subcontinent (from 700 to 1700) and Protestantism in Europe (from the 1500s) claimed equality before God and thereby in social life
6 Progressive movement in education: The Progressive movement in education was an offshoot of 'progressivism' a philosophical movement in the end of the nineteenth century. At its core was evidence-based decision-making, scientific reasoning in order to make society a better, a more just place, in order to collectively address everyone's interests. The offshoot to education is mainly Dewey's contribution. Dewey transferred the core principles of progressivism to education. The term *progressive* was a qualification to distinguish it from the traditional one as mastery of an individual over content or given skills and culminating in individual material success and privileged the upper class. 'Progressive education' is rooted in experiential, contextual, collaborative 'learning-by-doing' in order to achieve social justice.
7 The Great Depression: The Great Depression was a period of about a decade starting from 1929, when serious economic recession set in in the USA and affected many parts of the world, particularly the West. The causes are many but commonly agreed reasons are overproduction of goods, artificially inflated consumer spending without real capacity for purchase, massive trading, and risk-taking in the stock market that led to 'market crash' and loss of capital. This also led to devaluation of some banks, resulting in mass panic, pushing people to withdraw their savings. This set a cycle of recession, affecting a lowering of demand, low production, bankruptcy of industries, massive unemployment, and human suffering. The government, in turn, did not act in due time to provide basic support to the public or to revive employment and industry.
8 George S Counts (1932), *Dare the School Build a New Social Order?* John Day, New York.
9 John Dewey (1937), 'Education and social change,' *The Social Frontier* 3 (26).
10 John Dewey (1937), 'Education and social change,' *The Social Frontier* 3 (26).
11 Pragmatism as a philosophical tradition developed in the USA during the 1870s. In broad terms, pragmatists argue that one can explain the world by participating in it. Rather than explaining the social world in the realm of philosophical ideas, pragmatists advocate the scientific method of 'doing', experiencing, testing, and then explaining social phenomena. The 'social' is key, and that all action, whether individual or collective, is to be understood in terms of 'social experience'. Pragmatists argue against the binaries of mind and body or individual and social.
12 John Dewey and John L Childs (1933), 'The social-economic situation and education', in *Educational Frontier,* edited by William H. Kilpatrick, D Appleton-Century, New York.
13 ibid.
14 'Deliberative democracy is a system based on participation, rational discourse, and a politics centred on a strong conception of the public good. This exists as a critical response to the liberal conception of democracy that focuses on a vote-seeking or an interest-based model. In addition, we use democratic education to consider how these ideas manifest in education, scholarship, and practices

designed to empower citizens to promote a more democratic society'. Michelbach, P A (2015). 'Deliberative democracy'. In M T Gibbons (Ed.), *The Encyclopaedia of Political Thought*, pp. 842–851, John Wiley & Sons, New York.
15 Lippmann, Walter (1922), *Public Opinion*, Harcourt, Brace & Co., New York.
16 Social Efficiency: https://education.stateuniversity.com/pages/2426/Snedden-David-1868-1951.htmlDavid Snedden (1868–1951).
17 Skeel, D J (1995). *Elementary Social Studies: Challenges for Tomorrow's World*, Harcourt Brace and Co., Orlando.
18 Vinson, K D (1998), 'The 'traditions' revisited: Instructional approach and high school social studies teachers', *Theory and Research in Social Education, 23*, 50–82.
19 Martorella, P H (1996), *Teaching Social Studies in Middle and Secondary Schools* (2nd ed.). Vinson, K D (1998), 'The 'traditions' revisited: Instructional approach and high school social studies teachers', *Theory and Research in Social Education, 23*, 50–82.
20 E Wayne Ross, Sandra Mathison, and Kevin D Vinson (2014), 'Social Studies Curriculum and Teaching in the Era of Standardization', in *The Social Studies Curriculum Purposes, Problems, and Possibilities* (4th ed.), Edited by E Wayne Ross, State University of New York Press, Albany, NY.
21 Dr. Jeffrey Byford Valdosta State University and Dr. William Russell (2007) University of Mississippi, 'The New Social Studies: A Historical Examination of Curriculum Reform', Social Studies Research and Practice 2 (1). Retrieved from www.socstrp.org on 24 August 2021.
22 E Wayne Ross, Sandra Mathison, and Kevin D Vinson (2014), 'Social Studies Curriculum and Teaching in the Era of Standardization', in *The Social Studies Curriculum Purposes, Problems, and Possibilities* (4th ed.) Edited by E Wayne Ross, State University of New York Press, Albany, NY.
23 Bruner, J S (1969), 'Man: A course of study', in M Feldman and E Seifman (Eds.), *The Social Studies: Structure, Models, and Strategies*. Englewood Cliffs, NJ: Prentice-Hall. And Bruner, J S (1977), The process of education (Rev. ed.). Harvard University Press, Cambridge.
24 Dr. Jeffrey Byford Valdosta State University and Dr. William Russell University of Mississippi (2007), 'The New Social Studies: A Historical Examination of Curriculum Reform', Social Studies Research and Practice 2 (1). Retrieved from www.socstrp.org on 24 August 2021.
25 Maurice P Hunt and Lawrence E Metcalf, *Teaching High School Social Studies: Problems in Reflective Thinking and Social Understanding*, 1955 and 1968, Harper and Brothers, New York.
26 Dr. Jeffrey Byford Valdosta State University and Dr. William Russell University of Mississippi, (2007), 'The New Social Studies: A Historical Examination of Curriculum Reform', Social Studies Research and Practice 2 (1). Retrieved from www.socstrp.org on 24 August 2021.
27 Apple, M W and Teitelbaum, K (2001), *John Dewey, 1859–1952*. In J. A. Palmer (Ed.), *Fifty Major Thinkers on Education: From Confucius to Dewey*, New York: Routledge.
28 Dewey, J (1939), 'Creative democracy – the task before us', in *John Dewey and the Promise of America Progressive Education Booklet*, No. 14, Columbus, OH: American Education
29 Dewey, John (1897), My Pedagogical Creed, https://en.wikisource.org/wiki/My_Pedagogic_Creed, retrieved on 8 September 2021. 'I believe that the school is primarily a social institution. Education being a social process, the school is simply that form of community life in which all those agencies are concentrated that will be most effective in bringing the child to share in the inherited resources

of the race, and to use his own powers for social ends. I believe that education, therefore, is a process of living and not a preparation for future living. I believe that the school must represent present life – life as real and vital to the child as that which he carries on in the home, in the neighborhood, or on the playground. I believe that education which does not occur through forms of life, forms that are worth living for their own sake, is always a poor substitute for the genuine reality, and tends to cramp and to deaden'.

30 Brameld, T (1956), *Toward a Reconstructed Philosophy of Education*. Holt, Rinehart, and Winston, New York.
31 Stanley, W B and Nelson, J L (1986), Social education for social transformation. *Social Education*, 50, 528–533.
32 Jorgensen, C Gregg (2014), 'Social Studies Curriculum Migration: Confronting Challenges in the 21st Century', in *The Social Studies Curriculum Purposes, Problems, and Possibilities* (4th ed.), Edited by E Wayne Ross, State University of New York Press, Albany, NY.
33 Westheimer, Joel and Joseph Kahne (2004). 'What Kind of Citizen? The Politics of Educating for Democracy', *American Educational Research Journal*, 41 (2), Summer, pp. 237–269. Retrieved from http://www.jstore.org/stable/3699366 on 2 July 2009
34 Based on outline of Social Science Pedagogy course, Simantini Dhuru, Disha Nawani, Kuldeep Garg, and Rashmi Paliwal. Professional Development in Education, Curriculum framework for Pre-.

5
TECHNOLOGY, TEACHING, AND THE PRACTICE OF SOCIAL SCIENCES

Towards the end of World War II and with the increasing stress of global industrial competition in the USA during the late 1940s and 1950s, the ideas of John Dewey and social progressivism were seen as being responsible for creating an educational culture lacking competition and clear educational standards to face the Cold War[1]. As we saw in Chapter 4, for Dewey, Counts, and others, the key purpose of education was to create a politically informed and engaged citizenry as a check on government and corporate power and control. But there was opposition to this conception of education by those who saw education as a platform for facilitating competition, production efficiency, and capitalism. This ideology saw democracy only as a mere political apparatus to facilitate profit maximization. They saw the acquisition of disciplinary knowledge, and educational specialization as essentials by which to create a competent workforce to triumph in the Cold War. We will locate the issues of technology, education, social science, democracy, and justice in this context. The discussions in Chapter 4 will help during this process.

An educator recounts

The public address system came alive with its usual coughing sound just as the school was about to end on Friday. It was announced that no one from classes VIII to X should remain absent on Monday. Monday post-lunchbreak, we were marched off to the big assembly hall where we saw the big bedsheet-like screen and a bulky projector ready to whirr. Huddled together, chatting with excited anticipation, we heard the announcement that we were to watch the film carefully and our class teachers would talk about it later. Lights off, the screen came alive with a warm glow and a little foetus gradually emerged, nestled in itself. The film went in flashback from the moment of conception to birth and the audience of 350–400 students became one with the experience. After we returned to our class, teachers discussed the film with us. Over the next few weeks, we had a few classes about menstruation, conception, contraception, women's rights, sex selection, and birth control, and subtly, but strongly, the ideas, 'Sex is not a crime, but there are consequences that you need to be aware of', 'You have the right to say "no"!'. For me, the mixture of awkwardness, excitement, the 'I know it all' attitude, found a grounding when my mind replayed the film, but it may have just remained an experience were it not followed by those classes. This was around 1978.

What strikes me today is that while the experience of watching 'that' film is still etched in my mind, it was the selection of the film, coupled with the classroom follow-up that helped assemble the jigsaw puzzle of growing up. Most importantly, today I can understand the significance of our teachers' *conscious choice* to use the medium of film, to expose us to a theme that is still considered taboo. Technology has been an occasional part of a few schools in India and accessed a little more in the Global North since the 1970s but it was usually the educators who went looking for it. Compare this with today when, despite the unstoppable noise of digital media, teachers are usually not clear about when to use technology, how to use it, or situate it appropriately in teaching/learning. For most teachers today, technology is imperious, not enabling.

Technology[2] has existed in human societies right from the early stages. In context of this chapter we use it specifically referring to computational, digital, satellite-based technology. As explained by the American sociologist Read Bain in 1937, "technology includes all tools, machines, utensils, weapons, instruments, housing, clothing, communicating and transporting devices and the skills by which we produce and use them." (Bain, Read (1937).

Let us understand how and why this came to be, examine our ideas and responses in using technology in teaching social sciences, and see whether and how we need to revisit aspects of our role as educators – individually and collectively.

Historical context of digital technology

The worker, the artisan, the inventor, the controller

1671: Gottfried Wilhelm Leibniz, a German mathematician, develops a binary computing system, 'Step Reckoner'. (His innovation later inspired numerical codes that described objects with digits, like the American Standard Code for Information Interchange (ASCII).

1801: In France, Joseph Marie Jacquard invents a loom that uses punched wooden cards to automatically weave fabric designs. Early computers would use similar punch cards.

1822: English mathematician Charles Babbage conceives of a steam-driven calculating machine that would be able to compute tables of numbers.

The project, funded by the British government, is a failure. More than a century later, however, the world's first computer was actually built.

1890: Herman Hollerith designs a punch card system to calculate the 1880 census, accomplishing the task in just three years and saving the government $5 million. He establishes a company that would ultimately become IBM.

1936: Alan Turing presents the notion of a universal machine, later called the Turing machine, capable of computing anything that is computable. The central concept of the modern computer was based on his ideas.

In the late 1960s, The US Department of Defense funds the Advance Research Projects Agency (ARPA) to develop the Advanced Research Projects Agency Network (ARPANET). Its initial purpose was to link computers at Pentagon-funded research institutions over telephone lines. ARPANET was an end-product of a decade of computer communications developments, spurred by military concerns that the Soviets might use their jet bombers to launch surprise nuclear attacks against the United States. By the 1960s, a system called SAGE (Semi-Automatic Ground Environment) had already been built and was using computers to track incoming enemy aircraft and to coordinate military response.

From the 1980s onwards to the mid-1990s, digital communication systems rapidly begin to enclose our lives through the World Wide Web and later in so many other forms.

Think

- What motivations did the early inventors have in creating the technology they are known for?
- Why would the need for conducting a population census and two decades later large-scale computing to emerge?
- What connections can you see in the military use of computer technology and large-scale computing?

In the context of the developments above, think about the presence of digital technology in our lives today. What about the connection between expanding Western colonial empires, the growth of industrial capital, emerging state mechanisms, and the need to gather and interpret large data like from a population census? In Chapters 3 and 4, we have seen how the growth of knowledge was intertwined with centralisation, with the concentration of power ultimately taking the form of modern nation-states. We have seen how the initial search for resources and markets by largely private interests were later brought under the edifice of newly emerging democratic states and how the creation and use of knowledge played a vital part in strengthening global capitalism controlled by Western democratic states. World history of the nineteenth century is a tapestry of technological inventions, travel discoveries, scientific breakthroughs, new ideas about social norms in the North-Western hemisphere on one hand and violent capture, control, exploitation of other parts of the world on the other. This rush to control the world led to conflict amongst the Western empires finally peaking in the form of the two global wars – World Wars I and II (WWI and WWII).

Let us understand how these developments are linked with education and our work. We will go back to the period when World War II was winding up and the forces of colonialism were waning, shaping another new world ...

Decoding the knowledge economy – war, markets, knowledge control

The end of WWII was the incubating period for the growth of computer-based information technology. The 'League of Nations', established at the end of WWI had come to naught. The devastation during WWII was unprecedented and the need to restructure the global ecopolitical landscape was recognised by the economic interests controlling Western powers. The moment was full of irony – capitalism failed vs capitalism triumphant! It triggered a churning in value systems, rewiring ethical codes. Among many emerged two options; reconciling, dovetailing into each other – profit balanced with compassion versus profit at any cost. Thus was formed the United Nations (UN, 1945) with the object of 'development' based on peace, justice, and environmental sustainability. But the agenda of the forces controlling the powerful economic interests also took hold in the form of the General Agreement of Trade and Tariffs (GATT, 1948): state-sponsored capitalism making way for global capitalism. Whereas the former was bound by geographies and legalities of the colonial state, the latter was fluid, manipulating raw materials, labour, production, and markets for oligopolistic global capital – the state being a mere facilitator.

During the Cold War, Western super-powers and the oil-rich Middle Eastern countries directed the events on the global stage using multi-pronged strategies of capture, co-option, and control. Gradually, digital technology has become the pivot around which increasingly scarce natural resources are controlled, the ceaseless desire for consumption created, and public choice manipulated. Manipulating information and processing it into useful 'Knowledge' for market profits hold the key to the game. 'Today, data (information) is the new oil'.[3] It is no coincidence that, out of the five richest people in the world, four belong to the IT sector. With the GATT mechanism morphing into the World Trade Organization (WTO) in 1993–1994, the power of the top few multinational corporations (MNCs) has been greater than that of all the sovereign countries put together. For example, in 2007, the GDP of the first 2% of MNCs was 20 times more than the GDP of all the sovereign countries combined. This means the power the MNCs hold over world affairs is unfathomable![4] The NGO Global Justice Now, publishes rankings of the world's top 100 global economic entities – 69 of the 100 from this list are corporations, leaving room for just 31 countries.[5]

Today, the world recognises the rapidly depleting natural resources and the widening chasm of inequality, but the stronghold of the forces that disregard the cost of environmental and distributive justice are deeply entrenched in majoritarian thinking that goes by the name of 'development'. Just as 'knowledge' is key to manipulating raw material, it is also essential to manage labour, and this is intertwined with how the distribution of knowledge is controlled. At the onset of the Cold War, two economists (both of them Austrian- Americans) introduced a paradigmatic change in defining 'knowledge' and its place in restructuring societies. In 1959, Peter Drucker introduced and popularised the concept of a 'knowledge worker', while, in 1962, Fritz Machlup coined the concept 'knowledge economy'. They argued that 'knowledge' (collection, organisation, interpretation, and use of information) should be seen as 'productive asset', capital or as a 'business product', as a tradable commodity. These concepts have taken root in the context of ideologies that celebrate 'profit at any cost' and have emerged from theories nestled under the benign misnomer 'scientific management' as outlined in detail in Chapter 4. It's this school of thought that popularised and brought into vogue the ideas of 'redundancy' (of labour, for example) and introduced the concept of 'outsourcing' for profit maximisation. Post-industrialist, advanced economies at their basis have the problem of how to deal with mass production on one hand and profit maximisation for their home-grown business on the other.[6] While social hierarchy has been a part of traditional societies by maintaining mechanisms like caste in the Indian subcontinent, modern, industrial Western democracies are not an exception. Scholarship in political economy and sociology of knowledge has demonstrated that, in countries like Canada and the USA, where the social structure is not based on ascribed identities of caste, the education system is structured in subtle ways to expose children from different social classes to qualitatively different types of educational knowledge. For example, the late American educationist Jean Anon, through her study '*Social Class and School Knowledge*' (1980) argued how 'students from higher social class backgrounds may be exposed to legal, medical, or managerial knowledge, for example, while those from the working classes may be offered a more "practical" curriculum (e.g., clerical knowledge, vocational training)'. Modern societies use different means to control the flow of formal knowledge by means like weak legal measures constraining equitable access, allowing private profiteering or maintaining geographical segregation (Karabel and Halsey,

1977; Apple, 1979; Young and Whitty, 1977). Since the 1990s, education policies of sovereign states in the Global South have been manipulated to develop specific categories of 'human resource' – a few selected for leadership, some trained for middle-level jobs, a larger section for semi-skilled labour, and for manual labour (Sadgopal, 2009).

India is a case of particular interest with its productive population being the largest in the world. India has the world's largest population in the age bracket of 15–24 years, with nearly 500 million seeking education. Thus, the education market in India is huge and is slated to grow at a rapid rate. Post 1990s as India adopted the liberalisation model it diluted state support to higher education. As a result the share of higher education market in India is about 60%. Similarly, with lack of access and quality in school education the market share of schooling from early childhood to 18 years is about 40%. With a ripe ground for profitability, free and equal access to education does not suit the market-mongers. The presence of technology in education in direct or subtle ways has grown statedly over past two decades. But the National Education Policy 2020 (NEP 20) has brought focus on educational technology as never before, placing it on a pedestal. A specialised workforce is needed to convert and regulate the rapidly growing information into profitable 'knowledge'. Thus, for such a system, keeping control over the distribution of certain knowledge streams and regulating the size of 'knowledge creators' is also essential. Keeping this number proportionately small is necessary as this class commands higher prices in the market and the masses are at its receiving end as consumers or labourers. The larger the labour sector, the cheaper and more vulnerable they come![7]

But the problem here is that, although knowledge is vital for survival, it is not produced in a vacuum. If the environment is destroyed and societies are rendered hapless, so-called technological innovations will not put food on people's plates or produce water to quench thirst. Even if the top 1 percent-rich find solutions to survive in face of such a situation, the solutions are unlikely to be equitable and sustainable, as the world is facing challenges of basic human needs like water and food. With mounting evidence about the precarious nature of the world, about the highly strained resources, has made it imperative for the MNCs to capture resources faster than before and ensure that the markets make profit. Every possible risk in the link to profit maximisation needs to be mitigated.

The more our life gets integrated with technology, the more vulnerable we become. Data wars in today's world are hardly uncommon, and education space is not an exception to this.

'Hackers' steal or 'mine' data from competitors to be used for different motives. Post-COVID-19, technology has become entrenched in our life even further, making teachers, students, and parents more exposed to hacking. Government portals used extensively during lockdown for accessing materials and coursework were hacked, compromising the personal

FIGURE 5.1   Education in the digital age!

information of millions of students and teachers over a year. But with the lack of response from the government, such acts of vandalism become normalised.

Exercise

Reflect on what we have outlined thus far:

- You can write or draw a mind map, or write a poem, create a blog or vlog, reflecting on your experiences about technology. How have things changed? What do you feel about the changes?
- Do you feel the need to look at digital technology afresh in your role as a citizen? In what way?

We will look at using technology in social science education in the context of the challenges discussed so far.

Theoretical understanding of technology in education

> In theory, there is no difference between theory and practice. But, in practice, there is.
>
> Jan L.A. van de Snepscheut[8]

A new political party takes over after fresh municipal corporation elections in a city and decides to convert all schools into 'smart classrooms'. Blackboards are replaced by interactive screens, projectors, and laptops are provided. Teachers are trained by experts from a world-reputed company contracted to provide the hardware, software at 'reasonable rates'. The timetable is reworked and prerecorded programmes developed by an edtech 'start-up' are scheduled in classrooms. But most teachers are confused about how to manage 'regular teaching'. The training given to teachers was limited to the technical aspects of handling the hardware and software. While the students were initially excited, their enthusiasm is now wearing off and they are distracted when the prerecorded programmes or live lectures are played. Teacher unions have raised concerns about the technology replacing teachers. Students are unable understand the pre-recorded videos, the link often breaks, their teachers are often unable to clarify what the resource person said. They are supposed to use the tablets for solving 'homework', but in school hours. In addition to the Wi-Fi difficulties, they often cannot understand how to give right answers because, whereas the options of answers are already given in the programme, their choice of answer is often not available. Their already weak skills of writing are getting lost, because they spend time figuring out how to use the tablets in the limited time in schools and teachers are burdened with the additional responsibility of storage of the tablets. Teachers, students, and school heads are finding it hard, caught between the higher-ups and politicians, who want them to comply with the 'smart school' initiative, and the pressure of demonstrating good performance at the end of the year.

Such instances are not uncommon today. Technology claims to transform human limitations and help us become 'smart'. Has it? Can it? Should we reject it outright because of its limitations as seen in the scenario here? And what are the implications if we indeed do so?

As a result of the COVID-19 pandemic, education, like many other areas of our lives, was catapulted into digital mode. Although it seemed the best possible option under the circumstances, it brought to the fore various concerns and challenges. In addition to exposing the deep and wide chasm of the 'digital divide' which mirrors our unequal society, it raises serious questions of epistemic disconnect, teachers' place, and social nature of teaching/learning among others.[9] This has consolidated the already-prevalent strong resistance to technology in education. Advocates of technology, on the other hand, argue that these are mere teething troubles that will eventually even out. They look at it as a panacea and push for its increased presence.

But, between the two polarities, there are questions to be explored:

- Is technology sometimes a hindrance to teaching/learning?
- Should we use it selectively only as an option?
- Should we use it only when we are forced to?
- Most of us use digital technology unthinkingly in everyday life, so why do we feel intimidated when it comes to the use of technology in education?
- Can technology improve teaching/learning if the problems of equity to access and affordances are addressed?
- Are there other aspects to the issue of equity that are beyond the problems of access to technology?

Today, it is essential that each of us thinks about such questions because whether we advocate for or oppose it, technology has already entered education, and its influence is spreading in ways unknown to us. Technologies are neither neutral nor unbiased, particularly when they play out in education which is a socially rooted process. We need to think about technology in education in ethical, political, epistemic, and pedagogical contexts. The context of the brief history of the emergence and spread of digital technology with its entrenched presence in our lives today can provide some clues. We need to prepare ourselves to take positions, inform ourselves theoretically, and develop our capacities, focused in particular on the teaching of social sciences.

When it comes to technology in education, the focus is on familiarising ourselves with and mastering various applications and software. It is assumed that, once they master the skills, teachers will integrate and apply technology in teaching. Acquiring new skill sets is a time-intensive process in the busy schedule of educators. In addition, as technologies change rapidly and if the knowledge gained is not applied in everyday work, it can become redundant. Thus, merely introducing technology to the educational process is not enough. In addition to the systemic and structural issues of unequal access, the confusion about technology use in education is due to the lack of a theoretical basis required for understanding the complex process of integration. By understanding that different technologies come with their own distinct characteristics, affordances, and limitations that enhance/hinder different subject matters, teachers agency in deciding whether or not to use them, and when and how to apply them is vital. Developing this understanding is both a complex and enduring process.

In short, more often than not, neither a subject expert, for example a geographer, having advanced domain knowledge, nor a technology whizz developing a Geographical Information Systems (GIS) app will be able to teach certain fundamental concepts to young adolescents as effectively as a geography schoolteacher. Just as effective teaching cannot happen by separating content, pedagogy, and context, merely introducing 'technological solutions' cannot ensure the expected teaching/learning to take place.

Our ideas of teaching with technology are intrinsically linked with those about how we understand sensible teaching. In Chapter 4, we looked at the concept of pedagogical content knowledge (PCK), and, with help of this foundational model of teacher knowledge, we will build the theoretical technology integration in teaching/learning by understanding the Technological Pedagogical and Content Knowledge (TPACK) framework.

BOX 5.1 PEDAGOGICAL CONTENT KNOWLEDGE

In a very remote isolated, homogeneous Adivasi village in Chhattisgarh without electricity or TV/smartphones, the government decides to extend the primary school to cover grades up to class VIII. In such a situation *How can a teacher transact the concept of 'Diversity and Its Challenges' to children studying at the VI grade?*
   OR
In the same situation, transact a chapter on 'Air Pollution in Cities'? *What about prior knowledge or context? How can an abstract thing, like air, and an abstract concept of pollution be explained?*

Teachers constantly need to address these situations in schools. Let us see what array of knowledge, abilities, and dispositions they need in order to have optimal preparedness. In order to teach (any subject to students), teachers need to:

- Master the content to be transacted and understand the rationale behind including a certain concept/theme in the subject it is part of.
- Have clarity about how the knowledge in the particular subject is constructed and why the discipline is structured in a certain way.
- Have theoretical knowledge about how learning takes place including student's preconceived ideas and responses to certain concepts, keeping in mind age-appropriateness.
- Have knowledge about the group of children s/he is transacting the content to (their socioeconomicemotional context).
- Develop abilities to appropriately plan transaction of the given content in a way that will make it possible for the particular group of students to understand and process what is taught, including teaching as well as assessing.

Technology, teaching, and the practice of social sciences **141**

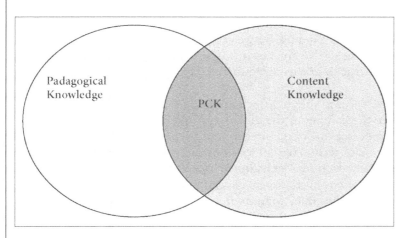

FIGURE 5.2   Pedagogical content knowledge (recreated with reference to Shulman, 1986).

It is here that the concept of pedagogical content knowledge (PCK), introduced by Lee Shulman, comes into play. Since its introduction in 1986–87 PCK has influenced both academicians and practitioners. Shulman in 1986 critiqued the way teachers were made to lay emphasis on 'content' or standardised textbook knowledge. Teaching was defined only in terms of accurate transfer of given content. But the stress on 'What is taught' (subject matter) in isolation from 'the way it is taught' (pedagogy), and without understanding the social context of learners leads to teaching-learning becoming emaciated and mechanistic, constraining both teachers' and students' role. While many 'good' teachers intuitively strike a seamless balance between 'content', 'pedagogy', and 'context', Shulman advocated a conscious approach to conjoining the different aspects in teacher education programmes, in order that educators develop capabilities to integrate various knowledge fields that interlace content, pedagogy, and context.

Teaching is a highly complex activity, demanding a dynamic composition of knowledge from different fields. It calls for cognitive as well as affective engagement. PCK represents the blending or 'amalgam' of content and pedagogy into an understanding of how particular aspects of subject matter are organized, adapted, and represented for instruction.

As we have seen, PCK represents a seamless integration of different knowledge fields essential in teacher's practice – content, pedagogy, and context. At the core of PCK is the way content is transformed into a pedagogical experience keeping in mind the level of development and social context of students. The framework of PCK not only draws attention to the issues regarding essential binding between content and pedagogy in context-specific teaching; it also underscores teachers' agency by placing them at the centre of teaching/learning rather than remaining a passive carrier of content.

As stated earlier, although technology has been present in classrooms since before the coming of the digital age, today, it is rapidly changing the prevailing processes and structures in education. The NEP 2020 demands an increasing role of technology in teaching/learning/assessment. The ideas in this chapter help us to further examine aspects of NEP 2020, to analytically study its implications in relation to education, digital technology, and society.

It is clear from the policy changes and from unexpected developments, like the COVID-19 pandemic, that the education landscape is about to change fundamentally, entailing changes in teachers' knowledge. Today, teachers' PCK demands the integration of technology, its potential, and limitations. With this as the basis, we look at the TPACK framework introduced by Punya Mishra and Matthew J. Koehler in 2008, building on the understanding derived from PCK.

Understanding TPACK in brief[10]

A close reading of the concept of PCK reveals highly complex cognitive, social, and motor domains of knowledge and capacities at work. As outlined in PCK, teachers draw upon many knowledge domains. Teaching is challenging, not only because it synthesizes diverse spheres of cognition and motor activity, but also because it takes place in ever-changing, contextually nuanced environments. To this synthesis of content and pedagogy is now added technology that requires teachers to think afresh and realign not just their understanding of technology but of all three components. In proposing the TPACK framework, Mishra and Koehler underscore the integration between the three components. In explaining TPACK, they unravel each component and their inter-relationships. For the purpose of clarity, this detailing and separation is an essential analytical exercise, while, in practice, technology, pedagogy, and content are expected to be organically interwoven.

TPACK – six knowledge components

Pedagogical knowledge (PK) – in line with Shulman's (1986) categorisation, representing 'teachers' deep knowledge about the learning theories and methods of teaching/learning, planning, and assessment. This also has the purpose of education, values, and aims as its basis.

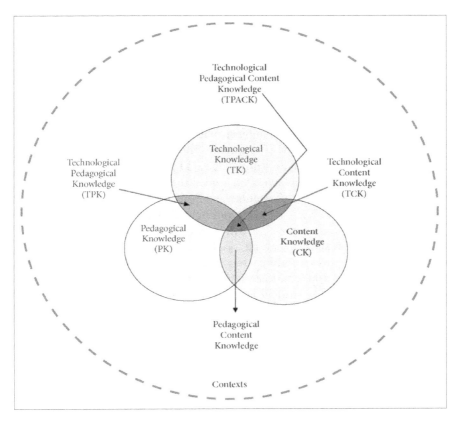

FIGURE 5.3 The TPACK framework (recreated with reference to Mishra and Koehler, 2009).

Content knowledge (CK) – also drawn from Shulman, this is teachers' knowledge about the subject to be transacted. Content knowledge thus needs to include 'knowledge of concepts, theories, ideas, organisational frameworks, knowledge of evidence and proof, as well as established practices and approaches towards developing such knowledge' (Koehler and Mishra, 2009).

Pedagogical content knowledge (PCK) – the *integrated knowledge* of pedagogy and content in an applied context-specific manner.

Technological knowledge (TK) – the element of technological knowledge is what sets the TPACK framework apart from PCK. Koehler and Mishra (2009) summarise this as being a productive working knowledge of technology, alongside a deeper understanding of how it can be used from a practical perspective. This is not limited to 'the traditional definition of computer literacy' but requires 'a deeper, more essential understanding', 'mastery', and the ability for adaptation (ibid.).

Technological Content knowledge (TCK) – this entails an understanding of 'the deep historical relationship' between technology and content, plus 'understanding of the impact of technology on the practices and knowledge of a given discipline' (Koehler and Mishra, 2009). Here, the highlight is the pairing of specific disciplines and certain types of content with specific technological choices. It requires teachers not only to make the appropriate choice of technology to teach certain types of subject matter but also to be aware of 'how the content dictates or perhaps even changes the technology – or vice versa'.

Technological Pedagogical knowledge (TPK) – Koehler and Mishra (2009) explain that this involves 'an understanding of how teaching and learning can change when particular technologies are used in particular ways' according to purpose, and disciplinary 'context'. Unlike TCK, where the *what* is being taught intersects with technology, the emphasis in TPK is on *how* technologies shape teaching and learning as they are used in specific ways. TPK thus requires an ability to reconfigure strategies for 'customized pedagogic purposes' and 'creative technology use, not for its own sake, but for the sake of advancing student learning and understanding'.

Technological Pedagogical Content Knowledge (TPACK) – at the intersection of the six categories of knowledge described above is the core of the TPACK framework. Technological Pedagogical and Content Knowledge is defined as 'an emergent form of knowledge that goes beyond all three 'core' components (content, pedagogy, and technology knowledge) and is based on their purposeful integration' (Koehler and Mishra, 2009[5]).

Serving as the basis for effective teaching, this 'professional knowledge construct' establishes 'a dynamic equilibrium' among all of its component parts, and they must all be brought into play'. Most importantly, there is a greater need for 'knowledge in action' or 'practice-based knowledge' before something can be defined as TPACK. When teachers choose to use technology beyond the aim of transferring content, when they actively engage students to create contextually relevant knowledge, what transpires is TPACK in action. For example, to explain the impact of international trade on local economy, teachers may set up interactive projects with students. A teacher from the Konkan region of Maharashtra where the famous Alphonso mangoes are grown can design a project with local students supplementing textbook content by interviewing mango growers about investment, risks, possible change in variety of mangoes due to market demand, dealing with fruit traders in Mandies trading within India, how increasing global market has impacted their situation, etc. They can virtually interact with their cousins from metropoles like Mumbai about the affordability or quality of the fruit in their small local market, virtually check rates at high-end mega-foodstore chains, observe the stock market, make predictions, etc., or students from Mumbai could do a similar exercise in reverse. The technological aspects can be selected by using virtual questionnaires and graphics to analyse and represent data, co-create virtual presentations, hold virtual meetings, source news, visuals, etc. This not only makes the subject matter accessible to students but provides opportunities in the cocreation of context-specific knowledge dovetailed with diverse expert inputs.

TPACK helps teachers to achieve 'expert' teaching/learning, going beyond the physical boundaries of the classroom. It enables inputs to be drawn from diverse knowledge platforms, it gives natural support to students to co-create knowledge, compare it, and refine their understanding. These abilities go beyond the specific subject matter. In short, for teachers, understanding TPACK is much more than using technology as a tool and as an 'input'.

The frameworks of PCK and TPACK form a vital part in understanding what is contained in teacher knowledge. Whereas PCK underscores a teacher's role in evolving teaching practices specific to the subject and the group of students being taught, TPACK makes us aware of the ubiquitous presence of technology in our life and underlines the need to be aware of possible changes in the cognitive processes shaping the construct of PCK.

Think

The TPACK framework builds on and highlights the common grounds with PCK. Do you think there are any differences? Of what kind?

Addressing limitations of TPACK[11]

As said earlier, the TPACK framework, and indeed the concept of PCK, are relatively new contributions denoting teacher knowledge, which is highly complex and context specific. In proposing the TPACK framework, Mishra and Kohler acknowledge that it is 'extremely difficult' to represent teacher knowledge 'within one overarching framework or theory' and that any such representation of knowledge needs to reflect its 'socially constructed and dynamic nature' (2006).

TPACK needs to be seen as an evolving construct mainly because, despite the massive spread of technology, its integration in teaching has remained largely passive, often at the level of use of ready-made software promoted by powerful corporations. Increased commercialisation of education has put a premium on assessment but reduced space for teacher autonomy. Teachers are neither given support to develop their capacities to adapt and integrate technology nor the freedom to contextualise and synthesise content pedagogy with technology. In addition to these challenges, there have been concerns raised about the initial conceptualisation of the TPACK framework (developed in 2006). The main concern was raised with the original detail in relation to the lack of importance given to contexts and sociocultural elements in TPACK (Figure 5.3: see the graphic representation of TPACK as proposed in Mishra and Koehler, 2009). TPACK's creators, in acknowledging these concerns, adapted TPACK to include 'Context Influence on TPACK Knowledge' (Mishra & Koehler, 2012) (Figure 5.4: see the graphic representation of TPACK with new elements and variables). This model takes additional set of variables and interlinks them in an outer ring composed of the labels **'teacher training'**, **'experiences'**, **'students'**, **'resources'**, **'objectives/aims'**, and **'attitudes'**.

Mishra and Koehler's (2009) TPACK framework, provides a suitable starting point in the search for the 'conceptual home' of technology in the social studies (Martorella, 1997). However, while Mishra and Koehler represent TPACK as three equal size circles representing the three bodies of knowledge, playing equally important roles towards 'good teaching with technology'. merging at the centre to form 'the complex interplay'; Hammond and Manfra (2009) prefer to represent it as suggested by Pierson (2001) as ovals, with the oval representing technology considerably smaller than the other two.

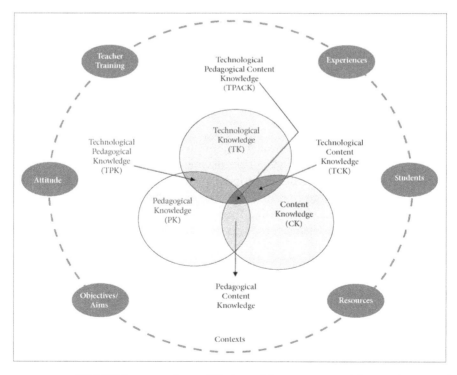

FIGURE 5.4 TPACK framework, modified to address contextual factors (recreated with reference to Mishra and Koehler, 2012).

Other commentators and those who have an applied understanding of TPACK look at it like this.

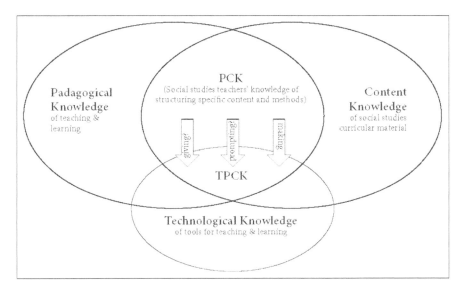

FIGURE 5.5   TPACK for social studies (recreated with reference to Hammond and Manfra, 2009).

Think

While addressing the 'drawbacks' of the original conception of TPCK, the creators added an outer circle of 'context' with elements of 'teacher training', 'experiences', 'students', 'resources', 'objectives/aims', and 'attitudes'. In your opinion, does this change sufficiently address the issues in relation to the key role of context specificity in teaching/learning? Can you try to list at least three concerns that need to be considered?

Let us look at some more concerns:
Access – to technology, to adequate technological instruction, and to culture-sensitive technological pedagogy. While, for the purpose of listing, we separate these three, in reality they integrate together to impact the quality

of teaching/learning. Let us look at them individually so that we understand how and why they are inseparable.

- **Access to technology.** Do all learners and teachers have sufficient and equitable access to all essential aspects of technology? Do factors of caste, gender, class, religion, race, region, or language impede access? This is particularly pertinent in face of the present state of technology that is highly sophisticated and which covers all aspects of our lives. What are the implications when access is abundantly available in one part of the globe or within a geographic region of a county, but is reduced or absent in most other places? What implications does this factor have on the existing inequalities on global and local scales? What implications does it have on the production and control of knowledge?
- **Access to adequate technological instruction.** This involves teachers and students. The nature of engagement needed for technology-based instruction is distinct from the conventional one. It requires re-aligning teaching/learning styles for synchronous and asynchronous instruction, self-study, doubt clarification, and adapting to different ways of assessment. Do teachers have sufficient support for capacity building for teaching with technology? Do they get support for capacity building addressing theoretical and practical aspects of a generic nature as well as those which are subject-specific? What kind of time-scheduling adjustments will teachers and students need to make? What does **adequate** mean? – will technology take over more of the school hours, reducing time for processing learning, planning, and reflection?
- **Culture-sensitive technological pedagogy.** Teaching involves two-way communication, and student feedback is crucial for the teacher. Communication is a socioculturally, contextually embedded process, both verbal as well as non-verbal. In face-to-face classroom situations, where technology is one of the options, teachers have access to many non-verbal, visual clues to understand students' responses. But in distant mode, even with synchronous instruction, this channel is highly restricted. This has implications on the teachers' ability to understand children's responses, children's role in knowledge creation, and thus to address and integrate equity in classroom culture. For subjects like social sciences/literature, etc., where cultural and contextual connections play a pivotal role, not having access to non-verbal clues from children can have deep implications on teaching/learning.
- **Teachers' beliefs about content.** This is overarching and fundamental in every facet of education, in its defining of teachers' role. Whereas

PCK addresses this and points at key ideas to think about by somewhat disavowing the 'sacrosanct', 'given' nature of content, this is an aspect that needs continuous revisiting. The TPACK framework also addresses this aspect in unravelling the TCK component, especially emphasising the meeting points when a certain type of content from a discipline comes in contact with a particular nature of technological option. But, does the teacher's role remain restricted only to understanding the relevance or clarification of content, its age-appropriateness, and in contextualising knowledge with help of the optimal technological choice? Does technology transform content, bringing in unexpected challenges, opportunities, and risks? For example, when students and their caregivers at home also have access to technology that bring in very different views about the same selected 'content' to be taught, what should the teacher do? What about the teacher's views of the 'given content' – particularly if they differ from both these positions? There are often manipulations of or disputes about historical events/places/personalities in relation to current political pressures. Although textbooks may be developed by relying on evidence-based history, they may attempt to portray an impassioned view of the past, revealing both positive and negative aspects of a dynastic rule, for example, the Mughal rule in the Indian subcontinent; sectarian forces may manipulate certain content through technology, seeking to either erase the very existence of this period or selectively reveal the negative aspects. This has to be understood in everyday terms when teachers, students, and their parents are continually exposed to social media where homogenized cultural identities and algorithms drive propaganda or unidimensional content, textbooks remain a mere formality for passing exams. This reality makes classroom discussions and ensuring in-depth evidence-based clarifications, extremely challenging, particularly given the limited time available in schools.
- **Teacher's beliefs about pedagogy**: Regarding the TPK component of the TPACK framework, the importance of teachers' clarity about the philosophy of education, their epistemic beliefs need to be further underlined because, consciously or unconsciously, it is these fundamentals that make them prefer one approach to teaching against another in defining their TPK.
- **Teachers' and society's understanding of the 'political economy' of technology.** This is the central point about the role of technology in education which cannot be sufficiently addressed by only looking at the entwining of 'technology' and 'teaching/learning'. It has serious implications on the very existence of our planet and our society with reference to equity and sustainability. With education

being speedily pushed on technology platforms, reducing campus-based/classroom teaching, the increasing role of artificial intelligence (AI) and disruptive technology like ChatGPT; TPACK, even with its outer ring of additional 'variables', needs further revision. In the hi-stakes exam-oriented, outcome-based nature of education, aberrations such as 'tuition classes' have already long been normalised. With technology entering the scene, these have been shifted to virtual mode, providing 'ready-made classes/tutorials' and pushing aspirational parents to purchase these packages. With a lack of political will to put in place mechanisms of checks and balances on such trends, the nature of knowledge, its equitable access, and the type of education seems like an unfortunate casualty.

With this awareness in mind, we move to the next key part of our deliberations – integrating technology in the teaching of social sciences.

Technology and teaching of social sciences

As we have noted earlier; the potential role of technology in education is inalienable from the nature and purpose of understanding about knowledge and society. We have looked at some foundational perspectives with reference to the place of social sciences in education in Chapter 4, for example John Dewey's pragmatism, George Count's social reconstruction, and Walter Lippmann's conservatism. We have also looked at the 'Social Darwinist' ideology and its impact on education. These serve as the basis for understanding the way a society views the role of schooling. Social sciences play the central role in this process. They help in communicating, clarifying, analysing, challenging, and redefining the nature of knowledge, the role formal education plays in solidifying iniquitous structures or challenging and transforming them.

In essence, we need to clarify for ourselves the perspectives and positions in teaching social sciences. We have seen the different approaches behind the construction and teaching of social science knowledge. In this context we can broadly sum up the ideas of Hammond and Manfra (2009) drawing upon Barr, Barth, and Shermis (1977) to understand the positions by which to look at the social sciences.

Cultural transmission – preparing the young to unquestioningly imbibe the dominant culture and accept socioeconomic structures in order that it carries forward without real changes for generations to come. The focus is on acquiring preselected content knowledge to be accurately reproduced and to develop 'technocratic skills' specific to the social sciences.

Social science – making students aware of how social science knowledge is constructed distinctly in each discipline. Formal education is structured on the basis of broad disciplines that are branched in school subjects. The focus here is on learning key concepts, the rationale for inclusion of these in the subject, how learning becomes an exciting and empowering experience when we have insights into use of the tools of enquiry and exploration of the grounding ideas that make this knowledge possible.

Reflective enquiry – mainly inspired by Dewey's conception of 'reflective action' and refined by others, is developing an enquiry-based, analytical, problem-solving way of thinking and taking action. Teachers support learners, encouraging them to use the subject matter (social sciences in this context) as an opportunity to experience learning as a process by which to reflect on their individual and social situation.

With reference to the possibilities and limitations of the theoretical framework of TPACK, social science educators must clarify to themselves where they stand in relation to the above. Essentially as social science practitioners, we need to ask ourselves the question which Counts raised: 'What should be the role of teachers, especially social studies teachers, with respect to the social order – transmission or transformation?' This needs to be addressed in the context of the prevalent social structure and its education system by developing critical contextual strategies. In immediate terms we may not be able to change the situation drastically – be it in terms of the dominant attitudes towards social science, the perspectives and content, or the forces that push programmes centred around using technology in isolation. But we can find ways to integrate technology in teaching/learning/assessment, to build supportive networks for peer-learning (for teachers and students) and generate possibilities for their refinement for theses processes to be meaningful, fulfilling, democratic.

In light of these analytical classifications we look at the intersections of education and technology. The conceptual contribution of the TPACK module in its cohesive integration of content, pedagogy, and technology has channelised work of other scholars and practitioners to expand and demonstrate the ways in which technology in education needs to be viewed. It underscores the point that 'thinking like a teacher', having clarity about purpose of education and perspectives about knowledge and society should take precedence over mere acquisition of technological skills.

We refer here to a three-part model developed by Hammond and Manfra (2009) for social studies teachers in using technology. Hammond and Manfra (2009) look at a range of pedagogical ideas, 'emphasizing the role of the teacher as the catalyst', illustrating different modes of instruction including both, 'transmission' and 'transformation' (Barr et al., 1977; Stanley, 2005) and providing 'social studies educators a common language with which to articulate their pedagogical aims'. Hammond and Manfra's work is relevant in this discussion for two main reasons. One their work is the theoretical

TABLE 5.1 Giving, Prompting, and Making in Social Studies Instruction

Examples	Giving	Prompting	Making
Expected Student Behaviour	To absorb and retain information: passive (or internally active)	To observe, detect patterns, create associations, or make inferences: active	To generate a product, create order, and describe and support a conclusion: active
Teacher Stance	To create structure, impart meaning, and assign significance; active: authoritative	To present, contextualise, paraphrase, invite elaboration, and juxtapose statements or evidence: active, facilitative	To supervise, challenge, offer feedback, and model: active, collaborative
Example (Theme: 'Child Rights')	Teacher uses textbook-based PPT to deliver lecture on child rights, and students are expected to accurately reproduce content	Teacher uses pedagogical strategies to understand what students think about child rights, proceeds to make available sampling of digitally sourced primary documents like constitutional provisions and relevant laws like 'RTE', 'POSCO', anti-child labour acts, the UNCRC, case studies in the media, photoessays, etc. and students are to present one example of a violation of rights	Students are asked to develop a project (video-recording case studies of working children, child rights activists, lawyers, secondary data from digital sources of businesses that typically employ children such as garment industry, hotels, brick-kilns)

Source: Hammond and Manfra 2009, 'Giving, Prompting, and Making in Social Studies Instruction' (the details in the column of 'Examples' is changed to suit the Indian context).

expansion of the concept of TPACK and the other is the practical application of TPACK in relation to existing discussion about approaches for teaching social sciences developed by Barr, Barth, and Shermis (1977).

Let us understand more concretely the model of 'Giving, prompting, and making,' Hammond and Manfra (2009) (see Table 5.1) that focusses on 'different expectations for student learning in the social studies classroom'. It is envisioned that teachers adopt modes that are complementary to the subject matter, to elicit and support the intended student response. The 'pedagogical aims' of the teacher are to be the starting point in making technological choices. Most importantly, 'the pedagogy should lead the technology, not technology lead the pedagogy'.

Giving: 'Tell it to me straight'

In this 'transmission' mode, the teacher looks at knowledge as a preselected, water-tight, ready-made product that is to be 'given' to students. The teachers' role is to make sure that knowledge is 'given clearly and efficiently, minimising uncertainty or confusion'. Thus, the teacher uses technology to present textbook information in an accurate manner to be reproduced by students without errors.

This way of teaching may make things efficient and keep order, but it does not necessarily ensure that the key objectives of social science are achieved. Invoking Dewey (1916), Hammond and Manfra (2009) call this approach passive and decontextualised. By 'mere amassing of information', it reduces social studies to 'a large number of statements about things remote and alien'. Paulo Freire calls this 'banking', where the teacher 'deposits information into students' minds who passively receive it', where learning is seen as faultless retention and dry cognition. Here learning is seen to be an impersonal, uncritical, and passive act without students reflecting on reality, without engaging with their independent conceptions and values that involve the element of feelings, so vital to social science.

Prompting: What do you see?

In contrast to the transmission or 'giving' mode, Hammond and Manfra (2009) draw from the New Social Studies movement (see Chapter 4), 'enabling the pedagogical turn'. Instead of being an interpreter or a 'filter' between given content and students, the teacher facilitates learning by carefully selecting material for learners to explore and construct knowledge (Vygotsky, 1978). Students are exposed to primary sources, enabling them to think like practicing social scientists.

For example; a topic like 'India in the Middle Ages – Emergence of the Bhakti movement' can begin with a filmstrip from a movie on a 'working-caste' poet-saint in conflict with powerful upper-caste men. Rather than a statement by the teacher that 'the film shows that…' which is usually followed by an explanation of what the film portrays, the teacher may prod, 'What did you see in this film?', 'What are the main points of the film?' and 'What do you know about caste-oppression from what you see?' The teacher's stance changes from the distiller and controller of knowledge to a 'scaffolder' (Vygotsky, 1978), 'prompting' students to explore their ideas, engage with resources, and express their thoughts. When students are called upon to analyse and reflect on their preconceptions about social stratification based on birth, they are able to own the process of meaning making by looking at primary resources, thereby enriching their skills, viewpoints, and knowledge base. In addition to carefully selected resources, the teacher in her role as a scaffolder sets a trajectory for deeper conceptual thinking by asking interesting questions which may not always have binary, 'right/wrong' answers, instead allowing students to feel less intimidated by adult expertise, build confidence in themselves and to construct their arguments on the basis of evidence. For instance, students could browse the digital space for 'Bhajans, Dohas' 'questioning social inequality'.

The teacher might provide material, such as timelines and maps, and give clear pointers in the form of simple exercises or statements to either complicate the discourse (e.g., views justifying caste as a 'division of labour' instead of as a hierarchical system of exploitation sanctioned by religion) or support the main point (e.g., decrees from the village heads about the types of houses allowed to be built by different castes, separate case-based water sources, exposing the water-tight constraints of caste and exploitation). Through group work and presentations, peer-group discussions can seek clarification, challenge viewpoints or use of certain sources. This experience can help students to step into the shoes of a social scientist.

Making: Show what you know

In this last pedagogical strategy Hammond and Manfra (2009) take the constructivist ideas to the next level of 'making' where, in addition to the kind of resources and approach used in 'prompting', students themselves 'make' a variety of artefacts, like blogs, websites, multimedia presentations, newsletters, slideshows, complemented by essays, skits, posters, surveys, etc. Teachers may ask students to conduct small sample surveys to see whether the impact of caste oppression has reduced, in what ways it has changed, whether people are aware of the impact the Bhakti movement had on changing caste oppression, etc. with help of technological tools. Students can present these data by integrating visuals of archaeological evidence like photographs of plaques on temples where entry to 'lower-caste' was barred , looking for poetry of Saints from Bhakti period, etc.

On another theme, like 'human-nature relationships', they can work on projects individually or in groups, for example 'floods' (or 'natural regions', or 'nature and habitats'). To begin with, students can be asked to develop web-maps/idea-webs to clarify and define the interconnections and scope of the theme, and refine it based on the teacher's or peers' feedback. For the theme of 'floods', along with the usual textbook information, the teacher may use a documentary or a news reportage about 'development and flooding'. With such triggers, students can explore ideas like a snapshot biography of a woman who, every few years, struggles to save her home and hearth against floods (in Bihar, Assam, or Kerala, or a slum dweller in Mumbai); they can construct a virtual chronological mural of the larger geography of her area with the help of 'Google Earth' and map the topographical changes which directly or indirectly cause flooding, like deforestation, dams, industries, changing cropping patterns, growing urbanisation, siltation and solid-waste dumping in rivers, land-refilling and construction in mangrove areas, etc. They can do an opinion poll in school, 'Floods: man-made or natural?', and/or initiate a signature campaign on a portal to demand broadening the textbook content to lay more focus on 'natural' disasters and the role of humans. Teachers can regularly review and offer feedback.

Project work, and specifically the act of student creation, provides opportunities for content knowledge formation and skill development, such as research, organisation, writing, or presentation, using valid web-resources, etc. Students not only develop a conceptual understanding about the 'geographical' factors that cause flooding but a nuanced understanding of the phenomenon, and are motivated to make lifestyle choices, develop empathy, and experience the need for alternatives. Most projects involve some element of student choice, allowing them to exercise their independence and their engagement, and that is why students will often recall the content and process of their project work, even years later. Finally, project work provides teachers with opportunities to engage students in 'powerful and authentic social studies' with a focus on enquiry, problem-based learning, and higher-order thinking (Newmann, 1991). Technology and web-based resources are being increasingly integrated into social studies for 'project work' which usually tends to be an assemblage of 'attractive' presentations. Instead, with broader, nuanced social geographical perspectives and creative use of technology for 'making', teachers can initiate profound changes in students' conceptions about geographical phenomena, geospatial skills, and value frameworks.

The giving/prompting/making model and TPACK

As we saw in the example at the beginning of this chapter, the technology tools available for social studies education have expanded. Social science teachers have already embraced some technologies – such as PowerPoint and digital video – so teacher-centred, passive pedagogies remain the norm.

Hammond and Manfra (2009) model – giving, prompting, making – can be visualised to work with TPACK, specifically addressing Mishra and Koehler's (2006) observation that 'Part of the problem...has been a tendency to only look at the technology and not *how it is used*'. Focusing on these three modes of teaching calls attention to the fit between teachers' pedagogical intentions (informed by their PCK) and their selection and use of technological tools (informed by their TK and TPACK). In Chapter 7, we will look at examples of technology use in teacher peer support and co-learning.

> TPACK does not – or ought not to – place the technological cart ahead of the PCK horse. Instead, TPACK is a nested expression: (T(PCK)). The pedagogical content knowledge is resolved first, and only then is the use of technology considered. The tool selection process is usually governed by the desired instructional pattern (see Figure 5.5).
>
> To be useful, a framework for technology integration must speak to all or many pedagogical stances and models of instruction. Technology is not inherently a behaviourist or constructivist tool. It can be effectively used within transmission models (giving) or for more transformative modes of instruction (prompting and making). Technology integration decisions should follow and extend from pedagogical decisions.
>
> *Hammond and Manfra (2009)*
>
> The TPACK framework can serve as a starting point to clarify that technology need not be deterministic. In contrast, statements such as 'The Internet promotes problem-solving skills' or 'The Internet promotes cooperative learning' fail to appreciate the role of the content and the teacher. Furthermore, individual tools can be used flexibly within a discipline. PowerPoint, for example, can be used for more than delivering "bullet point after bullet point of text." Instead, 'primary sources could be displayed, coordinated, projected and used as a mechanism for formative and summative assessment' (Hammond & Manfra, 2009).
>
> Finally, the example of *'giving, prompting, and making* has a special resonance for social studies education as an opportunity to discuss democratic teaching styles'. After all, a classroom in which the teacher is consistently engaged in 'giving', is not democratic. A classroom that has an organic balance among 'giving', 'prompting', and 'making' is likely to be more student-centred, more democratic, and better at preparing students for the 'engaged citizen' in the advanced sense.

Conclusion

Here, we briefly highlight the ideas in this chapter:

- The drive for invention and efficiency gave us early computer and digital technology which later has been the fuel to drive economic, political, and social control. Every aspect of the education system, from access to quality, is impacted by technology today.
- Since the 1980s, technology has been present in teaching/learning but the contribution to theoretical representation of the use of technology in teaching/learning has enabled the possibilities of its meaningful use. It has also made further analysis, criticism, and refinement possible.
- Practitioners and theorists concerned with social sciences have adapted the theoretical framework to explore and examine ways of integrating technology in relation to the ideologies and perspectives that define the purpose of the teaching of the social sciences.
- Finally, through the lens of social science, we need to look at all these aspects in a cohesive manner as this chapter attempts to propose.

Exercises

1. What were your views about digital learning or ideas about the 'knowledge economy' prior to the ideas explored in this chapter?
2. Can you think of any more affordances or limitations of the TPACK model, keeping in mind your context of work?
3. Look at web-based platforms like SCIM-C, APPARTs, 'WebQuests' Jackdaws, and 'Digital History' projects, resources for geography like Fathom, Google Earth, Gapminder, Mapmaker, Country Studies, Atlapedia, etc. (one each suited to history, geography and political science/citizenship education) and give an example how you would make use of these platforms in Indian context.
4. Develop a blueprint with at least one example of any theme/subject from social sciences using the conceptual model of TPACK and 'Giving, Prompting, Making'.
5. Look at Part III, 'Other Key Areas of Focus', Sections 23 and 24 of the National Education Policy 2020 of India in the context of the ideas explored in this chapter, with particular focus on the 'knowledge economy' and 'teacher education'. Can you note down at least two points of concern with reference to each of these aspects?

Notes

1 Woodford, P (2012), 'Dewey's bastards: Mursell, Broudy, McMurray, and the demise of progressive music education'. *Visions of Research in Music Education,* 21. Retrieved from http://www.rider.edu/~vrme on 9 September 2021.
2 "Technology and State Government". *American Sociological Review.* 2 (6): 860–874. doi:10.2307/2084365. JSTOR 2084365.
3 Khanna, Parag (2016), *Connectography: Mapping the Future of Global Civilization*, Random House.
4 Shrivastava, Aseem and Kothari, Ashish (2012), '*Churning the Earth – The Making of Global India*', Viking, by Penguin Books India.
5 https://www.weforum.org/agenda/2016/10/corporations-not-countries-dominate-the-list-of-the-world-s-biggest-economic-entities
6 A J Johnston (1986), 'The State, the Region and the Division of Labor', in *Production, Work, Territory: Geographical Anatomy of Industrial Capitalism*, Edited by Scott A J and Storper M, HarperCollins Publishing.
7 Gurumurthy, Anita and Chami Nandini (2020), '*The Intelligent Corporation: Data and the Digital Economy*', https://itforchange.net/intelligent-corporation-data-digital-economy-platform-governance (retrieved on 18 July 2021).
8 Punya Mishra and Matthew J Koehler (2006), 'Technological pedagogical content knowledge: A framework for teacher knowledge' *Teachers College Record Volume* 108, (6), pp. 1017–1054.
9 V Madhurima and Gurumurthy Kasinathan (2020), '*What Challenges Do Online Classes Pose?*', https://itforchange.net/what-challenges-do-online-classes-pose-the-hindu-v-madhurima (Retrieved on 18 July 2021).
10 Paul Breen (2018), 'Technology, Knowledge, and Workshops', in *Developing Educators for The Digital Age: A Framework for Capturing Knowledge in Action*, pp. 21–38, University of Westminster Press, retrieved from https://www.jstor.org/stable/j.ctv5vddjh.5
11 Paul Breen (2018), 'Technology, Knowledge, and Workshops', in *Developing Educators for The Digital Age: A Framework for Capturing Knowledge in Action*, pp. 21–38, University of Westminster Press, retrieved from https://www.jstor.org/stable/j.ctv5vddjh.5

PART 3
Challenges and possibilities

In the initial chapters of the book, we tried to examine the contexts of social science like social change, the role of the state, the role of consciousness of the people, and scientific approaches to the study of society, as well as its teaching/learning. In the concluding chapters of the book, we engage with reimagining of schooling in the light of classroom experiences, policy changes by the government, and the possibilities that could be opened up to enrich classroom transactions.

Part 3 is organised into two chapters. Chapter 6 ('Can classrooms transform?') looks into the challenges as well as possibilities of democratic teaching/learning. The dialectics between the reproduction of an unequal society and the democratic possibilities in the classrooms are examined through documentations of concrete experiences. Policy changes in education like the NCF 2005 are examined for its implications in curriculum and pedagogic changes, as well as the challenges that they face at the ground level that is prone to the reproduction of social inequalities in the classrooms.

As examples are brought in from local, regional, and national levels in the country, the recognition becomes evident that educational change in the country ensues only through a holistic approach involving policy, academics, pedagogy, and classroom experiences. This way, the onus of change as well as its implications and modifications rest not with particular parts of a system, but with the whole system itself. In this perception, the requirements of assessments take on an entirely changed possibility. Assessment would need to be a continuous process, not just of students, but of all the components of the system mentioned above. A collaborative change can develop

DOI: 10.4324/9781003449348-9

assessment practices that contextualise the cultural capitals and seek ways to address those social realities.

Chapter 7 ('Teachers, society and the classroom') looks into the possibilities of what teachers can do collectively. No part of the book aspires to be prescriptive for any segment within the educational scenario. But the focus on teachers in the concluding chapter is to enhance the reimagination of this key player in the classroom. It is of significance that the collective actions and consciousness of teachers in the neoliberal times have yielded relatively better wages to the para-teachers across the country. This chapter tries to focus on the potential collective strengths which can politically recognise how privatisation and neoliberal policies attempt to minimise the larger canvas of democracy that was expanding in the country up to the 1980s.

6
CAN CLASSROOMS TRANSFORM?

Introduction

In Grades eight to ten, I studied in a small school where some thoughtful retired government school teachers taught us. The school was located on a small hillock on the outskirts of Trivandrum City. There was an ambience of simplicity, from the uniforms we wore to the minimal fees, and to the pedagogies of the teachers. We talked in our own language, Malayalam, and our school principal taught us good English in the language class. The botany teacher took us out to the hillock where we learnt about the plants and flowers growing there. The social studies teacher came to class with a lot of magazines, maps, and a globe. We poured through colour photographs of temple and mosque architecture. It was the first time that I had seen a topographical map. The teacher gave us an exercise on that:

'In which place would you like to live? Give three good reasons for your choice'.

I remember how someone wanted to live by the riverside, while others preferred a hill slope. Some looked for road connectivity and others for forests and ponds. In this process, we were talking with each other and learning to decode the contours and symbols, and were excited at making our own choices.

Segregated benches for girls and boys were a norm. But the social studies teacher often pointed out that girls and boys should be friends. I remember that we hardly felt any examination pressure. I don't remember having studied late into the night. There was so much we learnt from the daily classes, that we just wrote the examinations.

DOI: 10.4324/9781003449348-10

Today, I wonder why those teachers used such different teaching practices. Surely, their shared critical perspectives on how schools usually conduct teaching must have been the core point. Across the country, we can find a wide range of attempts to change the nature of education Several organisations/ groups contextualise education of the marginalized sections of society like the Adivasi and fisher communities, women, Dalits, rag pickers, and so on. These attempts involve re-imaginations of content and pedagogies.

Larger changes in the education system attempted by organisations like KSSP (Shastra Sahitya Parishad) in Kerala and Eklavya in Madhya Pradesh have often been forced to take a back seat with political changes in state administration. The NCF (National Curriculum Framework) 2005 involved educationists and practitioners from across the country in policy-making as well as in the writing of the textbooks that followed. Some of these books made a watershed of sorts, as discussed in Chapter 3, but, with subsequent changes in the government, the progressive and inclusive perspectives in educational policies and practices were backtracked.

Amit of 'Adharshila' (an organisation/school for tribal students in the Barwani district of western Madhya Pradesh) mentioned in a conversation that the alienation of the Adivasi continues even in NCF 2005 and the subsequently written textbooks. Amit and Jayashree (Badhwar, 2015)[1] note that the experience of schooling has completely disempowered the Adivasi people. That is why, in Adharshila, children are encouraged to first learn to read and write in their mother tongue, Bareli, and their rich oral culture and storytelling become important and contextual pedagogic tools.

In contrast to such efforts, the knowledge in textbooks (for instance, Chapter 3: Mineral and Power Resources, Grade 8, NCERT) in our schools talk of resources and their extraction with a lot of pride and pay no attention to the tribal communities who live in such resource-rich areas. This gap is well expressed by journalist, Padmanabhan:[2]

> …I had grown up thinking of these places as heroic territories full of resources the nation needed to power ahead…and curiously devoid of any human presence. Not once had it occurred to us to ask if these areas were inhabited by people, which indeed they were…

We can contrast this with the real and vivid description of Raniganj, in Chotta Nagpur plateau, in a novel by well-known writer Sarah Joseph:[3]

> Even before reaching Raniganj, small heaps of coal could be seen in the streets. On reaching Raniganj, mined coal was seen heaped high like hills.

The atmosphere was filled with soot and dust. Children and adults were pushing sacks of coal tied to bicycles. Their faces, hair, and dresses were soot-like. Trees coated with soot had lost their greenness. The soil was also black.

In some places, like in Jharia, coal burns underneath, and it becomes extremely hot. Even as several efforts have been made to extinguish the fire, it continues to burn at temperatures reaching 700 degrees centigrade, and located just a few metres below the surface. People in Jharia have been advised to move out, but they often wonder where they would go to? What would be their livelihoods?

From Raniganj in West Bengal to Hazaribagh in Jharkhand, there is a stretch of coal mines. The Jharia coal mines situated in Dhanbad district have been burning for over hundred years. Mining of coal in Jharia had started in 1894 and the first fires in the mines were reported in 1916. People say that the fires were started when the mines were owned by private businessmen who did not care about the safety of the miners or life in the locality.

The fire underground has destroyed the soil, the trees, and the plants. Poisonous gases are released into the air. Sometimes, the land caves in, threatening and destroying people, roads, and railways. Mining continues in Jharia even as some rail lines have been declared unsafe. The local people are caught in a vicious cycle, with no alternative plans being made. Without livelihood options, they continue to work in the coal mines. Coal pickers often work inside the mines with the fire going on in a nearby underground tunnel. On the issue of rehabilitating the coal mine workers, who are the local residents of the place, the core issue burns down to the question of their lives and livelihood[4].

There is much need for textbooks to write about such aspects that make people suffer and deprived. Such 'development' activities bring huge profits for a few. If such issues are not discussed, how can students engage with the causes of poverty and the environmental problems?

164 Challenges and possibilities

FIGURE 6.1 Different sides of a development story.

Source: Sunny, Y (2022), *Sprout: A Story of Spaces and Geographia*, Eklavya Publication, Bhopal, p. 66

Think

- What sort of alienation do you think the children of mine labourers would experience if they are attending school and reading the chapter on mining that does not talk about the real-life context?
- In citizenship education, mainly achieved through the social studies subject, do you see the labouring people being discussed? Why not?
- Do we see questions on the economic and social system that creates poverty and hardships for large numbers of people, and wealth for some? Why not?

Given above is a debate on the displacement of local communities from their land (just as in the mining example given above) for a 'development' project. The prosperity and progress mentioned is not inclusive of all people. This is the key feature of the capitalist economy. As vividly articulated by Karen Haydock,[5] even the most progressive books of NCERT do not mention the word 'capitalism' in their social studies textbooks. She mentions that this word, as well as the concepts of socialism and communism, is essential for an understanding of economic development. 'Apparently, the unstated aim is that if capitalism remains ununderstood and unanalysed, it may not be questioned, and students will not realise that there is any alternative to capitalism' (Haydock, 2015, p. 109). She further emphasises that science is not a body of knowledge but a method of asking questions and searching for answers. This approach needs to be used in all subjects.

Educational practices become concretely played out in the class rooms, where all the above-mentioned themes converge. What do classroom practices, reveal about the presence or absence of transformative pedagogies? The perspectives, resources, and activities for transformations become crucial and, in the process, the meanings of assessment also become contextualised. These aspects examined below in the three sections below, elucidates these mutual relationships.

Classroom observations

In the classroom, the questions of students are one of the most important concerns and require ample space and time for those to be addressed by teachers. If teachers engage with the questions, they would be not only exercising a process of democracy in the classroom, but also opening up the doors for collective knowledge creation. Let us critically examine some concrete experiences from classrooms and think about how new pedagogies could be created for social studies.

Case 1: Dealing with inequalities

A study by Agarwal (2008)[6] was done through classroom observations in an army school in Nahan, Himachal Pradesh The school subscribed textbooks from a private publisher which followed the guidelines of NCF 2005. But the classroom transactions show a contradictory trajectory, as seen through her narration given below:

Teacher: 'Exploitation on the basis of caste is a thing of the past and now, because of government policies, there is much more equality. The inequality we see around is on the basis of class, the lower rung suffering because of their own laziness and incapability. If they want, they can also become more educated and raise their standard of living'.

While the teacher was explaining in this way, she came across an example in the text which contradicted this view. The text stated that, during the tsunami that impacted the coastal areas, Dalit people did not receive food supplies as the suppliers were often not ready to reach out to them. We got freedom in 1947 and untouchability was abolished in the 1950s but it is still practised today.

To resolve the contradictions between her own statements and that of the text, the teacher said that untouchability is being followed in the backward villages, but is hardly visible in urban areas. Though there might be some evidence of untouchability being followed in urban areas like not drinking water from a sweeper on the day of fast or having separate utensils for sweepers, these, she said, are rare occasions. She even asked students to find out if caste discrimination is done in their homes. Next day, no one said that it is practised in their homes. There was no space in the class to admit such things. Moreover, it seemed that students had not even asked their parents or grandparents about it. This question is not given the kind of weighting given to the questions given at the end of this chapter. It was assumed that all the relevant knowledge that is worth knowing has already been researched and has become part of the textbook. No debate was encouraged.

Teacher: Have you seen Ramesh *Bhaiya*, who sweeps in the school? His mother is a sweeper at the railway station. He is following his mother's occupation. Had he done some studies, he would have become something else, but he chose the easier way of not studying and following his mother's occupation. Their pathetic condition is the result of their own actions. The government has provided facilities for them and made provisions. It is their fault that they are not taking advantage of government policies.

The text stated: When an educated youth of a Dalit community goes to the employment exchange looking for a job, the application is made automatically for a *safai karamchari* (sanitation worker) or some such job. This is social conditioning. The teacher explained this as: 'SC went to the employment exchange and got himself registered as a safai karamchari, though he was educated. Why he did so is beyond my imagination!'

She completely misread the text and interpreted it on the basis of her worldview. According to her, the person himself chose to be a safai karamchari, though the text said it was the person in the employment exchange who registered him as a safai karamchari. This could have been a good example to illustrate how the caste system is still entrenched in the minds of people (including the educated people living in cities) and how, in spite of the constitutional provisions, it continues to be manifested in different forms. However, the teacher failed to recognise the role of the privileged section in contributing to the conditions of the Scheduled Castes.

The teacher discussed manual scavenging. 'They remove human excreta with their bare hands. Nobody wants to touch them. It is also not hygienic. Leave caste aside. We do not follow caste, but do you think you would like to take water from the hands that have cleaned toilets? We believe everybody is equal, but hygiene is something different'.

Here we can see that, though the teacher has said that categorising people as untouchables is bad, she gives an argument to reinforce it. She also said that, if that person wore gloves, then things would be different.

What is the role of the government? Are they there only to make laws? Who would see to their implementation? Who are the people who employ manual scavengers? Why do people undertake manual scavenging jobs? All these are questions that could have been discussed and debated, but there was complete silence on these issues. As noted by Kumar (1996, p. 7),[7] the school curriculum always shies away from such issues of conflicts. It is the resolution of such conflicts which leads to a deeper understanding of issues like untouchability; just saying that manual scavenging is banned does not help create any understanding.

The text states: In general, urban Indians are less particular about the caste system than the rural folk. The use of public transport and public places has become a necessity rather than a privilege enjoyed solely by the upper castes. It is one of the preconditions of city life that enables people to mingle with each other, but, in rural areas caste-based discrimination still exists.

The teacher emphasised this point, saying that caste-based discrimination is not practiced in urban areas but only in rural areas. Regarding gender-based discrimination, she said, 'In urban areas, the situation is different but, in rural India, there are lots of problems'. When I interviewed children, they also said that discrimination on the basis of caste or gender is carried out in villages that are backward, but not in cities. Discrimination on the basis of caste and gender is practised even today in cities, though the form might be different. Even in cities, people are not ready to accept inter-caste marriages; if one reads matrimonial ads in the newspaper, one finds ample examples. Similarly, even educated people discriminate. Female foeticide cannot be done without the help of doctors in cities.

The text states: Gender inequality also influences income disparity. Women get less remuneration in many areas of economic activities and the proportion of women in employment in the organised sector is still well below that of men. Women are paid an average 12–23% less than men for doing similar jobs. The higher women rise up the promotion ladder, the greater the pay gap becomes.

The teacher explains this as: 'Females are paid less in the private sector – not in the government or semi-government sectors. The sex ratio is low; therefore, the female employment percentage would obviously be low'.

A student (girl) said, 'Women are employed less because they have the responsibility of household work'. This could have provided the opportunity to discuss how gender division of labour forces women to give a higher priority to household work rather than being employed outside the home. Reasons for women being paid less could also have been discussed here. However, such discussions did not happen.

The teacher's opinions about why caste persists is that the so-called lower-caste people are not making enough effort, and it is their laziness that is the main cause. We hear such things often, and the teacher, embedded in society and not being critical about caste relationships, reflects a dilemma in social studies teaching. Kumar (2005, pp. 93–94)[8] notes that, 'as a member of the local community, sharing its culture and valid forms of knowledge, the teacher could well afford to scoff at the knowledge he was himself imparting in the school. It was not his job to make this knowledge meaningful. His personality was thus split into two halves – one representing the salaried employee of the education system and the other representing a literate, traditionally revered member of the local community'.

Think

Suppose you are to talk to the teacher, what evidence would you gather to convince her that her point of view needs to change?

Suppose you are to teach the students, what pedagogy would you use through which students' knowledge and questions would also become integral parts of the classroom transactions?

Case 2: The question of cultural diversity

Kapoor (2015)[9] observed classroom processes and interacted with students and teachers in a Central school in New Delhi. The ambience in the school starkly reflected the communal politics that was becoming more legitimised in the country by then. Given below is Kapoor's narration.

The chapter was on rulers and monuments. I tried to constantly encourage students to come up with well-thought-out answers.

A student said: 'In temples, there are idols of Hindu Gods but there are no idols in mosques. Why was there no idol of Allah?'

'Not all religions follow the same rituals and practices'.

This was a good opportunity for me to bring in the diversities of cultures of faith. I communicated that Islam believes in a spiritual strength called Allah which does not have a form. Followers of Islam do not believe in idols and their worship.

We talked about mosques. A girl from the class had gone to visit the Qutub Minar at the weekend. I told them that the Delhi Sultans and Mughal Rulers constructed these mosques and how the chroniclers described them as the Shadow of God. We referred to the inscription in Arabic on the Quwwat-ul-Islam Mosque which stated that God chose Allaudin as the king because he possessed the qualities of Moses and Solomon. Here, I could sense my lack of knowledge in communicating about Moses and Solomon, and a student came to my rescue. She described in detail about who they were as she had read about them in the Bible. It was great to see that everyone in the class listened to her very attentively. Here, it also acted as a way to incorporate children's experiences and, again, was helpful in celebrating diversity in the classroom.

We talked about the construction of reservoirs and tanks by the rulers, the examples being Delhi-i-Kuhna, Hauz-i-Sultaani, and the reservoir around the Golden Temple. A student also shared his experience of visiting the Purana Qila and having seen the lake there.

I had randomly selected two students and given them reading materials a day before the class.

- Chola Rajendra I, who had built a Shiva Temple in his capital and had filled it with prized statues seized from defeated rulers; and
- Mahmood of Ghazni, who had attacked temples of defeated kings and looted their wealth and idols

One by one, the two students came in front of the class. It was planned that the other students would interview them. The students came up with the opinion that, in both cases, there was disrespect shown to the defeated kings. They wished to show their power, gain the support of the public, and increase their territory.

'Is it good to do such destructions?'

'It was important to give the message that the king was powerful...'

'... while it must have created troubles for people, destroying their place of worship'.

'... hurting people who worked so hard building them, disrespecting God'.

I associated this with the idea of having opinions about facts in history and how the students could do it really well. Then, I focussed on how such experiences are seen, even during present times, like the Ayodhya dispute in particular. Although students did not talk of any concrete experiences, they did agree on the prevalence of communal conflicts in the country. It was a significant aspect to deal with as it represented how the idea of an uninterrupted past is problematic in a political sense.

I realised that we promote the view of the past and human life very narrowly as we focus on conquests and characterise groups of people in particular ways. Many textbooks talk about the 'advent of Islam' by discussing raids from Ghazni and Ghori causing battles and brutalities across the northern Gangetic plains. There is almost no mention of the years of peaceful living together of groups of people along the Malabar Coast. It is important for the teacher to deconstruct statements as curriculum knowledge essentially brings forward a particular perspective of legitimate knowledge, a particular worldview of the nation, identity, history, and so on. This needs to be taken into account.

Later, we discussed the architecture of Delhi Sultanate. We saw the prominence of column-like structures.

'These might be for the Imam to sit at the top and say the sermon so that the voice could reach far'.

I didn't have any idea about it so I asked whether the Imam sits at the same level as everyone else top. I asked if anyone had been there. At the same time, I heard some people teasing Mujibulla by saying, '*Bta jaldi bta jaldi*'. ('Tell, quickly')

He looked angry at that time. Mujibulla said that the Imam sits at the same level as everyone else.

The above-mentioned behaviour of children was a stark contrast with what happened earlier when a student offered to tell us more about Moses and Solomon; it was noteworthy that the entire class listened to her very attentively. Mujibulla (the only student in the class from a family of Muslim faith) looked very angry when others coaxed him to answer. I felt that I shouldn't have asked such a question. I also realised that he wasn't comfortable with his Muslim identity as the others were making fun of him. I discussed this with their teacher. The teacher responded as follows:

> Muslims are less in number in the school. They don't come out and be a part of the larger society, don't send girls to schools… They don't socialise much with others. Students marginalised Muslims in classes because they get to hear about news on terrorism which usually comprises Muslims.

She went on to say that it was only Muslims who invaded India and looted temples, causing destruction. We can essentially see how meanings are constructed in the classroom. Here, even though the textbook is supposedly quiet on the issues of communalism but such ideas are essentially being promoted through the way students and teachers constructed knowledge. The pedagogy with which the curriculum is transacted and the assessment methods used to examine learning also require scrutiny. Also, possessing superficial knowledge on the conditions of Muslims, and stating that they themselves are responsible for the same is hugely problematic.

The most glaring observation from the study was the strong reproduction of societal biases in the school spaces. The school ethos was one of homogenisation, for example, an idol of the Hindu Goddess Saraswati is seen at the entry of the school. This is talked about as representing the Goddess of Learning. Moreover, boards in the school which had quotes such as '*Hindi ka prachaar rashtriyata ka prachaar hai*' ('The propagation of Hindi means the propagation of nationalism') and so on. There were boards with Sanskrit quotations too. This is how the idea of nationalism was being promoted.

There were many positive learning experiences too. Students' interest in architecture of monuments could be utilised to teach them history in a more engaging manner. Students were interested in discussing rituals and religious practices. They had the opportunity to share their experiences of reading holy books and visiting places of religious importance. The students' interest in issues of differences in rituals and practices among different faiths could be utilised to address multiplicity/diversity.

- How does the classroom experience become very different when the teacher and students share their knowledge?
- Religious sites were sometimes attacked during conquests of feudal states in the past. Why was that done? How many different intentions can you derive from the above writing? Can you find more meanings from other sources, especially regarding the looting of wealth which was done by conquerors irrespective of their religion?
- It is not merely the texts, but also the meanings that teachers and students create that needs to be examined. From this case, what can you say about the operation of the hidden curriculum?
- Should the public school, as an educational site for all, promote any religion as is done in the above case?

It can be seen that Kapoor does not act like a teacher who knows everything. Being unpretentious gives her several advantages. It lets her relax and encourage students to put forth their questions. Any teacher would obviously not know the answers to all the questions. But the questions from students by themselves are important in creating new pedagogies and new knowledge. The teacher and students can make efforts to search for answers to questions. How can they do that?

Students are involved in the process of learning in which adult guidance as a crucial component is mentioned by Vygotsky (1978, p. 126),[10] who critiques the lack of sufficient recognition among educators of the many ways in which an experienced learner can share his knowledge with a less advanced learner. He points out how learning is socially and not biologically- facilitated. The dialectical relationship between the individual and society has been the core of his work in being able to change the processes of schooling. A dialectical relationship refers to the way in which two very different forces work together and how their differences can be resolved.

Social traditions and social science are two different processes. They come together in the classroom. They can be resolved through dialogue, evidence, and the methods of social science.

> Lev Semyonovich Vygotsky (1896–1934) was a Soviet psychologist. His sociocultural theory focusses on learning as an essentially social process. He elaborates how the support of peers, parents, teachers, and the wider society and culture enhance the development of fuller functions in the individual learner.
> - Find out from other sources the nuances of cooperative learning activities in Vygotsky's writings, where peer interaction is very significant.

Perspectives, resources, and pedagogies

If you are a teacher or educator, perhaps one of the first questions you can ask yourself is the sort of society that you would aspire to. Secondly, can social studies be adapted to engage with the idea of a just and equal society? Thirdly, what sort of pedagogy and resources would you need to transform your classrooms in that way?

Usually, schools in our country use textbooks as the primary resource. There are three main reasons for this:

1. Examinations or assessments are designed on the basis of the textbooks.
2. In most parts of the country, libraries, infrastructure, and reading materials are scarce.
3. Even where some resources are available, the flexibility of the school system to utilise them is limited.

In Figure 6.2, five components are shown which teachers can utilise to create new and collective knowledge in classrooms. The textbooks, as well as other sources, easily provide the teachers with the required resources. The teachers can interpret those and create new pedagogies. Let us take a few examples to illustrate the point.

Case 1: Enriching a given chapter

In the introduction of the present chapter, we discussed coal mining and how textbooks give only a fragmentary view of such procesess. Consider the chapter from NCERT Social Studies (Grade 8 Chapter 3: Mineral and power resources). If the teacher seeks to enrich the chapter, she could refer to other resources as well. For instance, she can use literature, like that of Sarah Joseph mentioned above. Questions can be formulated around it. For example:[11]

- Read the above-mentioned description of Raniganj. Imagine that you are a child living in the Raniganj coal mining area and your parents are labourers in the coal mines. Attempt to describe your everyday life. (Activity 1)
- How is your real life similar to or different from the everyday life of a child you have imagined and described above? (Activity 2)
- Can you make a drawing on the basis of the description of Raniganj? What aspects of environmental pollution can you see? (Activity 3)
- In terms of pollution, how is your own actual place of living similar to or different from the above picture? (Activity 4)

FIGURE 6.2 Collective creation of knowledge in the classroom.

174 Challenges and possibilities

A new film has just been released. It has received a great deal of publicity because it is based on a true incident of communal violence.

Through an interesting story, the film depicts a communal riot that has resulted in the deaths of a few hundred people, and makes an appeal for peace. Although it has been passed by the Censor Board, there is one group of people who feel that the film should be banned. They have not seen the film, but they feel that it shows one community in a bad light and will therefore lead to more violence. So they protest against the film by confronting the owner of a local cinema where the film has been released, and threaten him with violence. They also burn posters of the film, break some furniture, and warn the owner that if the shows are not stopped immediately, the theatre may be burned down.

Points for discussion

- Why do the protestors want to ban the film?
- Do you think it is acceptable to use violence to stop something that you don't like? Why?
- Do you think it is necessary to find out what a person is saying before disagreeing with him?
- If you disagree totally with another person, in what ways can you show your disagreement?
- Who do you think should decide whether a film should be banned or not? Why?
- Once a film has been given a censor certificate, should it be banned because some people find it objectionable?
- If violent protests force the owner to stop showing the film, then what will happen to other films in the future?
- Do you think there are some books which should be banned? Why? Who should decide whether a particular book should be banned or not?
- Do you think incidents like the one described here happen often? Why?

FIGURE 6.3 The reactions to a film.
Source: Avehi Abacus, 2003.

- If you are yourself living in a mining area, you can list out the problems faced every day on issues like health, drinking water, and so on. What measures do you think can change the health and other situations of the people? (Activity 5)

Case 2: Creating local knowledge

Given below is part of a writing[12] of the impacts of sand mining in a locality by the banks of the Narmada River. The issue was studied through observations, discussions with people, taking photographs, and also searching for more information from other sources.

Sand-nesting birds: Lapwings coexist with people who grow melons and cucumbers on the sands of the Narmada. They call and fly around and do not perch on trees like the egret. They stand on the ground as their feet cannot take a grip on tree trunks. They lay their eggs, like the curlew, on the sand without elaborate nest building. Egrets, storks, cormorants, jacanas, herons, and winter migrants, like ducks and the Siberian crane, live along the Narmada.

In summer mornings, solitary kingfishers feed from the river, needing a daily diet amounting to at least 60% of their body weight. So, they seek to have control over a suitable stretch of the river. Both female and male birds excavate burrows for nesting in stone-free sandy soil. The river flows slowly in the Hoshangabad Plains, and is ideal for kingfishers. But deforestation in the upper catchments, as well as water pollution, have diminished the aquatic life in the Narmada.

A fisherman named Narmada observed: 'We now wait longer to obtain a catch as compared with the past. We often travel upstream, away from the town, hoping for a better catch'.

The bee-eaters are active in summer, swiftly catching flying bees and thrashing out their stings or venom on tree trunks. Their nests are tunnels made on the vertical sides of sandy banks. They loosen the sand with their sharp bills and kick out the soil with their feet, completing the nest building in around 20 days.

The richness of flora and fauna along the river banks is sustained through deep interconnections, like the seeds of several trees getting dispersed through droppings of birds to become new saplings.

Livelihoods impacted through sand mining: Prior to the monsoons, people farm melons and cucumbers on the sands through lease or *patta* of the land from the Revenue Department. Often, the dams that open gates in the summer damage these crops. Donkeys led by young boys carry sand on their backs. Fisher folk catch fish for themselves and to sell some in the market.

The Narmada and other rivers in Madhya Pradesh have been sustaining thousands of sand farmers, fetching enough to survive the four monsoon months during which there is no income generated. Villages such as Devachar

176 Challenges and possibilities

in Narasimgpur District were well known for sweet cucumbers cultivated by the Majhi, Kushwaha, Mehra, and Kahar communities. Rampant sand mining has deprived the growers of their livelihoods as well as reducing the availability of good-quality cucumbers.

Sanju, who sells water melons in Hoshangabad town, said: 'Around five years ago, we had to stop cultivation because of sand mining in the summers. We now buy melons from other places and sell them'. New varieties of cucumbers and watermelons are being grown on non-sandy soil. A conspicuous decline in the livelihoods of landless people has been noted since the sand mining policy of 2015.

Mining has altered the landscape, the river flow, water availability, and sand deposit patterns. Streams now dry up from January onwards, including the Shed and the Shakkar in Narsinghpur District, which used to hold water all year round. Tributary rivers of the Narmada, such as the Dhudi, have dried up and changes in river ecology have have made sand to be deposited inside some farms, making it impossible to farm.

As large-scale mining destroys livelihoods that are dependent on sand deposits. The wages received for some time by labourers in mining sites are not sustainable options. Decisions are taken arbitrarily by the state without any consultations with the people whose livelihoods are at stake. Decisions on issues of development are governed solely by capital, with no control over the large scale of mining, including the illegal ones. People with no capital and voice in the system lose out on their relationships with nature.

Case 3: Reflecting upon a contemporary incident

Given below is an example[13] of how several happenings in our society, especially ones that involve contradicting views and violence, can be reflected upon using questions and reflections as pedagogies.

The table guides you to reflect on the three examples given above. Some of the boxes are filled. Please fill in the blank boxes:

TABLE 6.1 Reflection

Case/ Process	Resources	Interpretations	Pedagogy	Possible New Knowledge
Case 1: Enriching a given chapter		Lived experiences of people		
Case 2: Creating local knowledge				Sustainable development
Case 3: Reflecting upon a contemporary incident			Reflective and reasoned thinking	

As a teacher or educationist, it would be enriching to write about your own experiences and trials and discuss them with other teachers and peers, so that pedagogic possibilities are widened through collective action and sharing. Can you think of taking up such a step?

> Can you bring together other teachers, make a network for collective learning and sharing? This could be through a local level networking where teachers can come together or through some virtual network, like telegram or signals. Other ideas could be shared with other teachers and built as examples of cooperation to change the educational practices.

What is to be assessed?

In Chapter 3, we reflected on the relationships between the modern school, the modern state, citizenship education, and the political economy. Assessment is inherently a part of these relationships in the system. The individual students are assessed and graded which closes down or opens up the possibilities for further studies and for future employment in the modern production system. In this way, assessment becomes one of the core aspects of formal school system. It increases angst for parents and tensions for students, as well as for teachers.

Vasavi (2019)[14] writes on how school differentiation in India reinforces social inequalities. There are nine types of schools which vary by the cost of schooling, medium of instruction, type of board exams, and management structure: (i) Ashramshalas (for Adivasi regions); (ii) state-run government

178 Challenges and possibilities

schools (including municipal, corporation, and *panchayat* schools); (iii) state-aided but privately managed schools; (iv) centrally aided special schools, such as the Kendriya Vidyalayas, Navodaya Vidyalayas and 'Military Schools'; (v) low-fee-paying, state-syllabus private schools; (vi) expensive private schools including the 'Public School' chains; (vii) religious schools (Pathshalas and Madrassas run by religious institutions and trusts); (viii) alternative schools run by independent or non-profit organisations; and (ix) international schools. In sum, these constitute the most varied and most class-based schooling system in the world.

She points out that permitting a proliferation of schools and an education market has negated the possibility of fostering a democratic ethos that would be embedded within educational institutions. These combine to account for the widespread 'democratic deficits' that some scholars have pointed out as being glaring in the everyday private and public life of Indians.

In a study (Sunny, 2011) of classroom observations, a teacher of a government boys' school was interviewed. She responded that the 'good' students have left for private schools, leaving behind only the wards of the poor in the government schools for boys. She found it difficult to convey the text to them. These children are mostly first-generation learners and so did not have a tradition of schooling, rote learning, and parental support as middle-class children did.

Here the teacher voices the lack of 'cultural capital', three forms of which are identified by Bourdieu: economic, social, and cultural. Whereas the first one deals with money and the second one with the network of social relations, the third one is the product of education which is

> ...connected to individuals in their general educated character – accent, dispositions, learning, etc; connected to objects – books, qualifications, machines, dictionaries, etc; and connected to institutions – places of learning, universities, libraries, etc. (Grenfell and James, 1998, p. 21).

Cultural capital informs the relationships between schooling and family/social structure and this is also seen to shape the teacher's role in negotiating or not negotiating with students with different cultural capital (Sunny, 2011, p. 29).[15]

An example: Assessment bypassing cultural capital

In Eklavya's[16] school programme, which was running in the government schools of Hoshangabad District in Madhya Pradesh, there was a consolidated effort to restructure all the components of school education that together make an impact. These include the textbooks, teachers' orientation, classroom processes, setting of question papers for the examination, and the method of evaluation. The examinations used to be open book, and hence there was no point in rote learning. The assessment in such a system addressed the social realities of cultural capital.

The questions of the examinations were formulated in such ways to enable students to compare, summarise, analyse, reason, and so on. Prior to evaluation, teachers conducted a sample paper assessment. A few answer sheets were selected randomly to see the trend of responses of the students. Three broad categories of answers were elicited: those in which students showed (1) a fair amount of satisfactory responses, (2) median level of satisfactory responses, and (3) inability to handle the question, as the difficulty level was high.

On the basis of the above trends, the weightage of each question was decided. Questions that came under the categories 1 and 3 were allotted least weightage, and the questions that came under category 2 were allotted most weightage. Why was this being done?

If most students were answering well, this means that they have, as a group, grown above the expectation of the questions.

180 Challenges and possibilities

These levels are not perceived as some 'natural levels' students acquire, but the onus could lie in the textbooks and the classroom transactions. These were treated as feedback to the system that needed to modify the learning requirements of students. These were noted and appropriate changes were made in the proceeding round of textbook revision and teachers' training.

The nature of assessments and the perspectives on modification of the system, based on reflections of students, also mean that the system was responding to learning possibilities for all students in society. The unequal cultural capital at individual levels were restrained to some extent in impacting student assessment.

The students were not 'blamed' for the lack of satisfactory performance. Instead, it is understood that the system needs to change. The approach allows changes to be made in the system through realistic assessments. This also has a deep philosophical element of collective learning, that enriches peer interactions and teacher–student relationships.

Classrooms, debates, and the question of assessment

While teaching MAEE (Master in Elementary Education) in TISS (Tata Institute of Social Science), Mumbai,[17] the classrooms were a microcosm of the country. Students from regional, caste-class-gendered, and Adivasi contexts made our classroom interactions rich and vibrant. The course was on 'Pedagogy of Social Studies'. One of our favourite and most challenging reading used to be 'Writing ordinary lives' by M.S.S. Pandian,[18] who was then Professor in JNU. It is a concretely layered academic paper which utilises Tamil Dalit literature as its sources.

Pandian problematises the viewpoint through which caste is dealt with in academia. He notes that abstract academic writings are located far away from the realities of caste experiences. In the former, emotions and subjectivities are avoided. But at a time when caste-based reservations had become a hot issue in the country, he notes that upper-caste social science scholars did express their concrete feelings. At the same time, Pandian critiques Dalit scholars from esteemed universities in Delhi who articulated that Dalit writers should move into theoretical areas and away from poetry and emotional writings. Foregrounding these academic trends of social science, he uses two books of Dalit writers, Bama and Gunasekaran, to illustrate and contextualise everyday caste experiences of ordinary people. The strategies used by the two Tamil writers are examined by Pandian as being deeply contextualised and reflective of real-life social processes and therefore having a much deeper literary and pedagogic value than the abstract writings of social science.

In one batch, the presence of two vibrant students in the class, one a Dalit activist man (A), and another an upper-caste woman (B) from two different regions of the country, made the class more vibrant than usual. Prior to reading Pandian, some students had responded that caste is a thing of the past and that Dalit activists are reinventing caste in the present day. This comment, by one of the students, gave way to responses from several students who narrated their caste experiences from different parts of the country. Sexual exploitation of Dalit women, curtailing of schooling of Dalit students, and upper-caste resistance to Dalit persons procuring employment and wealth were some of the issues that were narrated.

Through Pandian's paper, the classroom conversations were further enhanced. 'A' pointed out caste-based experiences from his village. One of them concerned how the village was spatially organised on the basis of caste. Even a dog walking from the Dalit *basti* into the so-called upper-caste spaces, he said, created a lot of ruckuses. "How dare the dog walk into this area?" – such outbursts, he said, were hilarious as well as arrogant, and such attitudes still guide everyday lives in most parts of the country. 'B' had heated discussions with 'A' on these points.

As teachers, our role was to enhance informed debates. It was important to curtail neither A or B, yet we clearly explained our anti-caste stands. Some conversations ensued as follows:

B: You can't side with A. The teacher has to be neutral.

We replied that, as teachers, we take no sides, but we have our points of view. On the issue, we are not neutral. We had to assure the class that their opinions were important, and had to be articulated. There would be debates, but their stands would not impact the assessments of assignments. Assessments, we assured them, would be done on the basis of reasoning, evidence, and reflections. But B wrote long mails in the course Moodle group on how disturbing the social studies classes were.

Years have gone by. Today, both 'A' and 'B' are educators of repute in their own regions. 'B' has had several exposures to rethink on social stands; our course, too, must have been a small part of that. She takes inclusive stands and actions today. The point being made is that transformations happen through observations, reflections, readings, and so on that make students realise the contextual realities of our society. The ability to transform can be enhanced. This is perhaps the greatest potential value of education.

Another incident was of a student from Nagaland who wrote a long note on our course Moodle group that the course teaches only about Hinduism and does not talk about other religions. We were quite taken aback initially because we were not teaching about any religion. We invited the student to present the problem in the next class so that we could collectively look into the problem. She was referring to the range of discussions we had in class following the reading of Pandian's paper. In her context of an Adivasi society, there were religions, but no caste. She was Christian by faith and pointed out that Christianity has no caste system, unlike Hinduism. This led us to further examine social structures of tribal and feudal formations.

Even as the teaching/learning of other subjects also have their own tensions between the concrete and the abstract, in social science we are learning of social processes in which our own locations and perspectives become explicit when we engage with concrete knowledge. These become subjective by reflecting upon life experiences, but the holistic examinations of social structures and transitions show the embeddedness of experiences in the larger picture of social relationships. As elaborated elsewhere (Sunny, 2010),[19] it is noted that the scope for process-based understandings lies in the methods, information, and perspectives of social science.

> - What was the knowledge creation happening in the class through the debates among students?
> - In situations of disagreements, how can open discussions become a useful pedagogy?

Conclusions

In the school as an institution located in the modern (capitalist) system, there is an urge to look for the best students through distinctions conferred through examinations. Competition along with the social hierarchies of the caste-class-gender enhances classroom transactions to label and stratify students. Social science potentially helps to question these hierarchies, and to cast light upon the social processes in society that extend uncritically into the classroom. But we need critical engagements with both theory and practice in order to be able to actualise those potentials.

The main ideas emerging from the concrete changes and possibilities of improvements discussed in the chapter are not meant to be prescriptive for the reader. It is an indication of possibilities in a hierarchical system, of which both teachers and students are a part.

Dialectical relationships unfold in many ways for a teacher of social studies, as for instance, between:

(1) the unequal society and the democratic space legally promised in the modern school.
(2) the abstract writings about society in the textbooks and the actual life experiences of teachers and students.
(3) the hierarchical social notions held by teachers and students and the liberating potentials of contextualised contents in textbooks and of critical pedagogy.
(4) the framework of the examinations and the reality of cultural capitals.

This book began in the premises of consciousness. In the modern state, the teacher, as labour and as citizen, could, through collective consciousness, play a dialectical role in changing the system. Teacher unions have mobilised teachers to voice their rights to fair wages. There are examples of educationists, teachers, and policymakers coming together to shape educational policies and to rewrite textbooks in India, like through NCF 2005. Collective efforts from across the country and through intersectionality can develop transformative praxis.

Notes

1 Badhwar, Natasha (2015), 'The school on the hill', *Mint*, https://www.livemint.com/Leisure/hrgTu2CmdYZERoR1TaBc0M/The-school-on-the-hill.html accessed 3 December 2020.
2 *The Hindu*, 2 June 2012.
3 Joseph, Sarah (2022; 27), Budhini, Kottayam, D.C. Books, (Translation mine).
4 The section on coal mining is taken from Yemuna Sunny, 'Embedding GCED in Geography Text books', in *Global Citizenship Education: A Handbook for Teachers at Upper Primary Level in India*, Regional Institute of Education, Bhopal, 2019, pp160.
5 Haydock, H (2015), 'Stated and unstated aims of NCERT textbooks', *Economic and Political Weekly*, L, (17), pp. 109–119.
6 Agarwal, P (2008) Unpublished study of field assignment in TISS, Mumbai, for the course MAEE
7 Kumar, K (1996), *Learning from Conflict*, Orient Longman/Sangam Books Limited, London.
8 Kumar, K (2005): *Political Agenda of Education: A Study of Colonialist and Nationalist Ideas* Sage Publications, New Delhi.
9 Kapoor, B (2015) Unpublished study of field assignment in TISS, Mumbai, for the course MAEE.
10 Cole, M, V Jon-Steiner, S Scribner, and E Souberman, ed. (1978): *Vygotsky, LS: Mind in Society, the Development of Higher Psychological Processes* Harvard University Press; Cambridge, Massachusetts; London.
11 This is taken from Yemuna Sunny, 'Embedding GCED in Geography', in Pethiya, S and Sebu, S (eds), *Global Citizenship Education: A Handbook for Teachers at Upper Primary Level in India*, Regional Institute of Education, Bhopal, 2019, pp 158.
12 Sunny, Y (2020), 'How sand mining along the Narmada is choking web of life', *Down to Earth*, 5 Nov. 2020, https://www.downtoearth.org.in/blog/mining/how-sand-mining-along-the-narmada-is-choking-web-of-life-74100#
13 Source: Session 12 'Changes in Society' of 'Avehi Abacus Project',2003 (www.avehiabacus.org).
14 Vasavi, A R (2019), 'School differentiation in India reinforces social inequalities', *The India Forum* May 3, 2019, https://www.theindiaforum.in/article/school-differentiation-india-reinforcing-inequalities, accessed 2 December 2020.
15 Sunny, Y (2011), 'Teacher, society and modern school', *Economic and Political Weekly*, 46(17), 23 Apr, 2011, pp 26–31.
16 Eklavya is an organisation that started to work on education from the late 1980s. Up to 2000, it had the opportunity to seed innovative programmes of education in the government sector.
17 MA in Elementary Education which I had taught from 2006–2007 to 2015–2016. Dr. Manish Jain and I were co-teachers for a few years.
18 Pandian, M S S (2008), 'Writing ordinary lives', *Economic and Political Weekly*, 43 (38), 20 September 2008, pp 34-40.
19 Sunny, Y (2010), 'Communalisation of Education', *Economic and Political Weekly*, June 5, 2010, 45 (23), pp. 23.

7
TEACHERS, SOCIETY, AND THE CLASSROOM

The everyday image that comes to mind when we think of a teacher is placed in the confines of school and classroom, engaged in 'instruction'. (The increasing presence of digital teaching has also emphasised this 'delivery' aspect of the teacher's identity.) But the teachers we know do much more than playing the role of the instructor. Society looks at teachers mainly as a group of individuals in a certain school or as an amorphous, homogeneous collective. For most students and their parents, teachers represent a figure of authority to be obeyed, sometimes against the students' wishes. Teachers are commonly seen as a nebulous collective that underperforms but demands, blackmailing for privileges. Teachers themselves do not seem to have definitive ways of engaging with such narratives. It escapes most that teachers are not a homogeneous lot. The imagined power attached to teachers can at best be seen in classrooms or be visible in union leaders who themselves may not be practising teachers.

The diversity of teachers firstly represents a range of the hierarchy of schools as discussed in earlier chapters. Another point of separation in teachers can be seen in relation to the status of subjects taught in schools. Social sciences are typically perceived as 'non-utility' and 'soft' subjects and, in the hierarchy of school knowledge, stand in the 'lower place', just above arts-and-crafts and physical education. This status of social science attaches itself to the subject teachers (NCERT-NCF, 2005). On the other side of this heterogeneity, we find a common thread – the visible and invisible presence of the State.

Teachers are located in different relationships – with students, they are encased in carrying the mantle of social reproduction, transferring certain

DOI: 10.4324/9781003449348-11

knowledge-skills-norms through textbook-based content and structured examinations. In relation to the State, besides their identity as workers, teachers' character is constructed through the system of teacher education, providing a rationale for performing expected functions. A teacher's status as a citizen is subsumed in these roles. The State and society expects them to be 'non-political', their 'politics' restricted to their identity as 'workers' negotiating service rules, as part of a union for collective bargaining. Ironically, the Constitution of India distinguishes teachers' 'special status' as citizens with discerning character, legally enabling teachers to exercise executive power in shaping democratic polity[1] (Kingdon and Muzammil, 2001).

Although these issues should concern all teachers, social science teachers in particular need to seek clarity about where they stand in relation to the State and society, because they are the ones who deal directly with democratic citizenship education. As we have seen in earlier chapters, the nature of the State and conceptions of democracy are neither uniform nor static. In the context of India, the role of the State in relation to citizenship education has been changing, from colonial to post-colonial, and current neo-colonial times. It is imperative then to understand, how teachers' roles have changed through these phases. This understanding may help us delineate the possibilities and challenges in terms of our work as social science teachers.

Teachers in India: A brief history

In this section, we take a look at teachers in a historical perspective. The discussions here are not merely about teacher education and the specific component of social science teaching, but we position the teacher in the context of the evolution of the modern democratic state. We place the teacher within the reference points of the political, philosophical, economic necessities, and the priorities of the State.

Pre-colonial: From ancient and through medieval times in the Indian subcontinent, hierarchisation and control of knowledge through caste and gender segregation was one of the mechanisms of ensuring feudal power. The rulers did not directly interfere with education. The Brahmin teacher enjoyed freedom to decide what to teach, how to pace teaching, choose pupils and sometimes even expect sacrifice of life and limb from them. Teachers were assisted by senior students who could help the younger ones. (This came to be known as the 'monitorial system' when the British began their systemic intervention in education). In the medieval period during the ascendency of Mughal rule and other regional powers, trade with faraway places enlarged the content of education that was previously centred around matters of religion and ritual. It also began to include and emphasise aspects of administration and trade, but the Brahmin teachers' moral authority stayed intact. The 'cultural capital' of the community made it possible to take over bureaucratic positions in the royal courts. The British colonial empire changed this monopoly and status of educated Brahmins by fundamentally altering the meaning of civilisation, knowledge, and education.

Colonial: For the colonial rulers, educating Indians was both a compulsion and a choice. Whereas the East India Company spread its economic dominion through the subcontinent, it found it unsustainable to administer and strengthen it merely with help of British officials and a few Indians. After the Company's Charter was renewed in 1813, it began attending to questions of establishing systems to sustain and consolidate its hold. This process had its own dynamics in the political-economic pressures from the 'home country'.

The transition from feudalism to capitalism redefined the ideas of property and ownership – from joint to individual, informal to formal. Monarchies became democracies. The modern State emerged both as the competing player in economic activities as well as the mediator of public good. Competition replaced patronage and monopolies. The logic of the 'free market' became central to capitalist success, underlying which was the idea of private property. In the context of global capitalism and empire-building in the subcontinent, the dual character of the East India Company, as a trading monopoly and as a political, administrative entity, faced severe criticism. The pressure was to 'open up' the Indian economy, to facilitate British economic interests, both private and public. It was compelled to 'change its role as a business-house, acquiring profits for itself to a body in service of the empire' (Kumar, 1991). It became a 'quasi-state', administering control and keeping order. This necessitated forming alliances with the local elite, to enlist their traditional power of dominance to aid the functioning of the Company and the British State. Creating a 'civil society' was essential to this exercise, by co-opting the powerful sections, sharing gains of profit, and protecting private property of the local elite, rather than confronting them. The earlier conflicts and violence used to capture regions had to give way to developing common ground. This did not mean that 'violence' or force was totally abrogated, but, by creating common class interests with the local elite, the feudal class was 'sub-contracted' by the Company to rule on their behalf, if necessary, by force and subjugation of the 'uncivilized natives'. It is this 'pursuit of order' (Kumar, 1991) that led to the mirroring of the British systems of governance in the Indian Empire – judiciary, police, education, public works, taxation, etc.

Training the 'locals' to take up administration on their behalf meant not just passing on the technical know-how but instilling a new culture and value-set, preparing them to represent a 'superior' authority that was not merely economically powerful but seen to be culturally superior. The ideals of this civilisation were placed in the values of Reformation, rational thinking, and individual freedom, and were just a century old even for the British. Whereas, in their early encounter with the 'Indian civilization' the Orientalists, by viewing through the lenses of upper-caste Hindu males, imagined an advanced ancient culture, the 'Liberal' framework, on the other hand, sought to remove this blind-fold, exposing the social fabric woven with caste and gender oppression. In doing so, the 'Liberals' preferred to stereotype all local cultures as inhabitants of a 'dark continent', shadowed by 'oriental despotism'. In their eyes, the 'natives' needed to be 'civilised', correcting character flaws of their 'uncultivated minds' (like 'perjury', 'forgery', and 'narrow group interests'), and, moreover, rather than curbing their insubordination by force, it was seen to be better to educate them (Kumar, 1991; Jain, 2010).

A sampling of this strategy

> The later offences against the peace and happiness of society have indeed for the present been materially checked by the vigilance and energy of the police, but it is probably only by the more general diffusion of knowledge among the great body of people that the seeds of these evils can be effectively destroyed.
>
> *(Note by Lord Minto, Governor General, 1811, cited in Kumar, 1991,[2] p. 27).*

Think

- How do you view the relationship between 'vigilance and energy of the police' and 'spreading knowledge'? What role do each of these have in a modern State?
- What do you think the British meant by 'diffusion of knowledge'?
- Were the British administrators aware of the systems of formal education prevalent in the subcontinent?

The officers in different provinces commissioned educational surveys (Madras 1822, Bombay 1824, and Bengal 1835). One of the key reasonings for these surveys was to establish that the land was in want of enlightenment and upliftment. In the process, much of the information acquired by the colonial state was simplified and digested into monolithic narratives (Kakkar, 2016[3]). In particular, these surveys overlooked the complexities of the denial of education to 'lower' castes. The surveys (Adam, 1830; Arnold, 1857, 1858 in Kumar, 1991) revealed the existence of a large network of schools with their uneven regional spread. For the British, steeped in the zeal of 'enlightenment', 'scientific thinking', 'efficiency', and 'progress and happiness', all aspects of education in these schools were deemed to be lacking in real value. But, whereas the existing schools were seen as inept, the 'civilisation project' could be fast-tracked by supporting infrastructure and by training teachers in 'real knowledge'. Thus, in addition to bolstering the efforts for 'modern' education earlier initiated by European Christian missionaries, it was seen useful to give small grants to existing schools and to open 'normal schools' (teacher training institutes). For example, Lord Munro, the then-Governor of Madras, in his Minutes (1823), is known for having recommended ideas for improvement of existing schools by training teachers.

Munro's Minutes are considered a corner-stone in teacher education. But the primary rationale behind his motivation to spread education needs to be looked into.

Closely read the excerpts from Munro's Minutes about the rationale for advancing education amongst the 'natives'. You can look at more details by using the link provided here: https://www.indianculture.gov.in/rarebooks/major-general-sir-thomas-munro-bart-kcb-governor-madras-selections-his-minutes-and-other.

Excerpts from Major General Sir Thomas Munro, Governor of Madras, Selections from his minutes and other official writings, London, Kegan and Paul Co. 1, Paterson Square, 1881.

"A great deal has been said, both in this country and in England, regarding the liberty of Indian press; …I cannot view the question of a free press in this country without feeling that the tenue with which we hold our power, never has been and never can be the liberties of the people. I therefore consider it as essential to the tranquility of the country and the maintenance of our Government, that all the present restrictions should be continued. Were the people all our countrymen, I would prefer the utmost freedom of the press, but as they are, nothing could be more dangerous than such freedom. In place of spreading better useful knowledge among the people, and tending to their better Government, it would generate insubordination, insurrection, and anarchy."

(Munro's Minutes, 'The Danger of Free Press in India' 12th April, 1822, pp 287)

"By mild and equitable government, by promoting the dissemination of useful books among the natives without attacking their religions, by protecting their own numerous schools, by encouraging by honorary or pecuniary marks, of distinction those 'Where the best system of education prevails, by occasional allowances from the public revenue to such as stand in need of this aid; and, above all, by making it worth the while of the natives to cultivate their minds, by giving them a greater share in the civil administration of the country, and holding out the prospect of filling places of rank and emolument as inducements to the attainment of knowledge, we shall hy degrees banish superstition, and introduce among the natives of India all the enlightened opinions and doctrines which prevail in our own country."

(Munro's Minutes, 'The Danger of Free Press in India' 12th April, 1822.) pp 203-204)

Think

- When we look at the 'Contents' of Munro's Minutes we can see that the section on 'The Danger of Free Press in India' appears much earlier in main section and 'The Education of the Natives of India' is towrds the very end in the 'Miscellaneous' section. (22 July 1822, 10 March 1826, pp. 328–337).
- Why does the section 'The Danger of Free Press in India' appear before the section on education? (12 April 1822, pp. 287-297, particularly 292-295.)
- In light of Munro's ideas about 'freedom of the press' how do you place his suggestions about the spread of education among the 'natives', and the reasoning behind teacher training?

Today, we understand education as an essential condition for democracy, of which freedom of the press is an integral part. Taking the example of Minto's envisioning in and Munro's Minutes here, we can see how education was visualised to play the role of co-option, to contain dissent against an exploitative foreign rule, by controlling freedom of expression.

'Pursuit of Order' being the motivation underlying colonial educational initiatives, the rationale was to replace 'coercion' by 'socialisation' (Kumar, 1991). With the grants for infrastructure, salaries, materials, and teacher training, the teachers from the village and the physical space for schools made available by the village gradually became separated from the community and merged with the colonial state.

Dual role of education – colonial citizen and civil society: The 'framework of dual role' (Kumar, 1991), meant that colonial education functioned differently for different sections of society – making a 'colonial citizen' (Jain, 2008, 2010),[4] on one hand, and creating a 'civil society' on the other. Despite the colonial state's financial contribution being very low (Gokhale, 1911)[5], many of the administrators were not in favour of even the most meagre of expenses being paid. Educating the masses remained a very low priority – justifiable on the grounds as an investment in creating a class of cheaply paid, servile, dependable subordinate civil servants. 'Good citizenship' meant obedience, dutifulness, accepting one's position, amid gratitude to the rulers. The state's main role was the maintainer of order for the pursuit of individual happiness, protecting property and nurturing a 'civil society' amongst the natives.

Whereas for men from 'upper' castes or propertied classes who had access to higher education the content was wider consisting of literature, political philosophy, sciences, and logic, they too needed to be shown their place as colonial subjects, culturally subservient, required to learn the correct way to live from the advanced culture of their colonial masters and thus the overall tenor was weighted towards a moral agenda (Jain, 2008).

The task of shaping certain kind of citizens was placed in the domain of school social sciences, the subject of 'civics' was introduced from upper primary school and taught only to boys; the few girls who reached that level were taught 'home science' (Jain, 2008). (At this juncture even in their 'home country', women were not seen as full citizens, were denied voting rights.) A widely prescribed book for 'civics' was 'Citizen of India' which emphasised not only the role of British education in 'enlightening the natives' but considered that the very experience of colonial rule, its systems, and services were to be seen as a fundamentally vital educational experience.

In Chapter 3, with reference to the textbook for 'civics' by Sir William Lee-Warner, a British colonial administrator in the Indian Civil Service, we saw how opening schools and preparing teachers was seen as the gracious act of a benevolent patriarch.

> An effort ought to be made to teach our future citizens the ABC of their rights and duties. Who am I and who are my neighbours? How am I governed and what is expected of me? What becomes of the taxes I pay? What is done to keep me and my property safe and to protect me from disease and famine? (Excerpt from the Preface of 'The Citizen of India')
>
> We learn from history very clearly that there were three great dangers to which the lives and property of the people of India were exposed before British rule began. These were that the coasts of India were open to attack by sea, that the country was exposed to invasion by the passes in the North-West, and that the fighting classes, whose duty it was to defend the country, had become unable to do so by long residence in it ... Each one of these dangers and disadvantages has been removed by the coming of the English into the country. The seacoast is protected by the English navy... (Excerpt from 'The Citizen of India' Chapter – Races and Population)

As Manish Jain (2010) illustrates:

> To Lee-Warner, British rule was an educational experience for Indians. "Education" was not limited to school. For those who were unable to read or write, this education "began in the villages, in the municipal town, in the court of law, and on the railways" (Lee-Warner, 1900, p. vii). The public works of India were proof of the British "power of organisation and

> resource" and were the "best schools" to get the training of these skills (Lee-Warner, 1900, p. 163). Public justice, postal and telegraphic communication, jails, public offices, museums, hospitals, the press, and school, all had educational worth
> (Lee- Warner, 1900, p. 165). (Jain, 'Colonial Knowledge, Colonial Citizen: Civics in Colonial India.' (2010, p. 23)

Reformatting the teacher – from extolled guru to servant of the empire

Gradually, the empire solidified its administration by controlling production and trade, mandating high taxes, curbing insubordination by farmers, soldiers on the one hand and setting up 'modern' systems of governance on the other. The Wood's Dispatch (1854, popularly known as the Magna Carta of English Education in India) sought to expand formal education, not by investing in new schools, but by providing 'grant-in-aid' to existing village schools. This required teachers who could be trained to teach 'real knowledge' and thus requiring an expansion of the already existing number of 'normal schools' where teachers from local schools could obtain a certificate and were assured employment. Lord Stanley's Dispatch (1859, that came on the heels of the '1857 Revolt') recommended desisting from importing teachers from England and requiring that salary grants to schools be given only to 'trained teachers'. The 're-formatted' teacher became a key instrument of social control.

Think

- For the teachers, what did this label of training and qualification mean?
- How did it change the relationship between the community and the school?
- What did it represent for the society that held their Gurus and their knowledge in high esteem?

The emphasis on trained/'qualified' teachers underlined their separation, as well as that of the content in relation to what was being taught in the existing indigenous schools. Firstly, this signified the worthlessness of a culture that held its civilisation in high esteem. (Caste and gender discrimination had kept intact the exclusive status of such knowledge, and the 'Orientalists' interpretation of the 'golden' ancient past had left it uncritiqued). Secondly, in the indigenous culture, knowledge was not as strictly formalised and prescribed as was the case with the new schools opened by the colonialists. The teacher defined, selected, interpreted, and regulated the pacing of what was worthy of teaching. With the entry of textbooks prescribed by the new

State, this centrality of the teacher in the selection and transfer of knowledge was removed. The externally controlled examination system, the supervisory bureaucracy made the teacher a mere cog in the wheel. The official grants for infrastructure and government salaries alienated the teacher from the local community, marking him as a lowly servant of the Empire. As the Crown took over reins from the Company, the frequency and rigorousness of official measures to 'prepare teachers' increased by opening normal schools, colleges, courses for specialisation in teacher education at Masters level, and rules regarding sanctioning/withholding grants to schools tied to the appointment of trained teachers.

The position of school teachers at the lowest level of educational bureaucracy became further vulnerable with their low salaries. Earlier teachers could live a dignified life with cash/kind given by the families of the students, community, and feudal lords/religious bodies (Kumar, 1991), but now government school teachers' low status was reflected in their low salaries. The primary logic of underspending on education in general and on school education in particular communicated the State's position – its lack of enthusiasm about mass education. Supporting teachers in subject-specialisation for English language, physical sciences, and mathematics was seen as being vital for a technologically competent market economy and strong bureaucracy. Barring the 'dry positivist' stance in geography, school social sciences were devoid of scientific spirit (see Chapter 3). As was the case in other parts of the world, they primarily functioned as an avenue for constructing certain kinds of citizens to build the narrative of a benevolent State to prescribe a code of conduct sans criticality. Such a subject did not need specialists, anyone could teach the assemblage of information from the textbooks!

Post-independence

The spirit of the new country, with its need to build a strong sovereign democracy, necessitated reorganisation and expansion of education. The two stated aims were to retain the hard-earned political independence and to nurture and deepen the democratic ideals of justice, equity, and fraternity by refurbishing governance mechanisms. The Constitution the newly formed Indian state created a special identity for teachers that no other profession enjoys (see Box 7.1) However, a country does not exist in a vacuum: it is part of the global jigsaw. The end of imperial rule, the status of a sovereign, and its political independence doesn't necessarily mean it can completely change its economic trajectory. As we saw in Chapter 5, the end of WWII, freedom from colonialism, and the formation of the UN did not necessarily mean an end to imperialism. Newly independent India was placed in the 'new world order' with restructured global capitalism. We need to place the post-independence teacher in this complex context. It is in light of this that we can understand how the post-Independence education system, shaped by its 'structural and ideological contradictions', what Henry Giroux (pioneering contributor to 'critical pedagogy', professor and public intellectual) notes in the context of teacher training programmes: 'a larger social order caught in a conflict between the imperatives of its social welfare responsibilities and its functional allegiance to the conditions of capitalism'.[6]

BOX 7.1 THE CONSTITUTIONAL IDENTITY OF TEACHERS

The drafters of the Indian Constitution, after considered debate, provided for teachers' representation in the upper house of state legislatures; the upper house was created as a 'second line of defence' by including 'wise men' as its members to be nominated from sections of the intelligentsia, socially oriented, creative persons. The British, by withholding the right to universal franchise, had barred full citizenship to the majority of Indians excluding them from participating in political life. Thus, those without economic means or high social standing could not contribute to law-making and matters of governance. The framers of India's Constitution sought to enable active participation in policy-making by nominating public representatives from amongst scholars, talented, socially minded persons without the means or interest in contesting elections.

> Their experience, their mature judgment and their position in the society and country are such that they do not want to take the trouble of going through an ordinary election. But at the same time, they constitute the more sober elements in the society and it is a national loss if their experience cannot be availed of or placed at the service of the state.

Thus, Article 171 (3) (c) provided special political status to teachers in the 'second chambers' at State level. Although teachers' special status is not equitable across States and across different categories of teachers, it is notable that, among different service sectors (public/private), it is teachers who have special rights for participating directly in the democratic process, both for electing representatives and as executive functionaries (Kingdon and M Muzzammil, 2001, for more discussion).

The 'maker of nation's destiny' or the 'keeper of order'?

'The destiny of India is now being shaped in her classrooms' said the Education (Kothari) Commission (1968), placing teachers in a pivotal role – 'of all the factors which determine the quality of education and its contribution to national development, the teacher is undoubtedly the most important. Teacher, must therefore, be accorded an honoured place in society'. Commissions and policies in independent India addressed issues concerning teachers' roles, service conditions, and nomenclature in keeping with evolving understanding in the field. Things began changing visibly from the mid-eighties. The National Education Policy (1986/PoA92), while, on one hand, made specious statements – 'The status of [the] teacher reflects the sociocultural ethos of the society; it is said that no people can rise above the level of its teacher'. Although the policy made rhetorical statements for improving the quality of teacher education as a prerequisite for quality school education, it officially sanctioned non-formalisation of education by engaging semi-schooled instructors in Non-Formal Education centres run by NGOs. Rather than increasing the number of schools and filling teacher vacancies, subcategories of contractual 'para-teachers' were created. Despite the hyperbolic policy statements, the public education system remained underserved. 'Non-formalisation measures', instead of infusing flexibility, led to dilution. While teachers' salaries increased, their social standing plummeted as annual studies by mega-NGOs brought forth data of poor learning levels of students in public schools. Instead of drawing attention to systemic weakness, these studies often directly pointed fingers at 'incompetent, disinterested government teachers', further sullying their image and that of public education in the popular mind.

> **BOX 7.2**
>
> ...it is therefore no surprise that for the last two decades, the schoolteacher, as a former centrepiece of processes of social change, is reduced to a mere object of educational reform or, worse, a passive agent of the prevailing ideology of the modern state. A state that seeks to universalise schooling and the creation of a modern citizenry, through massive public investments in school infrastructure and the transaction of a standardised curriculum, pays only peripheral attention to the needs of its primary change-agent: the teacher. A state that seeks to be an IT and knowledge superpower of the twenty-first century, but uses a classical early twentieth-century paradigm of teacher education to "reproduce" millions of teachers who have few skills and lesser incentives to make this happen. (Batra Poonam 'Voice and agency of teachers: Missing link in National Curriculum Framework 2005', *Economic and Political Weekly*, January 2005.)

The overall degradation, dilution of school education, and obsolete teacher education systems resulted in a weakening of the knowledge base in the teacher cadre. So, while some policy documents infused a much-needed paradigm shift about issues concerning learning, teaching, and society, their vision has remained shackled by the iniquitous legal framework, superficial, inconsistent policy perspectives, and endemic structural challenges. The multi-layered nature of the education system has been further sharpened by market pressure and a neoliberal policy stance, resulting in withdrawal of the State's commitment. Teachers today are an alienated lot – who can be called for census, election, disaster management, and other duties like clerical work, at the expense of their primary role as partners and facilitators in knowledge creation. Thus, whereas the Independent state in its initial exuberance drew its ideals from the freedom struggle, it soon slid into stasis in favour of the traditionally privileged.

Think

- What are your views about changes in the 'expected role of teachers' post-Independence?
- Do you see the Constitutional vision about teachers' role in society (drawn from pre-Independence experiences) reflected in teacher education policies?
- How was the teacher's role as a citizen reflected in the envisioning?
- In what way do these issues impact the nature of social science teaching/learning?

With reference to historical perspective about the changing role of teachers, the nature of education, and its relation to the character of the State, it is possible to identify a few key issues:

- First, that the colonial administration's actions in the field of education carried a cultural agenda as well as political and economic compulsions, and, as a result, changes in the position of the teacher, from exalted mentor to a mere employee, had cultural, politicoeconomic dimensions.
- Second, the post-Independence Constitutional vision of society reflected the ideals for which freedom was fought for and won but the policies that followed, while retaining some of the vocabulary, did not vitalise education in challenging structural inequities and the role of teachers in redefining knowledge.

In addition to the function of preparing a certain kind of workforce, the British saw education as a mechanism of social control through socialisation. At the same time, looking at Munro's Minutes, it is clear that the British valued democracy and freedoms back home and viewed education as a means to bring gradual social change (preventing revolt) in places under their dominion. However, while colonial education functioned as a mechanism of social control, it also contributed to ideas of sovereignty, freedom, democracy, and equality in society. The contestation between these two sets of values is alive even today. Education in India today also functions as an apparatus, creating a malleable workforce for the global market, socialising individuals into unconditional acceptance, but at the same time it has the potential for critically questioning the system, to make it more just and humane.

We saw very briefly how 'training' teachers held a key when the British spread their education system and how the trajectory of teachers' positions and roles had been impacted by the way education shaped up in Independent India. In such a situation, teachers' understanding of the purpose of their work carries weight and the kind of teacher education they are exposed to thus needs to be examined. We will draw mainly from insights from Henry Giroux's contributions to the field.

Teacher: Tool of the State or transformative intellectuals?

We have tried to develop an understanding of the manner in which education and teachers are placed in the larger context of the State's development paradigm. Henry Giroux's insights about how the educational policy reform measures post mid-eighties affect teachers in the US have relevance for us as well. Outside family and close neighbours, children have relevant relationships with teachers as adults. However; when it comes to policy, Giroux draws attention to the 'lack of confidence in teachers to provide intellectual and moral leadership for the nation's youth'.[7] Teachers' role in preparing active, sensitive, and critically engaged democratic citizens and teachers' intelligence, judgement, and experience is ignored in policy-making. Teachers become mere objects of policy reform, implementing ideas of experts usually far-removed from everyday realities and complex contexts of diverse classrooms.

The social science teacher development is specifically charged with the responsibility to support teachers to enable future generations to learn the knowledge, dispositions, and skills necessary to build a principled and democratic society. In Chapters 3, 4, and 5, we have attempted to analyse the formal system of education in historical perspective related with the issues involving knowledge production. This analysis is necessary in order to understand how education functions as socialisation mechanism to reproduce a division of labour and distribution of resources, enabling or curtailing democratic citizenship. However, these perspectives are absent in teacher education programmes.

'Teacher education programmes are caught in a deceptive paradox' (Giroux, 1988). While they profess aims of developing a teacher cadre to nurture ethical and democratic citizenship, the participating teachers are treated as passive agents, subtly programmed to not reflect on confronting the challenges to democracy or the socioeconomic inequalities within which schools are placed. Invoking John Dewey, Giroux points to the importance placed on skill-building and methodological expertise, negating the need for critical thinking about the very purpose of education.

Giroux discusses the dominant modes in which most teacher education programmes are placed and suggests possibilities for change.

Obsession with methodology: It is essential to understand that the questions about meanings and purpose in teacher education programmes are political in nature. They symbolise the ideologies behind the socialising agencies with a set of rules and models of constructing and legitimising categories regarding competence, achievement, and success, as well as promoting specific hierarchical roles. The problems/challenges with regard to teaching are often viewed as having merely a technical nature. The State (often advised by multilateral/international agencies) produces and draws from research that legitimises the technical nature of challenges in education and advocates procedural reforms to address them without paying heed to complex contextual realities or imbedded structural issues.

> Most research tends to view teaching as a problem of human engineering and teacher education as the most efficient way to provide new recruits with specific behaviours and attitudes of the people who practise teaching ... the conduct of schooling, the system of status and privilege of the occupation, and the social and political implications of institutional arrangements are obscured through a process of reification. Teachers and teacher education are treated administratively.
>
> *(Popkewitz)*[8]

The overall effect on teacher education of the social engineering approach has been considerable and is far removed from the vision of John Dewey, George Counts, Freire, Tagore, Gandhi, or Ambedkar, who argued for critical, reflective, transformative, humane education, who stressed the need for ethical, experiential, and emancipatory dimensions of education. The 'methodological madness' (Aronowitz),[9] presents easy solutions advocating specific approaches or dimensions to curriculum. Such solutions aim at behavioural changes, first in teachers and, via them, in students. They skirt around addressing the assumptions embedded in these approaches, ignore the sociopolitical contexts that have birthed them, and, most importantly, overlook the ethical dimensions in everyday relationships, or the larger interests they represent.

In the Indian context, scholars and practitioners like Poonam Batra have argued that education policies, even if they are progressive, theoretically transformative, do not address teachers as whole beings. Both their potential personal agency in bringing about change as well as their biases and limitations are ignored. They are seen as 'passive agents of state to be "persuaded and trained" to magically translate the policy vision' (Batra, 2005).[10] As an example, Batra points to research about the tendency of many teachers:

> ...to simply accept poverty as the reason for the absence of many children and to see poverty as an unavoidable and inevitable factor that leads to high absenteeism and dropout rates...teachers see conditions such as that of bonded child labour, migration of children during school, the retention

of children for domestic chores...as unavoidable family circumstances that cannot be addressed by any policy or programme... (Vasavi, 2000, p. 36 in Batra, 2005).

The quick-fix of 'methods' downplays the politics underlying selection (or omission) of content that represents critical understanding to analyse and critique the political apparatus in subjects like 'civics/political science', or alternative conceptions of historical pasts, in History or dialectical perspective in geography. The potential of social science to enliven school life, to examine the social nature of knowledge creation is silenced by the isolated stress on cognition and imbibing accurate information. When the hierarchical education system 'fails' to produce expected 'outcomes', teachers become the problem to be fixed, by either giving them packages of modules (like 'life skills', 'value education', 'environmental education', etc.), or training them in new pedagogical methods or artificially controlling quality of teachers at entry-level, resulting in alienation of new teacher cadre, reminding them that they are to be mere cogs in the gigantic wheel of mechanisms beyond their control.

> **BOX 7.3**
>
> Dwarka has started teaching chapters on Constitutional Rights; the first of these chapters starts with 'Children's' Rights'. Today is a teachers' workshop about the recently introduced 'child-friendly' policy and revised textbooks. The theme of the workshop is 'Life-skills Approach for Child-Friendly Teaching' and Dwarka is eager to share yesterday's experience. During the class yesterday, as the section on child labour and exploitation was being discussed, the mood in the class changed. Everyone started staring at Rana and Jugal, the 'back benchers', the two boys had their eyes downcast. Everyone knows both these boys work in a hotel in the evening shift. During lunch break, as she passed by the class, she saw that Jugal and Rana were having a scuffle with a group of boys. When Dwarka went in, Rana said the boys always tease them about the work they do and today they blamed their parents for making them work, for exploiting them!
>
> During the workshop, after the expert's presentation, as the participants were allowed to raise questions, Dwarka narrated the incident, expecting a solution – the expert's advice was to look at the handout on life skills and the 'strategies for conflict resolution'.
>
> **Discuss, reflect, write, raise more questions:**
> - Why were Rana and Jugal avoiding eye contact during the class?
> - The group of boys teasing Rana and Jugal study in the same school and may have similar economic backgrounds – but why do you think they teased them, blamed their parents?

- How do you think Dwarka as a teacher looked at what happened during the class? Or the fight between the boys?
- Have you experienced similar situations in your schools? What has been your response or your thoughts about them?
- What do you think about the expert's advice to Dwarka?
- How does our educational material look at endemic issues like poverty? Are complex socioeconomic issues dealt within their multifarious dimensions? Are teachers sufficiently exposed to such issues?

Manufacturing consent: Another issue that needs attention is with the way the notion of 'culture' that permeates social science content in mainstream school/teacher education. In this view, culture is defined as simply a 'people's whole way of life', confined to politically defined geographical boundaries. Divorced from diverse realities of class, caste, gender, religion, region, languages, or ideologies, such a notion presents culture as a homogeneous, harmonious whole or at best 'celebration of diversity'. This results in silencing the very potential of critical engagement, of shutting out lived realities, heirarchies, contradictions, and contestations. Giroux argues that it is essential to address the issue of culture in terms of the inequitable distribution of power and resources, and, rather than speak of a 'common culture' or a 'multiplicity of cultures', it is essential to bring into focus the 'dominant culture' and/or 'minority cultures', which themselves are not homogeneous – not doing so is an imposition, an act of 'manufacturing consent'. For example; festivals or weddings are often celebrated accompanied by live music and drums. Do we think who the drummers are? Do they come from the same milieu as the dominant, privileged culture or do they belong to particular castes and communities? Are we aware that the troop of drummers usually belongs to those considered 'lower castes'? Whereas, in large metropolises, these traditions may have become obsolete, in many small towns and villages they still prevail. Our textbooks also sometimes have illustrations of a wedding or religious procession accompanied by a drumming troop. How do students/teachers from certain communities relate to such images? By not acknowledging such practices or by removing such illustrations from books, will discrimination and exploitation cease to exist?

Gramsci (1971)[11] explains it in terms of the power wielded by the State through a combination of force and 'consent'. We have discussed this in the earlier section of this chapter in context of the British rule. In order to maintain order, to reproduce itself, the modern democratic State refrains from using force or repression, rather relying on creating subtle hegemonic public consent. The State's hegemony can be seen by critically understanding institutionalisation of dominant cultural modes through 'citizenship education', that strips away/smooth over the contradictions and contestations vis-à-vis 'minority cultures' or opposing ideologies. The agencies and systems that are part of the 'ideological state apparatus' (family, schools, media, popular culture, religious bodies, judiciary, workplaces, even trade unions) function as negotiators between the 'powerful' and the everydayness of life. The modern States inequitably distribute not just economic goods and services but certain forms of 'cultural capital'[12] (Apple, 1979),[13] as well. Schools become the primary site of ideological control (Bernstein).[14] Not just textbooks but the 'hidden curriculum' (Apple 1977) like the photographs of social and religious icons, special days and festivals celebrated in school, songs sung during school 'assembly', communicate ideological messages. This raises questions about teacher education programmes (in general and in relation to the teaching of social sciences in particular) since they condition those 'intellectuals' who play a direct part in socialising students into the dominant social modes. The questions that need to be raised by educators then are:

> Whose culture gets distributed in the schools? Who benefits from this culture? What are the historical, social, economic roots of this culture? How is this culture distributed? How is it sustained in the curriculum?

BOX 7.4

Renuka Khandagale enters the school compound but has to wait to get to the stairs. There is a huddle at the entrance, with students trying to pray to the goddess in a small temple near the stairs. Renuka has come to the school today under duress because the exams are on. Her family has gone to Nagpur to celebrate the 'Dhammachakra-Parivartan' day; after the programmes at the Dikshabhoomi, they will go to her grandmother's house and she's going to miss all the fun. She consoles herself that she will visit her grandmother for a long break soon when the schools close for the three-week Diwali vacations.

- Will Renuka tell her friends about why the family has gone to Nagpur?
- Will her classmates and most teachers remember the significance of the Dhammachakra-Parivartan day? Will they think of it as a day to celebrate?
- What do you think about the fact that Renuka's school does not have a holiday or celebrations for Dhammachakra-Parivartan day but that the Diwali vacations are long?
- Imagine yourself in place of Renuka – think about how she may feel when she encounters content about 'celebrating diversity', 'composite culture of our country' in textbooks but, in the examples of different celebrations, festivals of her community are never mentioned?
- Renuka religion is neo-Buddhism; can you think of children or teachers of other communities who may share Renuka's experience, particularly as they pass by the temple of goddess in their school every day?

'**Culture of positivism**': Another phenomenon that dominates teacher education and schools is the way certain 'innovative programmes' are introduced to 'improve the system', to 'motivate teachers', by providing 'rational' solutions for teaching and assessment, indicating 'technocratic rationality'. Giroux explains this trend with reference to the 'post-Sputnik' mentality in USA as well as the 'Social Darwinist' ideologies (the influence of Bobbit and Spencer), and the 'scientific management movement' of the 1920s, that we saw in Chapter 4. Giroux outlines the misconceptions as follows. 1) knowledge that is worthy has to be 'empirically testable', i.e., empirical analytical research can identify regularities in the social world, just as the 'precise laws of nature'. (We have discussed this with reference to 'Scientism', Comte's insistence of applying the yardstick of physical sciences to study social phenomenon.) 2) Variables that cannot be measured in quantitative terms, i.e., feelings, insights, philosophical questions, or historical enquiry are seen as unworthy/'soft-data'. 3) 'Knowledge' in this form of rationality is reduced to those 'facts' that can be clearly examined and defined, i.e., it ends up separating the subject/'content' from variations in experiences and contexts. And 4) the idea that education can and must separate 'value' from 'objective fact' dominates selection of content, pedagogical options and assessment.

In the Indian context, the state and the international/bilateral development agencies have adopted these ideas, particularly from the 1990s when India changed its economic paradigm. As the result of economic liberalisation the State shifted its responsibility to provide universal quality education and instead began placing responsibilities on teachers and learners to demonstrate learning in terms of 'outcomes'. Absolving itself of the primary role of allocating sufficient resources to provide good quality education to all, it began to view its role as an financial investor, giving certain inputs, thereby demanding certain outputs. For example, the 'Minimum Levels of Learning' programme (MLL, NCERT 1993), was introduced after the UN agencies and the World Bank (WB) organised the Jomtien Conference, 'Education for All' and the school teachers were made to undergo 'SMART' training as part of the WB-sponsored District Primary Education Programme (DPEP). This mindset looks at education in terms of 'competency-based systems of instruction', behaviouristic models of pedagogy aimed mainly at standardised evaluation that leave no scope for contextual knowledge or individual experience and insights. Empathy, taking ethical positions fundamental for social sciences is devalued. 'Teacher education programmes do not give teachers the conceptual tools they need in order to view knowledge as problematic, as historically conditioned, socially constructed phenomena'. The objectification of knowledge takes the soul out of social science classrooms. The idea of 'professionalism' and 'expertise' is imposed on teachers but neither s/he nor the students are free to speak in an authentic voice. (Giroux points out that, while teachers and students are expected to display a willingness to change, the prevalent 'institutional structures and their embedded dominance remain the same').

BOX 7.5

These examples are drawn from Kumkum Roy's article 'Context, content and social science textbooks' (Economic and Political weekly, 24 Sept, 2011, 46(39))

After elections, the new government has brought in fundamental changes in the curriculum, the official body responsible for curriculum materials has re-written textbooks with real-life situations, problems, diverse socioeconomic contexts, emphasis on students' contribution to content, encouraging debate, analysis, and exploration. Assessment is to have a 'continuous and comprehensive' approach, laying an emphasis on 'formative' aspects, rather than merely 'summative'. The government body responsible for implementation and examinations has created a 'Manual for Assessment'. The following types of activities are indicative of the primary character of the 'manual'.

Example 1: With reference to a history chapter on 'Nazism in Germany', the 'manual' has an activity entitled 'Learning is Fun' which has a pyramid made up of blocks, each block having the first letter of an expected answer to given clues, which are; '*Most oppressed race in Germany *Party founded by Hitler * Purest race according to Hitler * First German Republic * Secret police *Youth organisation *German Parliament *Humiliating treaty was signed here'.

Example 2: This is with reference to a chapter in History, on 'Cricket'. The chapter brings out aspects of power and racism in colonial India and discrimination on the basis of caste, gender, class, or region in post-Independence. The activities the teachers are expected to conduct are: '*Organise a cricket match (or another option) * Hold a Commentary Competition'. The learners are to be evaluated on the basis of their knowledge of the sport, oratory skills, and confidence.

Example 3: Again, an exercise related to a history chapter. 'Women, Caste, and Reform' has an activity to stage role-plays with dialogue on 'Social ills in Indian society at different times' (such as sati, female infanticide, child marriage, and discrimination in education).

- These exercises are meant to be exemplars in teacher's manual. How do the makers of the manual perceive teachers? How do they look at the role of the social sciences in society?
- The NCF 2005 'National Focus Group on Examination Reforms' says '...it should be recognised that exam reform has the potential to lead educational reform. It has often been lamented that in Indian education the tail (assessment) has usually wagged the dog (of learning and teaching). The charge is a fair one and de-emphasising exams will certainly liberate the learning and teaching process from its straitjacket'. (NCF, NCERT, 2005, p. 23). What are your views about this?
- Teachers are in the implementing role of reforms. When they are expected to use textbooks that have possibilities of change, but the assessment or exams are still based on recall of 'facts', when supplementary resource

> materials emphasise the conventional modes of assessing given knowledge, skirting-around crucial issues, possible shades of feelings, opinions, contestations, ... what is the message given to the teaching community?
> - Kumkum Roy ruminates:
>
> In a situation where examinations still remain the central, if not the only preoccupation of parents, learners and school authorities, they are bound to be taken seriously... , teachers will in all likelihood, dip into the manual for ways and means of devising activities and tests to ease their burden. Factor in the situation where most schoolteachers in public/private schools in particular are upper-caste/-class women from the majority community, one can see how the manual can be used to simply reinforce the status quo, rather than developing skills of questioning and arguing, debating and discussing, what are perceived as contentious issues, liable to disrupt the sterile, fragile peace of the classroom.

In light of Roy's concerns as described above, and what Giroux terms a 'culture of positivism', how do you see the social science teacher negotiating desired change? What can be the reasons for assessment/evaluation systems resisting the desired changes, and the nature of knowledge to be valued, judged?

> - Arathi Sriprakash, in her study ('Being a teacher in contexts of change: Education reform and the repositioning of teachers' work in India', *Contemporary Education Dialogue* (2011) 8(1), 5–31), observes: 'Policy agendas need to engage with the social contingencies of reform and with the ways in which the multiple meanings of 'being a teacher' offer up conditions through which reform ideals are negotiated, resisted, and reshaped'. (The study shows how policy reforms with teachers at the centre of [the] action, need to be negotiated in relation to, teachers' authority relations, bureaucratic regulations, social status, and positions in the labour market.)
> - When [the] education system treats knowledge as factual bits, and teachers as homogeneous, acontextual implementing entities, when the complex interplay between knowledge, learner, teacher, [and] society is ignored, is it accidental, or is it symbolic of co-option or of resistance to change for equity and justice, with teachers playing key roles, examining, reframing their value-framework, pedagogic rationales, [and] ideas about knowledge and justice?

Teachers, society, and the classroom 205

Possibilities: In light of the above, it is essential to understand that over-reliance on or subjugating one's thinking to the ideology of 'technocratic rationality', it is essential to be able to bring in other forms of knowledge creation that are more contextual, empathetic, 'heuristic'[15] in nature, based on reflective thinking and derived from praxis. Some possibilities suggested here need not be seen as an exercise in exhaustive listing of solutions, but key starting points. Let us understand some of these ideas with help of a few examples;

Possibilities for Change	*Some Examples (Examine the following in context of discussions so far)*
Learn to think dialectically – to see schools as part of wider societal process. For this, it is essential to look at things in their interconnectedness, to acknowledge the process of the social reproduction through education.	Think about the school you are part of, the socioeconomic background of students and teachers. Do students in the school today represent a transition in socioeconomic standing from their parents' generation? Is there a hierarchy among students/teachers on the basis of class/caste/religion, language? In a critical look at the prescribed content or expected pedagogy, does it endorse, generate or ignore inequities of class, caste, gender/sexuality, religious, ideological relationships? Think about the students in your class, how are their lives positioned in relation to the textbook?
Interconnected nature of knowledge – whereas separate disciplines allow us to understand the world in certain ways, tight compartmentalisation stifles understanding. It is essential to see the interconnected nature of life, by allowing fluidity in knowledge streams, creating teaching/learning experiences that are integrated – between subjects other than social sciences (natural sciences, languages, the arts, sports) and between school and prevailing social conditions.	For example: in history, the chapter about WWII with reference to the use of atomic bombs by the USA on Hiroshima and Nagasaki, may have brief information about the devastation caused and perhaps a question about the impact of nuclear arms, but, in geography, there may be information about 'resources', 'uranium mines in India' or chapters in science on 'how atomic particles behave' These exists without any reference to the devastation they cause in lives of people where atomic tests are conducted, substances are mined, or processed for 'science'/'peaceful' purposes. There is a need to link these together for ourselves and students to develop a comprehensive and critical understanding of such inputs rather than allow them to remain segregated. This can be done by drawing from examples of people's struggles against nuclear mining/processing plants or anti-nuclear peace struggles, with the help of news clippings, documentaries, detailed visuals of the nuclear holocaust, and imagining what may happen in the time of nuclear war.

Possibilities for Change	Some Examples (Examine the following in context of discussions so far)
'Theoretical is not final' – by this it is meant that the mind-set of taking a given theory for granted needs to be changed. Theories (and educational programmes based on them) need to be understood in terms of the forces that give rise to them. They also need to be experienced/imagined in classroom situations that are not the same everywhere. Allowing for dialogue and openness to critique 'given theories' can be a starting point.	While there are several examples to illustrate this issue, the most interesting may be of 'constructivism' as a theoretical position endorsed in national policy documents (NCF, 2000, 2005). After the draft NCF 2005 was shared for feedback, many concerned academics, organisations, and public intellectuals raised concerns about the lack of clarity, absence of clear-cut conception of 'children constructing their understanding' without critical analysis of situation, a deeper reflection on what is right/wrong, fair/unfair, and nuanced understanding of specific contexts – our own and others', clarity that the 'knowledge/understanding' is not free of values, norms, includes making complex choices and that the process of knowledge creation is socially rooted, it needs to be problematised as well as sensitively handled. Taking a cue from the changing national mood to majoritarian dominance, subjugation of the marginalised, particularly the minorities, valorisation of violence, justification of hate; what knowledge can learners gain from a dominant 'construct' with reference to their limited social milieu, or what knowledge will students construct growing-up in segregated ghettos?
Understand teaching as an intensely personal affaire – Social science educators need to examine and question 'given knowledge' in relation to their own life, the social group they represent, and the values, ideologies they hold. Based on this reflection, they need to re-examine their own belief systems, the way they relate with students/teachers/others, and to critically analyse the pedagogical experiences they design.	Take an example of special Constitutional provision of 'reversions' (positive discrimination) for the historically marginalised castes, tribes. The teacher's social location and personal context is likely to have a great impact on the way the teacher relates with this concept and depending on her/his/their caste, where her/his/their empathies lie, whether s/he/they see the need for such a provision or feel its 'unjust' to 'open' categories ('upper castes'). (With regards to 'reservation for women' in governance, gender may be the point of consideration.) Regarding ideas of development and displacement for infrastructure building, it may be about whether the teachers/their families/communities have an experience of displacement or whether they are beneficiaries of a 'development project', even if it has caused a loss to others. This is not to say that one's caste/communal/gender identities prevent us from being empathetic to others. Nevertheless, without our being conscious that they may colour the way we process ideas and present them in class.

Possibilities for Change	Some Examples (Examine the following in context of discussions so far)
	Another example is of 'historical periods', how they are labelled, what does this periodisation represent in today's times? What is our relationship, our understanding about what these periods represent? What is the current discourse about what these periods represent? Are there aspects that are 'constructed' in a certain way by dominant forces today? (The British, while formally introducing the discipline of history to Colonial India, periodised India's past in religious frames, namely 'Hindu', 'Muslim', and 'Modern'. Whereas cultures of the Indian subcontinent like most other civilisations are a synthesis of outward and in-ward migrations, the British portrayed Muslims as foreign invaders, since it was their power which they had to combat before their take-over of India. The imprint of this organisation of historic phases has left a deep impact on the common psyche, glorifying so called 'Hindu' past and demonising so called 'Muslim' period.)
Placing knowledge in a historical context – It is crucial to understand that the organisation of the education system, the school, selection and organisation of knowledge into certain 'subjects', the entity of 'teacher' – all have emerged in certain historical conditions, they represent certain social structures and ideologies.	We have attempted to build this understanding in Chapters 3 and 4. To recognise that ideas about society, knowledge, justice, and equity are in a state of continuous contestation is vital for educators. Our education system and the subjects we teach today are a product of these historical processes. (For example, 'positivism' as central tenet of modernity, how 'social studies' as a subject evolved in the USA, how 'civics' was introduced to cultivate 'colonial citizenship', the way periodisation of Indian past has constructed certain ideas of Nationhood and stained the national fabric today, how, while 'determinism' has been contested as the primary rationale of explaining human-nature and spatial relationships, still dominates formal education content.) Understanding the evolution of disciplines and how they entered schools in historical perspective will help us understand that the textbooks we use reflect selective knowledge/positions within the larger discipline. Lack of awareness about the historical conditions in which a subject evolved, the different contestations and positions within each discipline, and the way the subject knowledge has been curated to represent worthiness through our textbooks binds us to larger ideas about society, knowledge, and justice, and constrains our agency as teachers.

208 Challenges and possibilities

Possibilities for Change	Some Examples (Examine the following in context of discussions so far)
Discourse, dialogue, peer support – The historical conditionalities of modern democracies have shaped teachers to accept themselves as a kind of collective, externally created for the state apparatus. This muzzles the agency of individual teachers and the potential of a purposefully engaged 'community of practitioners', but this does not have to be so.	This is the area of great possibilities. Teachers need to come together to create a culture of praxis. Organised spaces (either as formal, legally-bound collectives or as informal groups) to interact with peers to discuss the rational and motivations behind our work, understand and analyse what we teach, how, and how it connects to the society we are part of, is necessary for teachers. Today, we can also use technology to mitigate the limitations of geography and time, as we will see here.

It is worth it because it is possible

With education being one of the most organised fields, teachers are one the most organised workforces, through the mechanism of unionisation.

In the context of India, teachers' unions emerged almost a century ago, as formal education began to see a gradual spread. This is in line with the earlier discussion about the intertwining of teachers' identity with that of the modern state, resulting in a dilemma about the roles played by teachers as knowledge creators, as agents of empowerment on one hand, and as faceless workers bound by bureaucratic regulations on the other. But what is of particular interest is how society largely looks at teacher as a member of a workers' collective, in a position of bargaining.

Unionisation of workers has been an inevitable outcome of the industrialised world economy since its very inception. The nature of the state evolved as democratic polity, with sections representing distinctive political ideologies and political parties emerged embodying these ideologies. These developments are deeply linked with the way the education system is organised and how teachers and their unions are placed. Although the earliest forms of unions were 'guilds' of professional, specialised artisans or traders, from the eighteenth century onward, it was the working-class labourers who formed unions with a distinct political consciousness to negotiate justice and the rights of workers. Over the period, unionisation has not been limited to the 'blue-collar' workers but extends to 'white-collar' professionals. For most of this time, it has been the ideological 'left' that has provided an impetuous for unionism, infusing a distinct sociopolitical perspective. Thus, despite their own 'class interests' resting with the better-off section of society, it is common to find highly trained, well-paid professionals like doctors, technocrats, and teaching professionals supporting causes beyond their immediate interests.

Over time, political parties supporting 'capitalist interests' and sectarian, religious ideological organisations have also used 'union building' as a means to draw the labouring class into their folds, concentrating only on immediate benefits; as a result, the 'left' unions too have adopted such easier options to keep their membership intact.

Unionisation has been seen as a threat by the powerful class right from the beginning of the Industrial Age. Being labelled 'aggressive' or 'excessive', concentrating merely on raising immediate demands related to salaries and benefits, 'unionisation' has earned a notorious reputation. Added to this is the discourse of neo-colonialism, with the emphasis on privatisation and the weakening of justiciable entitlements, with the unions being unable to resist the dilution of workers' rights. In the context of education, the steady decline of the government-run school system, the dilution of norms, parallel schemes creating a cadre of 'para-teachers', and the emphasis on assessment and rampant privatisation – all this has intensified the unresolved confusion about the identity of teachers: qualified professional, a selfless, noble figure or a service provider?

Teachers' union: Case study from West Bengal[16]

In light of a case study of the teachers' union in West Bengal, we will take an opportunity to think about teachers' collective identity and their engagement with society and the State. We base our discussion on the analysis of documentation of programmes and positions taken by the All-Bengal Primary Teachers' Association[17] (ABPTA formed in 1935/37). What made this union take up causes beyond their immediate interest? What is at the root of their social consciousness that compelled them to address structural problems? Did their type of political inclination play a role in the demands they raised? Can political allegiance or party affiliation be both the driver for taking up wider issues on the one hand and, on the other, act as a constraint? The study places in context these questions for consideration.

The study, spanning a period of nearly seventy-five years, is based on the records of state-level conferences that are a testimony to the policy perspectives of the union as well as its programme and activities. The study by Sarkar and Rana of 'Pratichi (India) Trust' is divided into three chronological periods (1935–1947, 1947–1977, 1977–2010) set in the context of sociopolitical developments during these phases. Whereas the study is highly detailed, we draw only on those details that are representative of the character of the union in the given phase. The political allegiance of ABPTA has been with 'left-wing politics', and the Pratichi study critically considers how, while the organisation is not formally a 'party body', the stand it has taken during various historic phases has been influenced by the party ideology and positions on larger issues.

We will analyse the 'case study' of ABPTA with the help of a 'phase-wise' summary, providing overall context and supporting material drawn from archival records.

210 Challenges and possibilities

The context	The key highlights of the ABPTA conference resolutions
Phase 1935–1947: The ABPTA was born at a time when the Independence movement – both the Indian National Congress-led 'Civil Disobedience' and the radical armed struggle in Bengal – were at a pause. The world economy, particularly in the USA and Europe, were gradually emerging out of the 'Great Depression' of the 1930s. As a result of the three 'Roundtable Conferences', the 'Government of India Act, 1935', giving wider power to Provincial governments and increasing local representation, was about to come into force. Socially, consciousness about equal rights on the basis of gender, caste, and minority rights was on the rise. Education was being seen as a channel for socioeconomic empowerment. The British education system by the takeover of traditional Pathshalas had begun to spread but had been superficial. While most of the provinces of British India had passed their respective Primary Education Acts, for 'free and compulsory' primary education, the implementation was grossly inadequate, uneven, and tied to cess-tax. Overall, primary education was severely lacking in access, infrastructure, teacher deployment, salaries, and work conditions, particularly in rural areas. Along with teachers themselves, citizens from different fields were discontented with the situation. ABPTA was formed in this context with support from concerned citizens mainly to redress the situation about access to and quality of education, along with that of teachers' demands.	**"Resolutions-action, 1935–1947" Concern for public funding of education** The government spends [a lot] on law and order, jail and the police department as it considers this expenditure indispensable. Similarly, if the ministry considered free and compulsory primary education as indispensable, then it could be [supported]in whatever way, even by cutting down the salaries of the ministers. (Sir Hasan Surawardi, Vice Chancellor of the University of Calcutta (1930–34), in his inaugural speech to the 1937 conference) We used to criticize the foreign government for not making proper arrangements for education. But if, even after 180 years of foreign rule, when Bengal has achieved autonomy, the ministry could not afford to spend at least one crore out of the 12 crore rupees for lower education, then what is the use of getting autonomy of this kind? (Moulavi Idris Ahmed, MLA Malda, 1937)

Teachers, society, and the classroom 211

The context	The key highlights of the ABPTA conference resolutions
This period was rife with socio-political turmoil. Whereas, in the later part of 1930s, the Independence movement went into a partial lull, socially there was much churning. Different social groups were becoming aware of their rights and there were many reasons for this emerging consciousness. But the seeds of 'divide and rule' sowed by the British (partition of Bengal (1905), the supposed 'historic trauma of lost glory' of the upper-caste Hindus (Chapter 3), and threat to weaning feudalism and caste-authority) was evident in the birth of the Muslim League and Hindu Mahasabha. In 1930, Mahatma Gandhi's 'Salt March' galvanised massive civil disobedience, leading to mass arrests, inducting more people into the cause. Soon followed the three 'Roundtable Conferences' (1930–32), negotiating Indian 'self-rule' or dominion status in the empire and re-kindling the questions of the status of Muslim minorities and the 'depressed classes' (Dalits) in the Hindu majority state. The 'Poona Pact' (1930) between Gandhi and Dr Ambedkar, negotiating rights for historically discriminated castes, led to social upheaval. On one hand, caste-Hindus enabled temple and common water access to the 'outcastes', sparking violent opposition by sections of upper-castes towards the others. Attraction to Communist ideology, while on the rise, particularly in parts of Bengal, was politically suppressed by the British but the WWII alliance with Soviet Russia allowed the Communist sympathisers breathing space. As the possibility of Independence drew near, communal strife took a dreadful turn. Independence brought the violent rupture of Partition and, for the second time, Bengal was torn to pieces.	Universalisation of free and compulsory primary education in all districts of Bengal with immediate effect. Spending the maximum part of the revenue earned from the Central Government on jute tax for primary education. Improving the teacher-pupil ratio (TPR) by appointing more teachers, extending the 'Scholarship Exam' opportunities to girls, Providing more exam centres in convenient locations in subdivisions. Committees to have 'experienced primary teachers' to address errors in textbooks. If space allows, vegetable gardening to be carried out in schools to supplement nutrition. More schools for girls, appointment of female teachers to boost girls' education, people's participation in education to combat apathy about education (ABPTA Conference 1937). One teacher per class, adequate teaching equipment, arrangement of training for more teachers, training for the Urdu and Hindi teachers of Kolkata, teachers should select those textbooks which were favorable for the development of nationalism and patriotism among students, history, geography and physical education be made compulsory at the primary level, five years of primary education instead of a proposed four years. Forming a committee comprising of experts on education to examine the Wardha Scheme of Basic Education in Bengal instead of accepting it outright. Reducing the catchment area of each primary school to half-a-square mile from the then-prevalent norm of three square miles. Instead of imposing a 'general tax' for education, collect it on the basis of economic criteria and increase government spending (1945). Weekly school holidays in Muslim-majority areas to be Fridays instead of Sundays (1947).

212 Challenges and possibilities

The context	The key highlights of the ABPTA conference resolutions
Phase 1947–1977: Independence, the long-awaited dream, in its realisation brought pain and exposed the basest in human nature as India was partitioned. Soon after independence disillusionment began fomenting with respect to promises forgotten – one such being universalisation of school education which, instead of becoming a guaranteed Fundamental Right, remained in the 'Directive Principles'. After the India-China war (1962), the Communist Party of India saw a split (1964). Beset by severe food crises, the radical-left armed 'Naxalbari' movement (1967) rose up in West Bengal and spread to other states. Bengal was divided for the third time, separating East Pakistan (1971) and bringing a sea of refugees from the newly formed Bangladesh. West Bengal struggled with the continuing political conundrum between centrist-vs-left-wing political parties, the frequent collapse of democratically elected governments, and the imposition of President's Rule. Disillusionment spilled into city streets with lockdowns, protests, blockades, and violent skirmishes in villages and was responded to by brutal State power, reaching its worst during the 'Emergency' imposed by the Congress Party (lasting 1975–76). ABPTA faced an organisational crisis and underwent a split.	**Resolution-action, 1947–1977:** The demands placed before the British government at various times took on more concrete shape. The ABPTA was in one of its most vibrant phases during this period. **Financial resources:** At least 25% of the total State revenue should be allocated for education, of which at least 50% should be earmarked for primary education. The Central Government should spend 15% revenue on education, of which at least 40% to be earmarked for primary education. The Education Tax should be rationalised and the poor exempted from it (1953); instead, the wealthier sections, business houses, and various exportable items should be taxed. **Access and infrastructure:** Demand for one primary school for each half-square-mile, first raised in 1945, was further radicalised in 1953 to establish primary schools in all school-less localities. ABPTA's demands, raised in its 1962 conference, were for free textbooks, stationery, school uniforms, and midday meals to address hunger in the classroom, and monthly health check-ups for the children in primary schools and were crucially important for spreading education among all sections of children. The issue of TPR, raised during the colonial period, was taken up repeatedly during this period: one teacher for each class, and one teacher for every 30 children. In addition, repair and extension of school buildings, supply of teaching equipment, provision of drinking water were consistent demands. New and comprehensive legislation for primary education, combining both the rural and urban areas, and educational boards to function under people's participation.

Teachers, society, and the classroom **213**

The context	The key highlights of the ABPTA conference resolutions
	Content – pedagogy: Mother tongue to be the medium of education at all levels, provision of textbooks in languages in addition to Bangla – Hindi, Urdu, Santali, Nepali; scientific and pedagogically advanced curriculum, attractive textbooks, critical analysis of syllabus, teachers' involvement in textbook development, teacher training, Primary teachers' participation in decision-making bodies, demand for opening of pre-primary classes in primary schools.
Phase 1977–2010: At the beginning, the Left Front government (CPI-M) followed redistributive socioeconomic policies, particularly implementing land reform and improving educational infrastructure, and, while the relationship with the radical armed left on one side and the centrist forces on the other side remained uncomfortable, the State, despite its many economic and environmental challenges, remained relatively stable. While the 'opening of the economy' and 'liberalisation' in the 1990s, were opposed by the left parties at federal level, within the State, the same party, departing from its ideological stand, adopted land acquisition for controversial projects leading to its political debacle, ending its three-decades-old political rule.	**Resolution-action, 1977–2010:** **Financial resources:** Since its inception, ABPTA had been demanding 30% of State revenue for education but it kept largely silent on this after 1977, on occasions of deliberating financial allocations for education, the ABPTA remained silent on the educational expenditure in the State budget. During Left Front rule in West Bengal (WB), the expenditure on education increased and was closer to 30%, enabling free education till class 12, free textbooks and uniforms, the opening of new primary schools. Later, the expenditure on education decreased and, despite this, ABPTA did not raise this issue and never challenged the government's low allocation for primary education. **Access – infrastructure:** While the situation with regard to access to school improved during this period, many rural areas remained untouched. On the issue of midday meals, instead of adopting the national norm of a cooked midday meal, the State government decided to distribute dry rations, and ABPTA did not challenge this violation of its own decades-old demand.

The context	The key highlights of the ABPTA conference resolutions
	Content – pedagogy: The Left Front government's radical decisions – withdrawing English as a subject at the primary level and introducing continuous evaluation system with a "no-detention" policy replacing the conventional exams – faced resistance from society. While ABPTA supported these progressive changes, it did not oppose reintroduction of English in 1999. During this period, it did not critically engage with curricular pedagogic changes brought in by the State government, but it did oppose the National Curricular Framework of 2002 proposed by the NDA government, which was criticised for its obscurantist, narrow cultural agenda. **Privatization of education:** While notionally, the ABPTA continued its opposition to privatisation and critiqued the centre's policies pushing privatisation within the State, it turned a blind eye and adopted an apathetic attitude to the State's inability to improve the government schools, instead actively supporting private interests, or attempting to convince the middle-class about the progressive steps, i.e., attitude towards the use of the English medium and the 'no-detention' policy. Largely, its engagement with society and its anti-privatisation stance remained an unfulfilled agenda.

The context	The key highlights of the ABPTA conference resolutions
	Teacher service conditions: In this period, issues related to salaries and service norms were addressed by the State without the unions resorting to pressure tactics. The ABPTS membership saw an increase. While they could have leveraged taking-up systemic issues for quality and equity of education with greater fervour, the organisation remained largely inactive. Instead, it actively promoted the Left Front government, even passing resolutions to acknowledge its stance and did not critique government inaction or pro-privatisation moves.

Summary

This case study illustrates that ABPTA did not confine itself to sectional demands. The positions taken by the union, particularly during 1947–77, had a decisive impact in the development of primary education in West Bengal. The various resolutions and demands reveal that, from the very beginning, the organisation laid stress on improving school education holistically. Its larger social vision displayed an understanding about structural inequities, the role education plays in addressing these issues, and the State bearing primary responsibility for its delivery. However, in the post-1977 period, its alignment with the party in power changed things. Its ideological affiliation to the Party that shaped its larger critical vision, fuelled its struggle to strengthen the public education system, also resulted in its inability to critique/confront the party's policies, bearing open compromises the union made with its core principles. It is interesting that, while the ideologically left-wing party it supported was in opposition, the union's pro-people demands for educational and social causes were sharpest – the price-rise/food-shortage struggle, anti-war peace movements, solidarity with war refugees, and rallying for State-supported universal school education. Standing up for working-class people and women (while it lacked understanding of caste issues), it strived for scientific, pedagogically progressive education, and won many of its demands. However, after the Left Front assumed office in West Bengal in 1977, the union's strength flourished and some of the demands were addressed, many issues were diluted. During the early period, it had broader support outside of the 'ideological, party left' (in its 1937 conference, visionaries like Rabindranath Tagore and Jawaharlal Nehru had sent their wishes to the delegates) but, despite not being an official arm of the party, its uncritical support to everything the party did weakened the broader appeal it held.

There are unions in many countries which, in spite of their ideological leaning, do not take a partisan role. Whether partisan or not, the notion of social responsibility among the teachers' unions – or any trade union – is drawn from certain ideological resources. It is the ideological drive that has played a crucial role in the pro-people engagements of the teachers' unions which have had a profound impact, not only on the delivery of services in education, but also with respect to other social issues, a characteristic example of which can be found in this history of the teachers' union in West Bengal. It is not easy to measure the reciprocal influences – perspectives, actions of the teachers' unions, and conditions prevalent in the larger society. But, the fact that these two trends have occurred simultaneously cannot but have some connections. This recognition is important; but more important is to explore and strengthen this connection further. (Sarkar & Rana, 2010)

The case study here helps us clarify our understanding about teachers' unions. It is useful to think about the larger circumstances within which the phenomenon of unions evolved, defined their perspectives, shaped their character, and their programmes and actions. Over a period of time, the situation and our worldviews have changed – from holding the State accountable in realizing its duties towards citizens and fulfilling rights of different sections to the current times, when the conception of the State has changed to act only as a 'regulator' of institutions and systems, where individuals and collectives are expected to fulfil their needs on their own, citizenship largely reduced to the role of casting votes during elections.

Think

- The very basic question – why or why not unions?
- Do you think it's common to have teacher unions take up causes beyond their immediate interests?
- At the same time, do you think teachers' demanding their rights in relation to fair work conditions is unwarranted? Can teachers' rights be separated from a justice-oriented, vigorous education system?
- Do you think a teachers' organisation without a spelt-out ideology would function better? Will there be different ramifications of their engagement with larger structural and societal issues?
- In the case study, the ideological impetuous and political alliances of the union was instrumental in its action programmes or lack of them. Do you think the union would have done better without an ideological stance?
- Is it really possible to have a 'politically neutral' position? Is it possible to be political without being partisan? What can teachers through their unions do to impact the thinking of the political parties they ally with?

These questions are complex and may not have binary answers; they will need to be addressed in specific contexts. But it is worth raising them to clarify teachers' roles, claim agency, and indeed push for a meaningful education system. As we saw, unions in addition to engaging in favourable negotiations for their members, also help create narratives about important issues. The role social science educators can play in building critical perspectives about society and education is crucial in this process. Moreover, the understanding of education as a social experience is often limited to that between teachers and students and among students, but the need for teachers as peers to interact with each other is not sufficiently acknowledged. We will look at the efforts to give expression to this need and find ways.

> Exercise
>
> - With the help of teachers who you may know, or news-reports/internet, find out about different teacher unions/groups of teachers – the kind of work they have done, positions/campaigns taken while responding to sociopolitical or educational issues (not immediately concerning their benefits/work conditions). It could be in physical settings or on social/mass media.

Community of learners

Teachers' collectives, whether in the form of a union or subject/issue-based groups, are crucial for academic support, intellectual stimulation, and mitigating professional isolation. Teachers' everyday work is increasingly demanding, leaving little time even for classroom work. It allows no space for structured peer interaction unless the system initiates it. While there have been some policy measures towards this, they either get trapped in bureaucracy, or do not continue if policies themselves change. Another central issue in this is that most policies are silent about structural issues, glossing-over contestations in society and shrouding the political perspectives they represent.

As we have discussed, policy discourse around teachers' role is set up in a schizophrenic way – the exalted, all-seeing 'Guru' on one hand and the pliant worker on the other. Even policies and curriculum documents, that have attempted paradigmatic shift in favour of progressive-critical pedagogies, have greatly ignored the complex issues surrounding teachers' biases, misconceptions, and challenges they face. The role peer groups can play in addressing some of these issues requires more attention.

There have been policy directions (1986NEP/92POA and Sarva Shiksha Abhiyan (SSA)) to initiate 'cluster-level' meetings and forums of subject-teachers but these have largely remained on paper, functioning in an irregular manner or limited to bureaucratic meetings. These ideas have not articulated an understanding of teachers as peers with their own values, understanding, motives, experiences, and expertise. We saw an example of teachers ideologically organising themselves for common political vision. There have been other perspectives looking at teacher-collectives together as peers with expertise in a discipline, coping, supporting, learning, and sharing. This may sound like a purely professional grouping, as Giroux critiqued earlier, but envisioned as a 'Community of Learners' (CoL), it is meant to be wider. The starting points of the concept of teacher-peer groups as 'Community of Learners' (CoL), is as follows:

Teachers, society, and the classroom   **219**

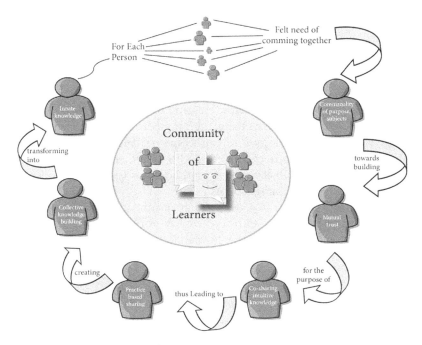

FIGURE 7.1   Community of Learners.

BOX 7.6 **'A Community of Learners'** (CoL) is a group of people who share values and beliefs and who actively engage in learning from one another—learners from teachers, teachers from learners, and learners from learners. They thus create a learning-centred environment in which students and educators are actively and intentionally constructing knowledge together. Learning communities are connected, cooperative, and supportive. Peers are interdependent in that they have joint responsibility for learning and sharing resources and points of view, while sustaining a mutually respectful and cohesive environment.

The very same principles that explain why students learn in communities of learners explain how teachers can learn in communities of teachers. Teachers must be in communities where they can actively and passionately investigate their own teaching, where they can consistently reflect on their own practice and its consequences, where they can engage collaboratively with one another, to investigate, discuss, explore and learn from one another about what happens when chance occurs in their teaching, and, thereby, where they can, as members of the community, generate a base of knowledge that goes beyond what any one of them could learn in the isolation which now characterizes their classrooms.

Ron Blonder, Weizmann Institute of Science, 2014

ICT and CoL

We will look at the work of an organisation, 'IT for Change' (ITfC) that works towards strengthening and improving public education. Their work demonstrates how ICT can be leveraged to facilitate and nurture teachers' collectives as learning communities. Taking clue from the NCERT National Focus on Educational Technology; with 'creating to learn' and field experiences, this case study shows teachers using digital media to connect with each other, using 'Web 2.0' technology to create contextual learning resources, remaining in touch by using text, image, audio-video, social media platforms and use, integrating subject- specific applications to support conceptual development, and accessing resources.

ITfC, in collaboration with the Karnataka government has facilitated the development and support of the 'Subject Teacher Forums' (STF) for high-school teachers. Financially supported by the state government, the STFs are formed to integrate ICTs for teacher professional development (TPD) to improve teaching/learning processes in classrooms.

> The key components of this programme include digital literacy, building collaborative networks of teachers for peer learning and sharing, with an online component called STFs, and integrating digital methods (tools and resources) for teaching/learning and resource creation. (Gurumurthy and Ranganathan)

Government high-school teachers have been trained as subject-wise master resource persons to support others to integrate ICT resources and pedagogies for teacher professional development. The master trainers have trained large number of peers. Teachers have become members of subject-wise virtual forums (mailing groups and other platforms), actively sharing ideas, resources, insights, and seeking/offering support.

During the first phase, ITfC worked with groups of teachers collaborating to develop, review, adapt, share, and publish "Open Educational Resources" (OER) with reference to the prescribed syllabus. Teachers have been collaborating to create supplementary, complementary contextual digital and non-digital resources for use in Kannada- and English-medium schools. These portals have generated great enthusiasm and is used massively by teachers across the State. The State government's teacher education institutes and colleges have been given resource support for well-equipped ICT labs. In addition to the in-service mode to create and nurture CoLs, capacities of teacher-educators have been built to integrate ICT in pre-service teacher education.

The programme seeks to develop teachers' TPACK by:

- Building teachers' capacity to use different software applications (TK)
- Providing them with access to varied sources of content appropriate for their subject, creating possibilities of enriching subject knowledge, helping teachers to learn (TCK)
- Supporting teachers to learn appropriate teaching methods to integrate digital technologies, such as showing a video and conducting debate and clarifying concepts by using ICT for simulation, etc. (TPK)
- 'Integrating digital educational resources for the subject with digital methods of teaching, such as a social science teacher showing a film on garbage disposal in cities to teach them about environmental issues arising from urbanisation' (TPACK). (ITfC) [18].

Learnings from ITfC's technology-enabled CoL of teachers – possibilities and challenges [19]

- Mitigate intellectual and professional isolation by facilitating sharing, exchange of opinions, suggestions for reflective teaching, and supporting each other. This can help develop a culture of the critical exchange of ideas.
- The facelessness of a teacher in a large system, absence of feedback to work can lead to inertia and cynicism that is self-destructive for an educator, unfair for students, and harmful for society at large. But the knowledge that other teachers elsewhere also face challenges can ease self-pity and frustration and instead build empathy. Technology-enabled CoL, by providing a platform for sharing classroom experiences, innovations, and challenges, can support interaction and exchange and can also help break 'textbook-culture'.
- Looking at one's peers' efforts, conversations initiated by other teachers can grow as individuals feel part of a collective. This can shape a democratic culture where expressing one's views, listening to others, and accommodating diversity and disagreements are valued.
- Taking class experiences to the group and applying what is learnt in the group can kindle meta-thinking about one's role as an educator.
- Flexibility of space and time allows interaction with synchronous and asynchronous modes.
- The conventional teacher meetings are typically 'expert' driven, one sided, and hierarchical, whereas a COL, on the other hand, is a collective of peers, where subject/domain 'experts' can be invited on a needs-based manner.

- The conventional teacher meetings are rare, irregular, lacking the continuity required for peer-exchange, to carry forward incomplete discussions/tasks, and set goals in a planned manner. Technology-enabled CoL can help maintain consistency in staying connected.
- It goes without saying that, with technology-enabled CoL, teachers can develop a comfort level with technology, integrate it for teaching/learning, and create and share TLRs, in turn developing their TPACK.

This is not to say that the TCoL is without any challenges. Some of the challenges can be – the participants may expect instantaneous response, all may not participate with equal enthusiasm, some may dominate the space or use the group only as a source of information/resources and not contribute. With the massive pressures of schoolwork and restraining personal circumstances, some teachers may not be able to spare the time and energy to participate, they may feel isolated and inadequate. Attitudes of teachers towards the education system at large may also impact their participation.

Despite there not being substantive evidence of experiences in Indian contexts, like the one referred to above, the idea is worth pursuing. 'As teachers learn from the community, over time they also sense a desire to support other teachers to learn in similar ways and reach out to them." (Radha and Gurumurthy).

Social science CoL – challenges and possibilities

It is possible to learn from these experiences while keeping in mind that the nature of subject or domain knowledge will undoubtedly shape the character of the group, i.e., the needs, issues, and challenges of a mathematics teachers' CoL will be distinctively different from that of a social science teachers' CoL (TCoL). Teachers need to develop critical, nuanced perspectives about the subjects they teach – shaping the way they view knowledge, technology, education, and society.

Social science teaching, while bringing these issues into a collective space itself can be challenging.

Teachers, school functionaries, and children are all social agents, representing and guarding the silos they live in. Scholars and practitioners have argued to pay heed to the substantive research available in the Indian context from the perspective of sociology of education. Policy documents (NCF, 2005; NCF-TE, 2010) have foregrounded the issue concerning how socialisation processes shape caste, gender, religious, linguistic, economic status, social interaction, and identity formation. Practitioners and social commentators have brought to notice how teachers' beliefs mirror social hierarchies in schools – in seating, sharing the midday meal, and scholastic expectations from children. More often than not, teachers do not address the age-old structural injustices of caste, religion, gender, and economic hardships and end up unquestioningly accepting discriminatory practices, justifying them as customary traditions or place blame on parents' illiteracy, poverty. Instances of teachers themselves discriminating students, their parents, and also colleagues owing to notions of superiority of caste, gender, religion, language, ethnicity, economic status, etc., are not uncommon. Schools are not insular: they are impacted by current events, political climate, the ideological make-up of ruling dispensation, and dominant social discourse fuelled by social and mass media. Schools are a microcosm of society – not merely mirroring it but reproducing it. Thus ... what is true of schools is also bound to be the case about collectives of teachers. While talking about a 'community of learners' teaching social sciences, these issues lie at the core.

Think

- What then can be the 'defining character' of social science TCoLs?
- Can social science TCoLs merely restrict their focus to given information and pedagogies to teach difficult concepts?
- What approach should the groups take towards textbook content?
- What role will technology play – particularly the ubiquitous 'social media' or unfiltered, unvalidated content available on interactive technology platforms like YouTube?
- Should there be specific attention paid to understanding the nature of information-communication technology? In what way?
- What attitudes should such groups have about contestations?
- How can issues of contestations be transformed into opportunities for breaking stereotypes reshaping teacher knowledge?
- What role can theoretical engagement with creation-crystallisation of forms of knowledge play in this process?

Whether in the form of teacher unions, or as TCoLs, there is a need to form alliances to end teacher isolation. By coming together, we can confront and unlearn our biases, debate to clarify purpose of teaching, re-shape the content and concepts we teach, de-construct 'given' knowledge and co-construct meanings within learners' context. This can be a personally enriching process giving real value to our work with the potential to transform social science education. Who will initiate such a process? The answer rests with each educator, not just individually but collectively.

Conclusion

We have looked at the construction of teachers' identity in modern times. Emergence of the modern democratic State, with its commitment to capitalism, has given a certain character to the way systems and institutions evolved. The education system developed giving central place to individual performance and the ability to pursue and accomplish material achievements. At the same time, the universal, omnipresent ideas of freedom and justice also became a hallmark of these times. During the same phase it materialized into India's struggle against colonialism, and the envisioning of the Constitution of Independent India. While the independent State continued to encumber the teacher, reducing her role as a worker, the values of justice, equity, fairness, have made society's need to question injustices, to collectively defend rights of the vulnerable within the education system or in the larger society.

It is common to see teachers of mathematics and sciences thinking beyond textbook content, seeking peer support to improve their teaching mainly because, whereas the content of those subjects is based on abstractions, it is tied to the concrete shape these concepts take in the form of technological solutions; although it ought to, it does not usually involve questioning one's notions of knowledge, society, ethics, and justice. For social science educators, the challenge is that we cannot separate content, processes, and conceptual clarity without looking into ourselves, questioning the social structures we are part of. Just as scholars have recorded biases and instances of discrimination by teachers, there are also cases where teachers overcome preconceptions to stand by fairness. There is a silent majority that believes in democratic values . The reality is made up of these diversities. Teachers are typically seen in a passive role, funneling 'given' knowledge. But teachers have also made substantive contributions to transformative policy frameworks, bringing life into teaching learning materials. The National Curriculum Framework for Teacher Education (2010) reflects these contributions. Its vision of social science education is summedup below.

> Teachers need to re-conceptualise citizenship education in terms of human rights and approaches of critical pedagogy, emphasise the environment and its protection, live in harmony within oneself and with natural and social environment, promote peace, democratic way of life, constitutional values of equality, justice, liberty, fraternity, and secularism, and caring values.
>
> *(NCF-TE, 2010, NCETE, Govt of India)*

It is a challenge to conclude this chapter, and the reasons for the challenge may be evident, as they are located in the nature of the kind of society that we are. The technological advances have made life easier for some but it has also come at an expense of marginalised groups and non-human life, upturning the forces of nature, challenging the very future of life on earth. The 'age of reason', the scientific advances and modern technologies began by challenging existing conditions, questioning ideas and values about society. The concept of 'reason' which is central to these processes is not sufficient to describe the underlying motivations – what it truly represents is 'Vivek', the word commonly used in many Indian languages. Vivek – reason with discernment, which includes compassion, empathy, and praxis. Today, while technology brings us challenges, it can also help connect with our peers to start a dialogue, help us reflect on our practices, and initiate changes in our classrooms to hope for a society that recognises the value of Vivek.

Think

- While teaching the concept of 'citizenship', a teacher stages a play/debate on the proposed changes in citizenship laws and is served notice by the administration. The reaction of other colleagues in WhatsApp groups is divided.
- While talking about 'types of houses and life in rural areas' in the State, the teacher goes beyond the textbook, creating an exercise to map the village where the school is located – bringing out caste and economic segregation.
- School authorities decide that no one will wear anything displaying one's religion. Many girl students from minority community are unable to attend schools. Teachers remain silent – while teaching about our Constitution, they deal with the concept of secularism from the textbook but do not allude to the reality in their school.
- Where do you stand in relation to the above?
- Can you add a few instances where teachers have taken a stand in favour of Constitutional, democratic, humanistic values?
- What role can teacher collectives or unions play in some of these situations?

Exercises

Based on discussions in Chapters from 1 to 7, construct at least seven questions/points for reflection to think about 'Teachers' identity and teaching of social sciences'

1.
2.
3.
4.
5.
6.
7.

Notes

1 Gandhi Kingdon, Geeta and Muzammil, Mohd (2001), *A Political Economy of Education in India: I: The Case of UP*, Economic and Political Weekly, Vol. 36, No. 32 (Aug. 11–17, 2001), pp. 3052-3063 Published, http://www.jstor.org/stable/4410974,Accessed: 11/04/2009 06:14
2 Kumar, Krishna (1991), *Political Agenda of Education: Study of Colonial and Nationalist Ideals*, Sage Publications, New Delhi/Newbury Park/London.
3 'Education, empire, and the heterogeneity of investigative modalities': a reassessment of colonial surveys on indigenous Indian education' Accessed 9 November 2021 (https://eric.ed.gov/?id=EJ1146435).
4 Jain, Manish.
5 Jain, Manish, (2010), 'Colonial Knowledge, Colonial Citizen: Civics in Colonial India.' Paper presented at the Annual Conference of the Comparative Education society of India, 15-17 November, 2010, Jawaharlal Nehru University (JNU), Delhi.
6 Giroux, Henry (1981), 'Teacher education and the ideology of social control' (revised version of an article in the *Journal of Education* 162 (1) in *Ideology, Culture, and the Process of Schooling* (Temple University Press, Philadelphia, USA and Falmer Press Ltd, London, UK).
7 Giroux, Henry (1988), Teachers as Transformative Intellectuals', in *Teachers as Intellectuals: Towards a Critical Pedagogy of Learning*, Edited by Henry A Giroux, Bergin and Garvey Publishers.
8 Popkewitz, cited in Giroux (1981).
9 Aronowitz, cited in Giroux (1981).
10 Batra, Poonam (2005), *Voice and Agency of Teachers: Missing Link in the NCD* EPW.
11 Gramsci, A (1971), *Selections from the Prison Notebooks*, (translated and edited Hare, Q and Smith G), New York International Publishers.
12 'Cultural Capital': 'That system of meanings, abilities, language forms, and tastes that are directly and indirectly defined by dominant groups as socially legitimate', i.e., worthy of possessing.
13 Apple, M W (1970), *Ideology and Curriculum*, Routledge and Kegan Paul, Boston.

14 Bernstein B (1977). *Class, Codes and Control. Vol. 3, towards a Theory of Educational Transmissions*; Basil Bernstein. Second revised edition. Routledge and Kegan Paul, London.
15 Heuristic (reasoning): The method of 'heuristic' reasoning is based on practical, hands-on experience of arriving at a conclusion. It is not necessarily a way to lead to accurate findings but often works based on trial-and-error, making an educated guess, based on strategies derived from previous similar experiences.
16 Manabesh Sarkar, Kumar Rana (2010), *Roles and Responsibilities of the Teachers' Unions in the Delivery of Primary Education: A Case of West Bengal*, © Pratichi (India) Trust.
17 From 1947, Paschim Banga Prathamik Sikshak Samiti. 'The ABPTA is not only the numerically strongest union but also shares the history of being part of the first teachers' union. The organisation has shown meticulousness in keeping many of the records of its past activities and has compiled them in three large volumes. The volumes contain reports and resolutions of various conferences of the organisation since its inception in 1935. The State-level conferences are the highest policy-making body of the organisation and the activities of the outfit are guided principally by the directions given in these conferences. Therefore, we considered it proper to examine in depth the reports made and resolutions adopted in these conferences in order to map the trajectory through which the organisation has travelled in the 75 years since its inception.'
18 https://itforchange.net/index.php/subject-teacher-forum
19 A 'Block' community of learning approach to teacher professional development-Role of ICT (https://www.google.com/url?sa=t&source=web&rct=j&opi=89978449&url=https://itforchange.net/)

BIBLIOGRAPHY

Agarwal, P. (2008). Unpublished study of field assignment in TISS. Mumbai, for the course MAEE.
Apple, M. W. (1979). *Ideology and curriculum*. London: Routledge.
Apple, M. W., & King, N. (1977). What do schools teach? *Curriculum Inquiry*, 6(4), 341–358, Curriculum theorizing since 1947: Rhetoric or progress? (1977), Taylor & Francis, Ltd.
Anurag, N. T. (2017). Influence of Brahminic hegemony on folk art Theyyam: Historical analysis of Theyyam myths and socio-cultural events in North Kerala. *International Journal of English Research*, 3(4), 38–42.
Auerbach, J. (2017, May 13). What a new University in Africa is doing to decolonise social sciences. *The Conversation*. Creative Commons.
Badhwar, N. (2015). The school on the hill. *Mint*. Retrieved December 3, 2020, from https://www.livemint.com/Leisure/hrgTu2CmdYZERoR1TaBc0M/The-school-on-the-hill.html
Barr, R. D., Barth, J. L., & Shermis, S. S. (1977). *Defining the social studies*. Arlington, VA: National Council for the Social Studies.
Bhatnagar, A. (2021). https://yuvaniya.in/2021/09/15/tribal-of-alirajpur-exploited-by-the-upper-caste-groups/
Blaut, J. M. (1976). Where was capitalism born? *Antipode*, 8(2), 1–11.
Blaut, J. M. (1989). Colonialism and the rise of capitalism. *Science and Society*, 53(3), 260–296. Retrieved July 29, 2013, from http://www.jstor.org/stable/40404472
Breen, P. (2018). *Developing educators for the digital age: A framework for capturing knowledge in action*. Technology, Knowledge, and Workshops, University of Westminster Press. https://www.jstor.org/stable/j.ctv5vddjh.5
Bruner, J. (1960). *The process of education*. Cambridge: Harvard University Press.
Bruner, J. S. (1969). Man: A course of study. In M. Feldman & E. Seifman (Eds.), *The social studies: Structure, models, and strategies*. Englewood Cliffs, NJ: Prentice-Hall.
Bruner, J. S. (1977). *The process of education* (Rev. ed.). Cambridge: Harvard University Press. (additionally *The social studies: Structure, models, and*

strategies. Englewood Cliffs, NJ: Prentice-Hall. And Bruner, J. S. (1977). *The process of education* (Rev. ed.). Cambridge: Harvard University Press.

Chattopadhyaya, D. P. (1992). *A study of ancient Indian materialism*. New Delhi: People's Publishing House.

Chakravarti, U. (2003). *Gendering caste: Through a feminist lens*. Kolkata: Mandira Sen for STREE, an imprint of Bhatkal and Sen.

Chakravarti, U. (2006). *Everyday lives, everyday histories: Beyond the kings and Brahmanas of 'ancient' India*. New Delhi: Tulika.

Chakravarti, U., & Krishnaraj, M. (2009). *Gendering caste: Through a feminist lens*. Kolkata: Stree, an imprint of Bhatkal and Sen.

Cherryholmes, C. H. (1980). Social knowledge and citizenship education: Two views of truth and criticism. *Curriculum Inquiry, 10*, 115–141.

Cherryholmes, C. H. (1982). Discourse and criticism in the social studies classroom. *Theory and Research in Social Education, 9*(4), 57–73.

Chinnakutty, M. Brahmanical thoughts affecting teaching profession. Unpublished work done as part of field assignment in TISS, Mumbai, as part of MAEE in 2009.

Cole, M., Jon-Steiner, V., Scribner, S., Souberman, E. (Ed.), & Vygotsky, L. S. (1978). *Mind in society, the development of higher psychological processes*. Cambridge, MA, and London: Harvard University Press.

Collected Works of Mahatma Gandhi, Vol 14, 16 (1965/1979), Vol 21 (1966), Vol 25 (1967). New Delhi: Government of India.

Counts, G. S. (1889–1974). Sociology and education, social reform, political activism, contribution. University, American, Chicago, and School – StateUniversity.com. https://education.stateuniversity.com/pages/1891/Counts-George-S-1889-1974.html#ixzz73cJALM8O

Dalrymple, A. (2019, October 3). 10 key cities along the silk road. Retrieved January 25, 2022, from https://www.historyhit.com/key-cities-along-the-silk-road/

Deshpande, G. P. (Ed.). (2002). *Selected writings of Jotirao Phule*. New Delhi: Left Word Books.

Dewey, J. (1916). *Democracy and education: An introduction to the philosophy of education*. New York: McMillan.

Dewey, J. (1937). Education and social change. *The Social Frontier, 3*(26), 472–474 (additional Education and Social Change John Dewey Bulletin of the American Association of University Professors (1915–1955), 23(6) (Oct., 1937), 472–474 (3 pages) Published By: American Association of University Professors).

Dewey, J. (1939). Creative democracy – the task before us. In *John Dewey and the promise of America progressive education booklet*, No. 14. Columbus, OH: American Education (additional details: Dewey, J. (1939). *Creative democracy— the task before us. In John Dewey and the Promise of America Progressive Education Booklet*, No. 14. Columbus, OH: American Education Press. (Republished in John Dewey, The Later Works, 1925–1953, Vol. 14.)

Dhankar, R. (2014). Making sense of the curriculum debate. Retrieved September 1, 2021, from https://www.deccanherald.com/content/420069/making-sense-curriculum-debate.html

Dubey, M. (2009). Education system in India. In *Debating education, IV: Against neoliberal thrust* (pp. 13–20). New Delhi: Sahmat.

Duverger, M. (1964). *Introduction to social sciences*. London: George Allen and Unwin.

Engle, S. H., & Ochoa, A. S. (1988). *Education for democratic citizenship: Decision making in the social studies*. New York: Teachers College Press.

Engels, F. (2010). *The origin of the family, private property, and the state*. London: Penguin Classics.

Fagg, H. (2002). *Back to the sources: A study of Gandhi's basic education*. New Delhi: National Book Trust.
Fenton, E. (1966). *Teaching the new social studies in secondary schools: An inductive approach*. New York: Holt, Rinehart, & Winston.
Fenton, E. (1967). *The new social studies*. New York: Holt, Rinehart, & Winston.
Friere, P. (1972). *Pedagogy of the oppressed* (M. B. Ramos, Trans.). Penguin: Harmondsworth, Eng.
Gandhi, M. K. (1966). *Collected works of Mahatma Gandhi, Vol 21*. The Publications Division, Ministry of Information and Broadcasting, Government of India, 38pp.
Gatade, S. (2011). *The saffron condition: Politics of repression and exclusion in neoliberal India*. Gurgaon: Three Essays Collective.
Gramsci, A. (1971). *Selections from the prison notebooks* (Q. Hare & G. Smith, Trans. and Ed.). New York International Publishers.
Giroux, H. (1988). *Teachers as intellectuals: Towards a critical pedagogy of learning*. Greenwood Publishing Group, Inc.
Gokhle, G. K. (1911). *The elementary education bill*. Arya Bhushan Press.
Government of India, Ministry of Education. (1966). *Report of the Education Commission, 1964–66 (Chairman D.S. Kothari)*. New Delhi: Govt. of India.
Gramsci, A. (1971). *Selections from the prison notebooks* (Q. Hare & G. Smith, Trans. & Ed.). New York International Publishers.
Gregory, D. (1978). *Ideology, science and human geography*. London: Hutchinson and Co.
Grenfell, M., & James, D. (1998). *Bourdieu and education: Acts of practical theory*. London and Bristol: Falmer Press.
Gurumurthy, A., & Chami, N. (2020, January). The intelligent corporation: Data and the digital economy. Retrieved July 18, 2021, from https://itforchange.net/intelligent-corporation-data-digital-economy-platform-governance
Hammond, T. C., & Manfra, M. M. (2009). Giving, prompting, making: Aligning technology and pedagogy within TPACK for social studies instruction. *Contemporary Issues in Technology and Teacher Education* [Online serial], 9(2). https://citejournal.org/volume-9/issue-2-09/social-studies/giving-prompting-making-aligning-technology-and-pedagogy-within-tpack-for-social-studies-instruction
Hammond, T. C., & Manfra, M. M. (2009). Giving, prompting, making: Aligning technology and pedagogy within TPACK for social studies instruction. *Contemporary Issues in Technology and Teacher Education*, 9(2), 160–185.
Harvey, D. (1996). *Justice, nature and geography of difference*. Oxford: Blackwell.
Haraniya, K. (2018). Meghalaya's ancient sentinels. Retrieved April 20, 2022, from https://www.livehistoryindia.com/story/eras/meghalayas-ancient-sentinels
Harris, J., Koehler, M., & Mishra, P. (2009). What is technological pedagogical content knowledge? *Contemporary Issues in Technology and Teacher Education*.
Hatcher, B. A. (1996). Reviewed work: *Classifying the universe: The ancient Indian Varṇa System and the origins of caste* by Smith, B. K. (1994) Review: Hatcher, B. A. Thematic issue on "Religion and American Popular Culture" (Winter, 1996), *Journal of the American Academy of Religion*, 64(4), 863–866, Oxford University Press. Retrieved July 1, 2021, from https://www.jstor.org/stable/1465626
Haydock, H. (2015). Stated and unstated aims of NCERT text books. *Economic and Political Weekly*, L(17), 109–119.
Heller, H. (2011). *The birth of capitalism: A twenty-first-century perspective* (pp. 33–34). The Future of World Capitalism. London: Pluto Press. Retrieved March 20, 2021, from http://library.oapen.org/handle/20.500.12657/3077
Hess, L., & Singh, S. (2002). *The Bijak of Kabir*. OUP, Oxford: Oxford University Press.

Hoare, Q., & Smith, G. N. (2009). *Selections from the prison notebooks of Antonio Gramsci* (Q. Hoare & G. N. Smith, Ed. and Trans.). New Delhi: Orient Blackswan.

Hoskote, R. (1996). Situation and symbol: A ritual identity and mode of expression under bourgeois cultural appropriation (with special reference to Warli art). *The Indian Journal of Social Work*, LVII(1), 79–90.

https://itforchange.net/teachers-community-of-learning-tcol-government-aided-high-schools-2018-21

http://mattkoehler.com/hybridphd/hybridphd_summer_2010/wpcontent/uploads/2010/06/history_of_tpack.pdf

https://thewire.in/government/bidar-karnataka-anti-caa-play-school-sedition

https://www.bbc.com/news/world-asia-india-51441549

https://www.eklavya.in/pdfs/Sandarbh/Sandarbh_74/01-08_We_and_The_Socially_Marginalized.pdf

https://www.google.com/url?client=internal-element-cse&cx=0903a1a109a46b6e5&q=https://www.indiatoday.in/india/story/school-headmistress-mother-arrested-as-child-participates-in-play-against-caa-nrc-1642019-2020-01-31&sa=U&ved=2ahUKEwiMt-iN-cH1AhX-zzgGHQQLAJkQFnoECAEQAg&usg=AOvVaw2fdgjH_bRzGhWXgk5TVEA9

https://www.weforum.org/agenda/2016/10/corporations-not-countries-dominate-the-list-of-the-world-s-biggest-economic-entities

Hullfish, H. G. (1924). Looking backward with Snedden. *Educational Review*, 67(February).

Hung, H.-F. (2001). Imperial China and capitalist Europe in the eighteenth-century global economy. *Review (Fernand Braudel Center)*, 24(4), 473–513. JSTOR. www.jstor.org/stable/40241528

Hunt, M. P., & Metcalf, L. E. (1955/1968). *Teaching high school social studies: Problems in reflective thinking and social understanding*. New York: Harper and Brothers.

Ilaiah, K. (2005). *Why I am not a Hindu: A Sudra critique of hindutva philosophy, culture, and political economy*. Calcutta: Samya.

Ilaiah, K. with illustrations by Durgabai Vyam. (2007). *Turning the pot, tilling the land: Dignity of labour in our times*. New Delhi: Navayana Publishing House.

Indus Valley Civilisation: Interview with Shereen Ratnagar. (2017, March 27). Retrieved April 15, 2021, from https://www.sahapedia.org/

ITfCh. https://itforchange.net/index.php/subject-teacher-forum

Jain, M. (2008). 'Inflections of Gender: Civics and Citizenship in Colonial India' Paper presented at the research students seminar organised by the Centre for Women's Development and Studies, University of Delhi, March 7, 2008.

Jain, M. (2010). 'Colonial Knowledge, Colonial Citizen: Civics in Colonial India.' Paper presented at the Annual Conference of the Comparative Education society of India, 15–17 November, 2010, Jawaharlal Nehru University (JNU), Delhi.

Jaffrelot, C. (2005). *Analysing and fighting caste: Dr. Ambedkar and untouchability*. New Delhi: Permanent Black.

Jorgensen, C. G. (2014). Social studies curriculum migration: Confronting challenges in the 21st century. In E. Wayne Ross (Ed.), *The social studies curriculum purposes, problems, and possibilities* (4th ed.). Albany, NY: State University of New York Press.

Jorgensen, C. G. (2012). *John Dewey and the dawn of social studies: Unraveling conflicting interpretations of the 1916 report*. Charlotte, NC: Information Age Publishing.

Joseph, T. (2018, December 30). How ancient DNA may rewrite prehistory in India. *BBC News*. Retrieved May 29, 2021, from https://www.bbc.com>world-asia-india-46616574

Joseph, S. (2022). *Budhini*. Kottayam: D.C. Books.
Lee-Warner, W, (1900). *The citizen of India*. London, Bombay, and Calcutta: Macmillan and Co., Limited.
Kapoor, B. (2015). Unpublished study of field assignment in TISS. Mumbai, for the course MAEE.
Karabel, J., & Halsey, A. H. (1977). *Power and ideology in education*. Oxford: OUP.
Khanna, P. (2016). *Connectography: Mapping the future of global civilization*. Random House.
Kingdon, G., & Sipahimalani-Rao, V. (2010, March 10). Parateachers in India: Status and impact. *Economic & Political Weekly, XLV*(12), 59–67.
Kliebard, H. M. (1986). *The struggle for the American Curriculum, 1893–1958*. New York: Routledge and Kegan Paul.
Krishnamurthy, S., & Tiwary, S. K. (2016). Origin, development and decline of monolithic pillars and the continuity of the tradition in polylithic, non-lithic and structural forms. *Ancient Asia*, 7(1), 1–14. http://dx.doi.org/10.5334/aa.78
Kumar, K. (1996). *Learning from conflict*. London: Orient Longman/Sangam Books Limited.
Kumar, K. (2005). *Political agenda of education: A study of colonialist and nationalist ideas*. New Delhi: Sage Publications.
Kumar, K. (1991). *Political agenda of education: Study of colonial and nationalist ideals*. New Delhi, Newbury Park, London: Sage Publications.
Kumar, R. (1993). *The history of doing: An illustrated account of movements for women's rights and feminism in India 1800–1990*. New Delhi: Kali for Women.
Kumar, R. (2009). Neo-liberal C consensus and the agenda for schooling. In *Debating education, IV: Against neoliberal thrust* (pp. 74–78). New Delhi: Sahmat.
Kuruvachira, J. (2008). *Politicisation of Hindu religion in post-modern India: An anatomy of world views, identities and strategies of Hindu nationalists in Bharatiya Janata Party*. Jaipur: Rawat Publications.
Lerner, G. (1986). *The creation of patriarchy*. New York: Oxford University Press.
Levitas, M. (1974). *Marxist perspectives in the sociology of education*. London: Routledge and Kegan Paul Ltd.
Lippmann, W. (1922). *Public opinion*. New York: Macmillan.
Long, C. H. (2020, October 20). Creation myth. *Encyclopedia Britannica*. Retrieved April 20, 2021, from https://www.britannica.com/topic/creation-myth
Mandal, D. (2019, January 9). Why Indian history has forgotten Fatima Sheikh but remembers Savitribai Phule. *The Print*.
Martorella, P. (1997). Technology and the social studies—Or: Which way to the sleeping giant? *Theory and Research in Social Education*, 25(4), 511–514.
Matthews, M. (1980). *The Marxist theory of schooling: A study of epistemology and education*. New Jersey: Harvester Press, Sussex/Humanities Press.
Menon, V. (2018, January 9). Fatima Sheikh: The woman who reshaped Indian education with Savitribai Phule. *The Print*.
MHRD (Ministry of Human Resource Development). (2008). Sarva Shiksha Abhiyaan. New Delhi: Ministry of Human Resource Development. http://pib.nic.in/archieve/others/2008/apr/r2008042401.pdf
Mishra, P., & Kohler, M. J. (2006). Technological pedagogical content knowledge: A framework for teacher knowledge. *Teachers College Record*, 108(6), 1017–1054. Copyright by Teachers College, Columbia University 0161-4681 1018 Teachers College Records
National curriculum framework for school education. National Council for Education Training and Research, 2000.
National Council for Educational Research and Training (NCERT). *National curriculum framework 1975*, 19–24; *National curriculum framework 1988*,

26–28; *National curriculum framework 2000*, 38–40; *National curriculum framework 2005*, 50–54.
NCERT (National Council of Educational Research and Training). (2005). National curriculum framework. New Delhi: National Council of Educational Research and Training. http://www.ncert.nic.in/rightside/links/pdf/framework/english/nf2005.pdf
National ICT Curriculum. (2013).
NCTFE (National Council of Teacher Education). (2010). National curricular framework for teacher education. New Delhi: National Council for Teacher Education. http://ncte-india.org/ncte_new/pdf/NCFTE_2010.pdf
Nehru, J. (1989). *The discovery of India (Centenary edition)*. New York: Oxford University Press.
Nehru, J. (1961). *The discovery of India*. Bombay: Asia Publishing House.
NEUPA. (2009). Elementary education in India: Where do we stand? New Delhi.
Newmann, F. M. (1991). Higher order thinking in the teaching of social studies: Connections between theory and practice. In J. Voss, D. Perkins, & J. Segal (Eds.), *Informal reasoning and education* (pp. 381–400). Hillsdale, NJ: Lawrence Erlbaum.
Ollman, B. (1998). Why dialectics? Why now? *Science and Society*, 62(3), 338–357.
Omvedt, G. (2003). *Buddhism in India: Challenging Brahmanism and caste*. New Delhi: Sage Publications.
Pandian, M. S. S. (2008, September 20). Writing ordinary lives. *Economic and Political Weekly*, 43(38), 34–40.
Paper presented at the Annual Conference of the *Comparative Education society of India*, 15–17 November, 2010, Jawahar Lal Nehru University (JNU), Delhi. This paper is based on the doctoral research (2009), *Civics curriculum and the idea of citizen since late nineteenth century*.
Parita, M. (1994). *Upholding the common life: The community of Mira Bai*. Delhi: Oxford University Press.
Peluso, N.L (1995), *Whose woods are these? Counter-mapping Forest territories in Kalimantan, Indonesia*, https://doi.org/10.1111/j.1467-8330.1995.tb00286.x accessed 3.6.22.
Periera, F. (2018). Theyyam: The dancing Gods. *Journal of Anthropological Films*, May 2018 2(1), 1369.
Pethiya, S. and Sebu, S. (2019). *Global citizenship education: A handbook for teachers at upper primary level in India*. Bhopal: Regional Institute of Education.
Pierson, M. (2001). Technology integration practice as a function of pedagogical expertise. *Journal of Research on Computing in Education*, 33(4), 413–430.
Poonam, B. (2005). EPW. Locating the agency of teachers in a changing Indian educational context.
Rajeevan, B. (1999). Cultural formation of Kerala. In P. J. Cherian (Ed.), *Essays on the cultural formation of Kerala: Literature, art, architecture, music, theatre cinema*. http://www.keralahistoryac.in/publicationhtm
Ramanujan, A. (1992). Talking to god in the mother tongue. *India International Centre Quarterly*, 19(4), 53–64. https://www.jstor.org/stable/23004008
Rangarajan, U. (2020). The legacy of Andal: Exploring the impact of Andal's poetry on the identity of the modern Tamil woman, confluence. *Journal of Interdisciplinary Studies*, iv. Retrieved July 5, 2021, from https://cjids.in/vol
Ravikumar, D., & Anand, S. (2007). *Ambedkar: Autobiographical notes*. Pondicherry: Navayana Publishing.
Reviewed work: *Classifying the universe: The ancient Indian Varṇa System and the origins of caste* by Brian K. Smith, Review: Brian A. Hatcher. *Journal of the American Academy of Religion*, 64(4), Thematic Issue on "Religion and American Popular Culture" (Winter, 1996), 863–866. Oxford University Press. Retrieved July 1, 2021, from https://www.jstor.org/stable/1465626

Rodrigue, J. (2020). *The geography of transport systems.* London: Routledge.
Rohan, V. (2020, October 31). Interview: Romila Thapar on the history of dissent and how it shaped Hinduism and India. *Scroll.in.* Retrieved June 5, 2021, from https://scroll.in/article/977026/interview-romila-thapar
Romila Thapar on the history of dissent and how it shaped Hinduism and India. *Scroll.in*, October 31, 2020. Retrieved June 5, 2021, from https://scroll.in/article/977026/interview-romila-thapar
Sadgopal, A. (2003). *Political economy of education in the age of globalisation: De-mystifying the knowledge agenda.* Bharat Jan Vigyan Jatha.
Sadgopal, A. (2009). Education policy and RTE bill: A historical betrayal. *Combat Law*, 8(3 & 4).
Sarkar, M., & Rana, K. (2010). Roles and responsibilities of the teachers' unions in the delivery of primary education: A case of West Bengal. Pratichi Occasional Paper No. 3, Pratichi (India) Turst.Sarkar, M., & Rana, K. (2010). *Roles and responsibilities of the teachers' unions in the delivery of primary education: A case of West Bengal.* © Pratichi (India) Trust.
Sarup, M. (1978). *Marxism and education.* London, Boston and Henley: Routledge and Kegan Paul.
Sarup, M. (1982). *Education, state and crisis.* London: Routledge and Kegan Paul.
Scott, J. C. (2009). *The art of not being governed: An anarchist history of Upland Southeast Asia.* Yale University Press. https://www.jstor.org/stable/j.ctt1njkkx
Session 12 – 'Changes in society' of 'Avehi Abacus Project'. www.avehiabacus.org
Shor, I., & Freire, P. (1987). *A pedagogy for liberation.* New York: Bergin & Garvey.
Shrivastava, A., & Kothari, A. (2012). *Churning the earth- The making of Global India.* Penguin Books India.
Shulman, L. S. (1986). Those who understand: Knowledge growth in teaching. *Educational Researcher*, 15(2), 4–14. American Educational Research Association, Stable. http://www.jstor.org/stable/1175860
Singh, K. S. (Ed.). (1995). *People of India: Mizoram vol XXXIII.* Calcutta: Anthropological Survey of India, Seagull Books.
Skeel, D. J. (1995). *Elementary social studies: Challenges for tomorrow's world.* Orlando: Harcourt Brace and Co.
Smith, B. K. (1984). *Classifying the universe: The ancient Indian Varna system and the origins of caste.* Oxford University Press.
Snedden, D. (1868–1951). Education, educational, social, and vocational. StateUniversity.com. https://education.stateuniversity.com/pages/2426/Snedden-David-1868-1951.html#ixzz744A0tRq4
Snedden, D. (1907). *Administration and educational work of American Juvenile reform schools.* New York: Teachers College, Columbia University.
Stanley, W. B. (2005). Social studies and the social order: Transmission or transformation? *Social Education*, 69(5), 282–286.
Stanley, W. B., & Nelson, J. L. (1994). The foundations of social education in historical context. In R. Martusewicz & W. Reynolds (Eds.), *Inside/out: Contemporary critical perspectives in education* (pp. 266–284). New York: St. Martin's.
Stanley, W. B., & Nelson, J. L. (1986). Social education for social transformation. *Social Education, 50*, 528–533.
Sunny, Y. (2006, January 21). Analysing current practices in geography education. *Economic and Political Weekly, XLI*(3), 270–278.
Sunny, Y. (2008, June 14). Experience and science in geography education. *Economic & Political Weekly, 43*(24), 46–49.
Sunny, Y. (2010). Communalisation of education. *Economic and Political Weekly, 45*(23), 21–24.
Sunny, Y. (2011). Teacher, society and modern school. *Economic and Political Weekly, 46*(17), 26–31.

Sunny, Y. (2014). 'Knowledge and the politics of education', *Economic and Political Weekly*, *xlix*(52), 32–35.
Sunny, Y. (2019). Embedding GCED in geography text books. In S. Pethiya & S. Sebu (Eds.), *Global citizenship education: A handbook for teachers at upper primary level in India* (pp. 154–162). Bhopal: Regional Institute of Education.
Sunny, Y. (2020, November 5). How sand mining along the Narmada is choking web of life. *Down to Earth*. https://www.downtoearth.org.in/blog/mining/how-sand-mining-along-the-narmada-is-choking-web-of-life-74100#
Sunny, Y. (2020). National Education Policy 2020: Realigning the Bhadralok. *Economic and Political Weekly*, 17–20.
Sunny, Y. (2022). *Sprout: A story of spaces and geographia*. Bhopal: Eklavya Publication.
Thapar, R. (2002). *The penguin history of early India: From the origins to AD 1300*. New Delhi: Penguin Books.
Thapar, R. (2020). Interview by Venkataramakrishnan, R, Romila Thapar on the history of dissent and how it shaped Hinduism and India. *Scroll.in*. Retrieved June 5, 2021, from https://scroll.in/article/977026/interview-romila-thapar
Thomas, J. (2021). The "Uru"s of Beypore, the largest handicraft in the world. Retrieved October 3, 2021, from https://theroadsandbeyond.com/the-urus-of-beypore-the-largest-handicraft-in-the-world/beypore-uru/
Toffler, A. (1980). *Third wave*. London: Macmillan for Pan Books.
TPACK.Org.
Urban, H. B. (2011). The womb of Tantra: Goddesses, tribals and kings in Assam. *The Journal of Hindu Studies*, 4, 231–247. Retrieved January 20, 2020, from https://www.researchgate.net/publication/270529066
Vasavi, A. R. (2019, May 3). School differentiation in India reinforces social inequalities. *The India Forum: A Journal-magazine on Contemporary Issues*. Retrieved December 2, 2020, from https://www.theindiaforum.in/article/school-differentiation-india-reinforcing-inequalities
Vaswani, P. (2021). Mythological trial of Manav Sangrahalaya: The Gond origin myth. Retrieved June 29, 2021, from http://www.dsource.in
Vijisha, P., & Raja, E. K. G. V. (2016). Existence of untouchability towards Maari Theyyam—A traditional art form of Kerala. *Open Journal of Social Sciences*, 4, 260–263. Retrieved April 22, 2021, from http://dx.doi.org/10.4236/jss.2016.43032
Vinson, K. D. (1998). The 'traditions' revisited: Instructional approach and high school social studies teachers. *Theory and Research in Social Education*, 23, 50–82.
Vygotsky, L. S. (1978). Interaction between learning and development. In M. Cole, V. Jon-Steiner, S. Scribner, & E. Souberman (Eds.), *Mind in society, the development of higher psychological processes*. Cambridge, MA and London: Harvard University Press.
Vygotsky, L. S. (1978). *Mind and society: The development of higher psychological processes*. Cambridge, MA: Harvard University Press.
Westheimer, J., & Kahne, J. (2004). What kind of citizen? The politics of educating for democracy. *American Educational Research Journal*, 41(2), 237–269. Retrieved July 2, 2009, from http://www.jstor.org/stable/3699366
Williams, T. (2015). Mapping the silk roads. Retrieved June 9, 2021, from https://www.researchgate.net/publication/280096308
www.ibef.org/indusmy/education-secron-india.aspx
Youn, M., & Geoff, W. (1977). *Society, state and schooling; readings on the possibilities of radical education*. The Falmer Press.
Zinn, H. (1980). *A people's history of the United States*, Harper and Row, New York.

INDEX

Note: Page numbers in italic refer to figures and bold refer to tables.

access 64, 88; access to technology 139, 148–50
Adharshila 162
Agarwal, Payal 168
ahoms 43
Ajivaka 46
Ambedkar, B. R. 65, 198, **211**
Andal 47–48
Anon, Jean 135
Anurag, N. T. 44
Apple, Michael 99, 107, 136, 201
archeology 29–30
artefacts 29, 33, 109, 154
ashramshala 177
assessment 142, 173, 178; class room 165, 181–83; continuous 159–60; critical 91; and cultural capital 179–80; manual for 203–4; methods 171; in NCFs 107–8; and teacher 145, 209; and technology 148, 151, 156
Auerbach, Jess 69
Avehi Abacus *102, 125, 127, 174,* 126–27
Ayodhya **111–12, 116,** 170
Ayyankali 64

Badhwar, Natasha 162
Bama, F. S. 181
barelvis 49
Barr, Barth, and Shermis 103, 150, 153, 147; approaches about citizenship education 60, 72, 82, 90, 103, 105, 109, 110, 177, 186, 200, 224; cultural transmission 103, 152; informed social criticism 103, 107; and Martorella 102, 146; and personal development 103; reflective inquiry 103, 106; social science 103
Basavanna 48
Batra, Poonam 195, 198–199
bhakti 46–48, 90, 128, 153–54; *see also* sufism
Bhatnagar, Amit 60
Blaut, J. M. 54–55
brahmanism 43–45, 48
British State 187; and also quasi-state 187; Company's Charter 187; East India Company 6, 187; Indian Empire 24, 135–36, 187, 192–193, **211**
Bruner, Jerome 104, 187; Fenton, Edwin 104; modes of empirical inquiry 104; structure of discipline 105, 121
buddhism 24, 46, 202

capitalism 13, 14, 82, 131; european 53, 56; in neocolonial states 68; proto capitalism 54; in text books 165, 193, 224; transition to 90, 131, 134, 187
caravans 26, 54
carbon dating 28

caste/castes 34, 37, 135; caste system 10–11, 64, 98, 182; caste-gender 39–41; and class room transactions 74, 167–70, 182–83; and colonial citizens 186, 188–89, 190, 192; and culture 200; and democracy 89, 108; knowledge 71–72; pedagogy 148, 154–55, 203–6; and policy documents 222–23, 225; resistance to 44, 46–49, 57; and school 64–65, 73; and teachers' association 209, **210–11**, 216; *see also* chaturvarnya
cave paintings 26–29, 53
Chakravarti, Uma 10, 27–28, 69
Chanana, D. R. 69
charvakas 45; *see also* ajivaka; bhakti; Buddhism; sufism
chaturvarnya 37, 40
Chinnakutty, M 73–74
christianity 24, 54, 182
citizenship education 60, 72, 105, 177; and democracy 89–91, 102–3, 120; policy 76, 106, 109–10, 119, 186, 190, 200; as social studies 75, 77, 165, **207**; and state 63–64, 70; and teachers 193, 197, 217, 224–25; *see also* social studies
civil society 77, **116**, 186, 190; educational surveys 188; Lord Minto 188; Munro's Minutes 189–90, 196; 'pursuit of order 187, 189, 190, 194; *see also* Jain, Manish; Kumar, Krishna
civilisation: ancient 49–52, 55–56, 71; colonial 188, 190–91, 194, **207**; urban 31
classroom transactions 166, 168, 180, 183
climate change 56, 70
Cold War 83, 103, 106, 131, 133–34
colonialism 12, 33, 53, 60, 68–69; and capitalism 56, 99; and democracy 95; freedom from 193, 224; neo- 184, 209; and world wars 134
common education 66
community 9, 34, 92, **111**, 227; and cultural capital 189; and curriculum 127; dalit 73, 166, 201; empowering the 94; of learners 218–20, 223; minority 225; and school 93, 106, 168, 191, 193, 201; teaching 204, **208**, 224; tribal 10, 15, 20, 28, 37
Community of learners (COL) 218; Ron Blonder 219

Comte, August 67–68, 202; Culture of positivism 202, 204; 'determinism' **207**; 'Scientism' 202
constitution of India 77, 197; Article 21 of the Indian Constitution 87; and Article 171 (3) (c) 193; and Convention on the Rights of the Child (1989) 87; and democracy 60; and education 65, 110, 188; preamble 14
constructivism **116**, 154, 156, 206
countermapping 69–70
Counts, George 91–99, 107, 133, 149, 198; social reconstruction 92, 100, 107, 150
creation legends 15, 20, 37
critical examination 64, 68–69
cultural capital 74, 96, 183, 187, 201; and assessment 179–80

Darwin's 'On The Origin of Species' 96
deccan 28, 41
decolonising 69–70, 72
democracy 50, 62, 77, 91–92; approaches 95–99, 102–3; and citizenship 70, 90; in classrooms 165; colonial 189, 196; and education 88–89, 119, 193, 197; electoral 60, 67; and ideology 131; in NCF 110, **109–17**, 120; and schools 64, 66; and social science 120, 186; teaching 93–94, *100*, 106–7, 109
deobandis 49
Dewey John 91–99, 106–8, 133, 152–53, 155, 199, 200; deliberative democracy 94, 96; and progressive movement in education 91; reflective thinking 108
dialectics/ dialectical 57, 172, 183, 199, **205**
Disciplinary and integrated 120; R. Pring 122
DNA 30
Drucker, Peter 135; knowledge economy 135, 157–59; 'knowledge worker' 135; Machlup, Fritz 135
Duverger, M 67

Education (Kothari) Commission (1968) 66, 111, 194
egalitarian/ egalitarianism 41, 43, 98
Eklavya 162, 179
Engels, Friedrich 10, 14

ethics/ ethical 30, 69, 82, 107, 197; codes 98, 134; dimension 200, 202, 224; and technology 139

fascist 66, 82
Freire, Paulo 94, 99, 107–8, 198; banking education 63, 153; critical pedagogy 94, **177**, 205; dialogical method 108

Gandhi, M. K. 64–65, 73, 198, **211**
ganga valley 40–41, 52
GATT 134; MNCs 134–36; WTO **114**, 134
Giroux, Henry 99, 194, 197–98, 202, 204, 218; deceptive paradox 197; methodological madness 198; NCF-TE-NCETE 2010 222; structural and ideological contradictions 192; and transformative intellectuals 197
global warming 56
Gramsci, Antonio 66, 200
Great Depression 91, 104, **210**
Grenfell and James 178
Gunasekaran, K. A. 181
Guru, Narayana 64

Habib, Irfan 30, 71
Hammond and Manfra 144, 146, 150–51, *152*, 156; Giving, Prompting, and Making in Social Studies Instruction' 152
Harappa 31–32, 52
Haydock, Karen 165
Heller, Henry 56
hidden curriculum 74, 171
honour killings 39
Hoskote, R 20
human resource 88, 91, 136; human engineering 198; structural issues 139, 198, 218
Hunt, Maurice and Metcalf, Lawrence 106

ideology: bhakti 48; caste 37; darwinism 96; education 103, 108, 131, 150, 195, 205; NCFs 109, **110**; political 209, **211**, 217; social efficiency 98–99
Ilaiah, Kancha 72
islam 22, 24, 47, 52, 169–70
IT for Change 220; National Focus on Educational Technology 220; TCoL 222–23

Jain, Manish 45, 76, 188, 190–91; civics 76–77, 190, 198, **207**; 'Citizen of India'; Sir William Lee-Warner 190–91; Wood's Dispatch 191
Jha, V. V. 69
Jharia 163
Joseph, Tony 49; Sarah 162, 173

Kabir 47
Kalibangan 31
Kamakhya 41, 43
Kamarupa 43
Kapoor, Bhawna 168, 171
Kaveri 41
Kilpatrick, William 108; project method 108
knowledge 22, 24, 45, 47, 63, 199; and capitalism 133–36; citizenry 103, 131, 195; class room 169–73, *177*, 183; colonial 191; in community of learners 219; constructivism **206–8**; contextual 202; creation of 68, 88, 90–91, 94–95, 165; and criticality 99, 224; curriculum 124, 126; decolonising 69–72; of disciplines 121, 123, 131; and dominance 89; economy 157; enriching 221–23; ethics of 30, 100, 105; experience 107–8, 118–19; local 175, 177; and market 96–97, 134; NCF **110, 111, 113, 114, 117**; and power 133; scaffolding 154–55; and school 64, 66–67, 75, 77, 87, 122; social science 104, 106, 122, 151, 182; and teachers 119, 186–89, 192, 195–97, **254**; and teaching 140–42, 145–47, 153, 168; and technology 143–44, 148–50, 156, 224; in text books 162, 165–66, 203–5; in union resolutions 215
Kosambi, D. D. 69
KSSP 162
Kumar Krishna 167–69, 187, 188–90, 192; Radha 71, 73

Lippmann, Walter 95, 150; democratic realism 95, 99; public opinion 95, 99, 109; Web 2.0' technology 220

MAEE 181
Manufacturing consent 200; and Bernstein, Basil 201; co-option 134, 190, 204; District Primary Education Programme (DPEP)

114, 202; Education for All 202; (MLL, NCERT 1993) **115**, 202; Sarva Shiksha Abhiyan (SSA) 218; 'SMART' training 202; World Bank (WB) **113–14**
manusmriti 37, 39, 64
Marx, Karl 14, 67
marxism 67–68
marxist 14, 73
matriliny 39
megaliths 28
mesolithic 27–28
migration 21, 30–33, 53, 198, **207**
mining 5, 51; coal 163, 165, 173; nuclear **205**; sand 175–76
Mira 48
Mohenjo-daro 31
Mussolini, B. A. A. 66

National Curriculum Framework (NCF) 104, 107–8, **112–117**, 118; citizenship education 76; policy document 206, 222; and teachers 186, 195, 203, 224; and text book writing 162, 166
The National Education Policy (1986/PoA92) 196; the National Education Policy 2020 (NEP 20) 20, 136, 142
NCERT 186, 204–5, 220; NCF **110–12, 116**; text books 74, 162, 165, 173
Nehru, Jawaharlal 45, 216

oligopolistic/oligopoly 134
Omvedt, Gail 46, 48
oral traditions 21–22, 37
Orientalists 187, 192; historical periods 207; Liberals 188; oriental despotism 188

Padmanabhan Chitra 162
Paine, Thomas 73
Pandian, M. S. S. 181–82
participatory democracy 92; creative democracy 107
patriarchy 12, 47
Pedagogical Content Knowledge 87, 140; Shulman, Lee (1986) 141
pedagogy 75–76, 87, 103, 109, 202; child-centred 98; in class room 119, 121, 159, 169, 171–72, 177; critical 86, 92, 105, 193, **205**, 224; in NCF **117**; of social studies 181; and teachers **213–14**; and technology 140–45,149–51, 151, 153

Peluso, N. L. 70
periodisation 33, **207**
Periyar, E. V. R. 64
Periyar valley 41
Phule, Jyotirao 40, 64, 73; Jyotirao and Savitri 64; Savitri 40
political economy 135, 149
Poona Pact **211**
positivism/ positivist 67, 107, 193, 202, 204, **207**
Pragmatist 93; pragmatic method of intelligence 93
Prakrit and Pali 69
praxis 60, 63, 73, 184, 205, **209**, 225; democratic 60, 63; marxist 73; transformative 184

Rajeevan, B 40–41
Ranade, Gopal Krishna 64
Ratnagar, Shereen 31
reflection 92, 97, 98, 107, 127, 149, **177**, 206, 226; reflective enquiry 151
reinterpretation 48, 68–69
religion 33, 45, 48, 53, 57, 82, 148; and authority **116**, 182; in class room processes 169, 172; and creation legends 20; and culture 200; and education 187; and exploitation 154; and school 201, 205, 223, 225; spread of 26; and state 37, 50–51; and tradition 72–73; tribal 52; vedic 47, 49
renaissance 67; and efficiency 91, 96–99, 131, 157, 193; enlightenment 81, 189; Reformation 188
Rousseau, Jean-Jaques 67
Roy Mohan 64; Kumkum 203–4

Sarup, Madan 66, 78
schooling 73, 136, 195, 198; and adivasi people 162; class based 178–79, 195; common 66, 77; elementary **110, 113**; and knowledge 122; in modern state 62–64; and society 74–75, 77, 150, 172, 181
Scott, J. C. 52
Sengupta 20
shaiva 49
Sharma, R. S. 69
Shiekh, Fatima 64
Shinde, Tarabai 64
silk road 24, 26, 54
slave 53, 97
Smith, B. K. 37, 66; Drucker, Peter 135; knowledge economy 135, 157–58;

'knowledge worker' 135; Machlup, Fritz 135
social reconstructionism 100
social science 15, 34, 85, 131, 153, 157, 186; approaches to 99, 109; as citizenship education 75–76, 90, 102–3, 190; class room 172, 181, 182–83, 202; in collective space 222–24; critical examination 71, 107, 181, 186, 217; decolonial 69; and democracy 92, 95, 98; digital methods 221; ideologies 100, 157; knowledge creation 199–201; methodology 67, 197; and NCFs 109–17; perspectives 182–83; role of 103–4, 106–7; and social darwinism 96; and society 86–89; specialisation 66, 68, 103–4, 151, 193; teaching of 118–22, 196–98, 226; and technology 134, 140–41, 150, 152, 156; text books 203–4, **205–7**; and traditions 172
social structure 2–3, 6, 19; knowledge creation 201–3; teacher development 196–97, 204–6, 221
social studies *147*; and citizenship education 63, 75, 90, 99, 165; class rooms 168, 176–73, 181–82; curriculum 99, 101, 103–4, 106; socialisation 64, 87, 190, 196–97, 222; teachers 151, **152**, 153, 161, 183; technology in 155–56, **207**; *see also* social science
socialist 14; *see also* social structure
society 22, 30, 34, 54, 67–68, 189, 192; band 10; capitalist 13–14, 96–98; of caste-gender 39–40; and change **207–8**; civil 187, 190; and community 9; critique of 70–72, 78, 87, 90, 94, 96, 138, 196; democratic 106–9, 120, 197; dialectics in 184; feudal 11–13; ideologies and 100; marginalised 162, 168; in NCFs 109–17; and patriarchy 12, 48; and school 64, 66, 74–77, 104, 170, 172, 223, 225; and state 36, 37, 44, 46, 51, 88, 103, 186, 194; teachers in 185, **214**, 216–18, 221–22, 224; teaching-learning on 49, 53, 57, 87, 89–90, 92–93, 95, 99, 121, 127, 176, 180, 195, 203–4; and technology 142, 149–51; tribal 10, 12, 21, 33, 39, 51, 182

sociology of knowledge 91, 135
sovereignty 68
Sputnik 104, 202
state 109; capitalist 13–15; city 46, 50, 90; colonial 77; and constitution 87; democratic 89, 91, 102, 134; feudal 11–12, 40, 57, 73; formation 34, 36, 41, 43, 51, 53; and gods 37; and kings 21, 53; modern 51, 60, 62–63, 67–68, 70, 75, 88; nation 54, 82, 90, 102–4, 133; policy **109–110**, **112–13**, **117**, 120; and private property 10; religion and 49–50; resistance to 44, 46, 47; tribal 52; and varna 52; view 76
sufism 47–48
Sunny, Yemuna 65, 71, 164, 178–80, 183

Tagore, Rabindranath 188
teacher unions 138, 183, 208, 217–18, 223; All-Bengal Primary Teachers' Association (ABPTA) and Sarkar, Manabesh and Rana, Kumar of Pratichi (India) Trust 208
technology 83, 103, 131, 132, 140, 145, 208; (AI) and disruptive technology like ChatGPT 150; computing 132; Digital Age *137*, 142; digital technology 83, 132, 134, 139, 142; educational technology 136, 220; and GIS 140; and information technology and ICT 134, 220–21, 223
Thapar, Romila 33, 38, 41, 46–49, 69
theyyam 43–44
TPACK framework 140, 142, *143*, 144–46, 149, 156; CK, PCK 145; Mishra, Punya and Koehler, Matthew J. 142, 147, 156; PK 143; TCK 144; TK 143; TPK 144
transformative 88, 156, 165–66, 198, 224
travelogues 22

Urban, H. 39, 43

vaishnava 49
Vasavi, A. R. 178, 188
Vygotsky, Lev 153, 172; scaffolder 154

WWII 82, 98, 103, 105, 134, 193, **205**, **211**

Zinn, Howard 70

Printed in the USA
CPSIA information can be obtained
at www.ICGtesting.com
LVHW011123310724
786911LV00009B/199